BREAKING THE SILENCE

Mariette Hartley

and Anne Commire

A SIGNET BOOK

NEW AMERICAN LIBRARY

A DIVISION OF PENGUIN BOOKS USA INC., NEW YORK

SIGNET
Published by the Penguin Group
Penguin Books USA Inc., 375 Hudson Street,
New York, New York 10014, U.S.A.
Penguin Books Ltd, 27 Wrights Lane,
London W8 5TZ, England
Penguin Books Australia Ltd, Ringwood,
Victoria, Australia
Penguin Books Canada Ltd, 10 Alcorn Avenue,
Toronto, Ontario, Canada M4V 3B2
Penguin Books (N.Z.) Ltd, 182–190 Wairau Road,
Auckland 10, New Zealand

Penguin Books Ltd, Registered Offices:
Harmondsworth, Middlesex, England

Published by Signet, an imprint of New American Library, a division of Penguin Books USA Inc. This is an authorized reprint of a hardcover edition published by G. P. Putnam's Sons.

First Signet Printing, September, 1991
10 9 8 7 6 5 4 3 2

Printed in Canada

ACNOWLEDGMENTS

There's this guy sitting in a bar talking to a priest.
"Hey, Father," he says.
"Yes, my son?"
"Forgive me, Father. I know it's none of my business, but you've got it all wrong about this God stuff. God doesn't exist. I oughta know."
"Why's that, my son?"
"Well, a while ago, I was ice-fishing in the Arctic, about twenty miles from the nearest village, when a blizzard came up, a real doozy—wind, blinding snow—I was a goner. I got down on my knees and prayed harder than I've ever prayed in my life. I begged God to help."
"And did He, my son?"
"Hell, no. God didn't lift a heavenly finger. Some Eskimo appeared out of nowhere and showed me the way."
And so, this is my space to thank my Eskimos—visible and invisible—who have helped me out of even the littlest storms and some real doozies.
First of all, I have to thank my dear friend Annie Commire for living in my shoes for the last two years, and for not getting bored and still

speaking to me. Thanks also to Gail Schermer in Vermont, who went through these chapters in the larval stages, blue pencil held high; and Neil Nyren, my editor at Putnam, who continued to encourage, even while enduring my stubbornness.

This book could not have been written without another dear friend, my manager, Arlene Dayton, through whose support and loyalty I have stayed visible, often in spite of myself. Her decisions and belief have been gold for me.

I'd like to thank my theater Eskimos: Claire Oleson, Eva Le Gallienne, and John Houseman; also Dr. Victor Monke, Joye Weisel, and dale Sowers for opening up the past to me and pouring sunlight into dark corners; Iris Bolton, Charlotte Ross, Karen Maxim, and all my survivor friends, who forced me to speak about a subject that made my knees weak; all my friends at MADD, whose courage astonishes me; the people I meet daily, who remind me that life is to be lived; and most especially my incredible husband, for his patience, humor, loyalty, and love; and my children, adopted and not, who—through their unique beauty, joy, and humor—continually teach me that legacies can be changed. Last of all, to my mother, who has finally allowed me to talk about her journey. No holds barred.

**To my beloved family—
past, present, and future**

It all started January 7th, 1980, at 11:23 P.M., but who's counting? Patrick and I had gone on a second honeymoon, had just arrived in Palm Springs, and were racing through the aisles of the local 7-Eleven, getting our various eggs and milk, hoping we could hole up the entire lascivious weekend and never come out, when my grocery cart screeched to a halt and I nearly fell into it.

There, on the covers of—not *Star*, not *Us*, not *Family Circle*—on the covers of *Time*, *Newsweek*, and *Life* magazines, was Meryl Streep, and underneath her picture it said, "Actress of the '80s." *Time*, *Newsweek*, and *Life* magazines: "Actress of the '80s." And I said to myself, "Well. There go the eighties."

It was not a good weekend. I was depressed; I was forlorn; the Jacuzzi felt cold. We didn't . . . I didn't . . . smile much. And I felt so petty that I couldn't talk to anyone. So who do you talk to when you can't talk to anybody? You talk to God, right? I talked to God a lot.

I'd say . . . "God. Okay, even if she is the actress of the '80s, I bet she never gets married. She's obviously a compulsive worker, and somebody that compulsive doesn't have time to develop a relationship. I, on the other hand, who have not been compulsively working much at all, have a wonderful relationship." By Sunday, God was answering back:

"Mariette. Meryl Streep just married a successful sculptor and is blissfully happy."

That's everybody's dream, right?—To marry someone who's not only creative, but making a small fortune at it. Anyway, there she was on the cover of *Time, Newsweek,* and *Life* magazines, Actress of the '80s, married to a successful sculptor; but I got past it, I was really okay, then. . . . Wanna hear the review? *Los Angeles Times* on *Sophie's Choice:*

> Nothing you know about acting quite prepares you for the amazing Meryl Streep as this sensual, feverish, kittenish, beautiful, tragic woman. Even though he thought it was a risk, Alan Pakula gave Streep the part. She was given a Polish coach, studied an accent for two months, and reported, 'Mr. Pakula? I'm beginning to feel the character.' . . . The only regret about Streep's matchless work is that *it ends.*

Well, I figured, even if she does get an Academy Award, I'll bet she never has kids. Her husband's obviously very creative, but what? He sculpts all day. She's constantly on location, constantly shooting movies at the end of some sea-sprayed jetty. How can they ever have kids? I, on the other hand, who have not been working at the end of any jetty at all, have two wonderful kids. I was actually feeling sorry for her. But God kept talking back, a voice that boomed from the heavens, sounding a little like Stan Freberg.

"Mariette."

"Yes?"

"Mariette, Meryl Streep and her husband, a successful sculptor, *have begotten two gorgeous children. A boy and a girl."*

"When!"

"On hiatus."

Well, I thought, at least I've nursed my kids. I didn't want to sound judgmental, but how could Meryl Streep find time to nurse her children? I'll bet they're career orphans, latchkey . . .

"Mariette."

"Hm?"

"Meryl Streep is a terrific mother. Her children get equal love and attention; never eat with their mouths open; and will never blame their mother in analysis, twenty years down the road."

"Never blame their mother!"

"There's more."

"Gosh."

"Meryl Streep's son will graduate from Yale with honors and be weaned the following week. Meryl Streep's daughter will marry Prince Harry and bequeath her two royal grandchildren. A boy and a girl. Want to see the wedding photos?"

"Not particularly."

Okay, so I was thrown. But I finally got past it; I was really all right. Then I noticed they were doing a remake of *Gone With the Wind.* I ran to the phone to call my agent, practicing all the way. "Oh, fiddle-dee-dee, Melanie, aren't things bad enough without you talking about dyin'?"

"Mariette!"

"Yes?"

"Sit down, Mariette."

"Scarlett O'Hara! Meryl Streep will play Scarlett O'Hara?"

"Better than Viv."

"Swell. It says here Paramount's shooting the life of Sonja Henie. She can't be playing Sonja Henie."

"Not only that, but she does her own skating."

"What about Esther Williams?"

"Does her own swimming."

"Maureen O'Sullivan?"

"Does her own vines."

"What about Joan of Arc? Does her own burning? Hell, what's left? Wouldn't surprise me if she did *The Story of Barbie and Ken.*" God was silent. "Who plays Ken?"

"Robert Redford."

"Tell you what. Just stop me if she's *not* going to play these parts, okay? Okay?"

"Roll 'em."

"Alida Valli, Dame May Whitty, Minnie Pearl? You can jump in anytime. Gisele MacKenzie, Lena Horne? LENA HORNE! She couldn't. She can't. It's against Screen Actors Guild. Actors can't play blackface anymore."

"Doesn't have to. She'll just study her color for two months. Want the rest of it?"

"Sure, why not?"

"Sandra Dee, Lu Ann Sims, all the presidents' wives, Audrey Hepburn, Kate Hepburn, Ruth Hepburn . . ."

"Ruth Hepburn?"

"Isn't famous yet."

"What about Larry, Mo, and Curly?"

"Does her own hitting. Zasu Pitts, Faye Emerson, Mariette Hartley, Zizi Jeanmaire . . ."

"Hey!"

"Hm?"

"Would you back up a little, third from the left there? Mariette Hartley?"

"Right."

"The life story of Mariette Hartley?"

"Right."

"Mmm . . . mmm . . . mmMeryl Streep will play my life?"

"That's right."

"But she can't do my life! That's not fair! That's my part!"

"Can't be helped."

"Why?"

"You're too tall."

"Anything else you want to tell me?"

"Can you take it?"

"Sure. Roll 'em."

"Meryl Streep will take over the Today Show; *chair a round table on advanced metaphysics; be the first American awarded the OBE; and on July 22, 1998, Dame Meryl,* and her successful sculptor husband, *will go on* Tattletales *and win for the banana section."*

"Boy, I mean, I gotta tell ya. Sometimes I think (I mean, I have a terrific career, I know that) but sometimes I think, well . . ."

"You know, Mariette. When someone's in the position that I am—with so many children . . ."

"Oh, I know that . . ."

"So many animals . . ."

"I respect that."

"So many mountains, so many rivers . . ."

"I know all that, but . . . well . . . Do you like her better?"

"Yes, Mariette. I've always liked her better."

"Is that why she gets to stay up later?"

So here it is. The story of my life. Soon to be a major motion picture starring Meryl Streep.

No holds barred.

PROLOGUE

When I was born I was five-foot-eight and had my father's chest and legs. The only person in the world that was taller than I was my mother. It wasn't until I was well into my thirties, after five years of analysis, two husbands, two children, that I found out I was taller than she was.

I was lying in bed reading a book called *Touching*—feeling very alive, very fresh in my body, having just finished nursing my daughter, Justine—and was fully sympathetic with Ashley Montagu's emphasis on the importance of touch. He wrote of baby monkeys that had been known to die from lack of it. He discussed child-raising theories popular in the twenties—antiseptic theories that greatly influenced psychology, theories that claimed that any show of love or close physical contact made the child too dependent.

> Pediatricians advised parents to maintain a sophisticated aloofness from their children, keeping them at arm's length, and managing them on a schedule. . . . If they cried [between feedings], they were not to be picked up, since

> if one yielded to such weak impulses the child would be spoiled. . . ."

I thought to myself, how times have changed. Both Sean and Justine were strapped to my front from birth by a blue Snugli. They went where I went: to a Paramount soundstage, to the Galleria, to the bottom of the ocean. Here I was nursing both my children on demand. Mom said she tried to nurse me, but my grandfather, Big John, had frowned on it. "I got too nervous; I couldn't do it. I didn't have any milk."

I returned to Montagu: Children were mechanical objects at the mercy of their environment, and parents could make them into anything they wished.

> The child's wishes, needs, feelings were treated as if they did not exist.
>
> Unsound as this thinking is, and damaging as it has been to millions of children, many of whom later grew up into disturbed persons, the behavioristic, mechanistic approach to child-rearing is still largely with us.

The man responsible—wrote Montagu—the man to thank, was "Professor John Broadus Watson of Johns Hopkins University."

I dropped the book and got chills.

John Broadus Watson. My mother's father. Big John. My grandfather.

> The child's wishes, needs, and feelings were treated as if they did not exist.

As the founder of "behaviorism," my grandfather had an enormous influence on psychology—

pioneering in child development, animal research, and learning. He became the first "pop" psychologist—selling "behaviorism" in magazines, books, and on radio. Established in the public eye as an expert on everything from child-rearing to teeth, he was even sent a grandson of Queen Marie of Romania to be "reconditioned" with kingly qualities. His 1928 book, *The Psychological Care of the Infant and Child,* was the bestselling "Spock" of his generation—rebutted by Spock in his generation. In it, my grandfather wrote:

> Children should be awakened at 6:30 A.M. for orange juice and a pee. Play 'til 7:30. Breakfast should be at 7:30 sharp; at 8:00 they should be placed on the toilet for twenty minutes or less 'til bowel movement is complete. Then follow up with a verbal report. The child would then play indoors 'til 10:00 A.M.; after 10:00 outside, a short nap after lunch, then "social play" with others. In the evening a bath, quiet play until bedtime at 8:00 sharp.

He was convinced that children could be trained to be clean from very early on, could be trained not to suck their fingers, not to touch their genitals, not to be too noisy. By the age of three, "children should begin to dress and act like youthful young men and women." They should have an early knowledge of the facts of life, freely discussing sex. He argued that institutions like the Boy Scouts and the YMCA could lead to homosexuality. Girls were even in more danger because they held hands, kissed, and slept in the same bed at pajama parties. "Our whole social fabric is woven so as to make all women slightly homosexual."

In Big John's ideal world, children were to be

taken from mothers during their third or fourth week; if not, attachments were bound to develop. He claimed that the reason mothers indulged in baby-loving was sexual. Otherwise, why would they kiss their children on the lips? He railed against mothers whose excessive affection made the child forever dependent and emotionally unstable. Children should never be kissed, hugged, or allowed to sit on their laps. If there has to be kissing, let it be on the forehead. Parents would soon find they could be "perfectly objective and yet kindly."

My mother's upbringing was purely intellectual. The only time my mother was "kissed on the forehead" was when she was about twelve and Big John went to war. Although she was reading the newspaper by the time she was two, there was never any touching, not any at all.

Grandfather's theories infected my mother's life, my life, and the lives of millions.

How do you break a legacy? How do you keep from passing a debilitating inheritance down, generation to generation, like a genetic flaw?

ONE

Heavenly Hurt, it gives us—
We can find no scar,
But internal difference,
Where the Meanings, are . . .

—EMILY DICKINSON

Sandy Gjuresko, ignore the "G," was my Meryl Streep in kindergarten.

I'm not talking about envy. Envy I can live with. I'm talking about spending the better part of my life deeming people perfect, then using them as a measuring stick—measuring my insides with their outsides. And I could never, ever, measure up. Sandy Gjuresko might have been quaking, too, but I didn't know it.

I saw a class picture from kindergarten recently. There we are, all my friends dressed in Halloween costumes underneath the arches of Horace C. Hurlbutt School in Weston, Connecticut—one Chinaman, two skeletons, one gypsy, two clowns, one unidentified schoolmate in blackface, and John Kalaskey in drag. There's my good friend, Marcia Cassedy. There's Keith Basso, there's Reid Hiles, there's Faxon Green. Then there's me—sticking up out of the back row taller than everybody including Mrs. Johnson, our teacher, like a Sequoia in a forest of saplings—with my Lone Ranger mask dangling down around my chin, my

Hopalong Cassidy hat, my Tom Mix vest, and my Ralston-Purina Periscope-Decoder ring.

And there in the front row, dressed as Snow White, stands petite little Sandy Gjuresko, ignore the "G," with her perfect bow, perfect smile, perfect braids filing perfectly down her back. Tiny little Sandy Gjuresko wearing a white taffeta dress sprinkled with red roses, a red taffeta train, and a hem so perfectly gathered that her Rinso-White crinoline peeks out perfectly from underneath. She was gorgeous, a sweet kid, and very kind. God, I hated her. Not because of her taffeta dress and taffeta train—although, I'd have died for a dress like that—but because her socks stayed up. She could go eight spins on the merry-go-round, three flips on the monkey bars, five Nadia's on the horizontals, and her socks would still be up. Sandy Gjuresko was like a Timex commercial.

So was Susan Grondona.

Whenever Susan Grondona ran to the bus—which was never, because she was never late—her knee socks stayed up. Mine never did; mine went down into my heel, my arch. I was always clutching my lunch box in one hand and a wad of sock in the other. That's when the unattended sock would notice I was distracted and take a dive.

This is how I judged my life: by the actions of these seemingly perfect beings and the nonaction of their socks. (Although I must admit, my socks were a lot tidier than Marcia Cassedy's.)

Not too long ago I saw a little girl walking down a street in Manhattan and she was livid—one knee sock was heckling her, giving her a hard time. In disgust she stopped in her tracks, pushed both socks to her ankles, and marched on. Just turned her knee socks into anklets. Just said, "Screw it." It never occurred to me to attend to my socks. I was their victim; I had to wait for them to fall, and I never knew at what precise moment that might be. It was like living with Damocles' socks. By the time I rounded first base, I could feel the slow descent—the wad of cloth collecting beneath my arch—and I knew that as I hobbled for second I was doomed.

I was thrilled when cat collars became popular. A cat collar around your right ankle meant you were going steady; a cat collar around your left meant you were available; though by seventh grade, it meant you were desperate. I buckled that cat collar around my left ankle so tight I lost oxygen, but my sock stayed up. Unfortunately the style called for one cat collar, not two. So I still didn't match. That meant my right sock stayed down and my left leg was blue.

I was born Mary Loretta officially—Mariette to some, Aunt Mariette to others—in a New York sanatorium during the summer solstice on June 21, 1940, the same day as the fall of France. It was the year that fraternity brothers swallowed live fish, Russia swallowed Finland, Germany swallowed half of Europe, and my great-uncle Harold vainly swallowed his enmity for Wendell Willkie while stumping for FDR's third term. It was the year that Leon Trotsky was assassinated, a middle-aged horse named Seabiscuit beat out three-year-old upstarts, my husband fled Paris in diapers, and my grandfather urged America to start using underarm deodorant.

Though I spent my baby years as a New Yorker, I don't remember a lot. My brother, Tony, was also born in New York. Ask him.

When I was two we moved to my father's house in Westport at Charcoal Hill. Four years earlier, a divorce settlement had split the proceeds between Dad and his first wife, but by 1942 the house was still on the market. Feeling the pinch of alimony and his two "new" kids, Dad determined to move in and sell it.

Charcoal Hill was a magical place: a stone house nestling in the hills, wild with wisteria, a stream babbling in the back with matching waterfall. Sad to say it quickly sold, clearing just enough for us to move to a rented house on Woodbine Avenue in Larchmont.

Remembrances of my childhood come in splashes—splashes of color, splashes of conversation, feelings, a face, a smell, a tone of voice. Seeing my first blimp. Sitting on Big John's lap while he fed me oysters on the half shell from Grand Central Station. Seeing my mother and Pearl Belchetz emerging from the house with tears streaming down their faces the day Roosevelt died. Stone steps slippery with moss under my feet; cat's eyes growing and shrinking in the light. I remember caressing the cats' fur, grounding myself in their softness. But most of the time—in the darkness of my memory—most of the time, I didn't feel safe.

There were wolves in my curtains in Larchmont. It was hard for my mother to talk me out of it because I knew they were there. They lived just behind the valance, a family of wolves, and they had bright red eyes. As dusk came, I'd lie in bed and stare at them while playing with my navel.

Otherwise, I was the perfect baby. Mom followed a lot of the teachings of Big John; when I was around two—if I got out of bed at night to go to the bathroom—I'd follow up with a semiverbal report. I'd walk into the master bedroom and kiss my mother on the cheek, "Good night, Mom, I love you," toddle around the bed, kiss my father on the cheek, "Good night, Dad, I love you," then walk back to bed. Mom continued the Watson Master Plan: she hated messiness and I stayed clean. I couldn't suck my thumb, I couldn't touch my privates—so I played with my navel until it bled. But the other mothers marveled; Mom beamed. I was perfect.

In the summer of 1945, we moved to Weston, a few miles inland from Westport, into what we called the "big house." Situated on the Newtown Turnpike, the main street of Weston, it was exactly one mile from Cobb's Mill, a marvelous restaurant at the foot of a waterfall that had swans and ducks all over the lawn, all over the pond, and lined like Rockettes on the edge of the falls.

Otherwise, Weston was and is a town without a town, relying on Westport for its village green, stores, newspapers, movie houses. Its unofficial "downtown" is the Weston Town Center, a tiny shopping plaza built out on the Weston Road when I was in high school. It contained the Weston Market, the barbershop, Peter's Spirit Shop where Mom once worked, and the drugstore that had its own little luncheon counter. It's still there, pretty much the same, minus the barbershop. A town with no curbs, no place to hold a parade.

I spent my school years here—in a charming old country house with five bedrooms and five fireplaces upstairs and down. Now a landmark—not because we lived there, but because it was built in 1787 by Joe Something (Mom kind of sloughs off details)—our house was golden. Here's where the memories began to stick. Here's where the tiny kitchen held an old Hotpoint icebox, a linoleum table edged with steel, and chickens that had free access including our favorite, One Gone, who had one eye. Here's where I learned to love wooden floors that creaked and gave with each step, where the windows of original blown glass waved as I walked by, where all the doors had latches. I always knew everyone's whereabouts because of the sound of the latches.

Resting on ten acres, the property had been divided by the owners—the Tates. Our side of the street, five acres. The other side of the street, five acres, where they rented the barns to Mo Percy. Lainie Tate loved coming down to the "renter's house" to have "hartichokes."

Although the house was charming, we only had a few charming pieces of furniture to fill it, so we put the outdoor picnic table in the dining room and friends loaned us a couple of antiques. Dad was convinced that color had an emotional effect, so he painted each room carefully. The kitchen was pale blue and bright red with one of his paintings on the wall: a magnolia in a white vase against the same bright-red background.

I was clothed, I was fed, I was well cared for. But strangely, in most parts of the house, I still didn't feel safe.

I felt safe in the attic. In the center of the deep brown eaves, I'd spend hours alone with my wooden dollhouse, playing out my other life, peripherally aware of a magical old racing oar hanging in the rafters above the beams. It was a life filled with fantasy, interrupted only by "dinner time!"

I felt safe in Dad's studio where he would draw by the hour or take photographs. He was a talented painter and a careful, artistic photographer, sitting us in front of pistachio-green sheets to commemorate our growth—face to face or back to back, holding vases of garden-fresh gladiolas or new generations of cats—each phase of our lives religiously recorded.

I felt safe in my bedroom, a small, second-story cocoon next to my brother's. It was all very feminine, crammed with stuffed animals and dolls, a vanity with a three-sided mirror, and a secret drawer hiding behind its skirt. My front window looked out on three noble maple trees, gold in autumn. My side window framed a rock-stone fence ambling over a hill.

I felt safe at church.

I loved waking up Sunday mornings to go to church when no one else in the family was going, sitting in the wooden pews of the Norfield Congregational Church or singing in the choir (unless I had a solo). Dad was shyly religious; Mom never. She always said mythology was a lot more romantic, beautiful gods sweeping her up to Mt. Olympus. Besides, her father, Big John, had spurned religion. "The idea of Jesus and all that stuff," she'd scoff. "I tell you, I can't buy it."

But Tony didn't feel safe. My brother's proximity to my bedroom was tantalizing, seductive. He was an easy victim on moonlit nights when I was restless and longed for trouble. Since we had adjoining windows over the front porch, it was easy to climb out on my roof, creep along the shingles to his room. While poor Tony was sound asleep, my hunched body would whisper past his large window with the stealth of a robber, the Freddy Krueger of Newtown Turnpike. What are sisters for? It took Amazonian effort to veer left and climb the arched roof, crawling to the less predictable tiny window just above his head. He still remembers the fingernails scratching down the screen, the terror evoked by my primal whispers, "I'll get youuuuuuuuu, Tony; I'll get youuuuuuuuu." He still remembers and can't forgive. What are brothers for? But I remember, too. I remember the feeling of power.

I felt safe at school. Until I didn't.

While we were in Larchmont, Mom had sent me to one of the few Montessori schools in the country. I can't describe it; I just remember loving it—there was a lot of working with hands. It wasn't the teacher's role to correct, to label "right or wrong," so we could explore the classroom and pick and choose what we wanted to work with. My busting from Montessori to a Weston public school was like a riptide. Everything became linear and I became a crazed child. I felt as if I had a vise around my head. The Montessori people had sent a letter urging the school to have me skip kindergarten, but I was denied because of my age.

I was a bully, I was bored, I was a year ahead and hated school. I hated waiting in line for a slide; I hated sharing. Tony wasn't my only victim. I was always the tall one, always falling in love with or beating up tiny little boys.

I began to have trouble learning. Mrs. Johnson remembers me as a good little girl. She says I came to school bedecked with beads and bracelets like Little Lulu, very feminine, very theatrical. That's not what I remember. I remember being more like Sluggo. Once when a boy infuriated me I jumped on him and got him down. A gang of kids gathered round, cheering and shouting, while I straddled him, punching. Then they started to snicker. As a favorite teacher pulled me up, I asked, "Why's everybody laughing?" Somebody said, " 'Cause you've got a hole in your underpants." It obviously had an effect on me because I'm still talking about it.

I don't remember much else about that early schooling. I remember that Johnny Ekkleberry wore bottle-bottom glasses, came up to my chest, and was always asking me to dance. I remember that Mrs. Tarbox, the Gypsy Rose Lee of Horace C. Hurlbutt, wore short-sleeved Ship 'n Shore blouses with little pearl buttons—the round pearl, not the flat—so her blouse kept popping open. She also wore arm bracelets, slip straps that dangled. We'd watch them, taking bets on how far they would drop below sleeve level before she would notice and pull them up. It was hard to concentrate on our *Weekly Readers* as we'd watch the slow descent of her straps while Reid Hiles hummed stripper music, "Bah bump bah, bah bah bump bah . . ."

But school wasn't the only problem.

In the back of the house was the master bedroom where my parents had this wonderful big bed, designed by my dad, painted high-gloss hospital green. The headboard had little cubby holes: a place for a radio, a pull-down desk, a shelf that pulled up and in where you could put pillows. It was a romantic bed, a bed where one pictured '20s and '30s people kind of lying there like Noel and Gertie, a bed that was the center of our home—built up on a platform with two doors underneath, so you could get inside, you could get lost in it. Mom would let me convalesce there, listening to "Lorenzo Jones," when I got sick. "And now smile awhile with Lorenzo Jones and his wife, Belle. Funiculi, Funicula, Funiculi, Funiculaaaa."

Memory distorts, but one memory that keeps coming back about that bed was of an evening in

Connecticut. I was about six, Tony was five, and Mom was kneeling on the floor, giving us our bath. It was an old bathroom: pedestal porcelain sink, oversized tub, stainless-steel faucets. The water was warm, luscious and warm, as she washed it over us with her soft washcloth. I was behind Tony, my legs spread around him, and I remember him looking back at me quizzically. A yellow hue began to surround him. I had peed in the warmth and comfort of the water.

What happened next comes to me like a sped-up black-and-white movie, except that I remember my mother's long, sharp, polished-red fingernails. I remember them in my arm as she grabbed me out of the bathtub. I was naked, still wet, and cold in the fall chill. She dragged me through the hallway, up the stairs, into the master bedroom, and threw me on that green bed. If I could have stopped time, if I could have disappeared, I would have. But I knew where she was going, and now fast motion became slow. Her body left me and went over to her dressing table. She came back slowly with her hairbrush visible, raised, attacking. My screams got lost somewhere in my history, only to emerge, again and again, much later on, when screams could be heard.

The silences began in Larchmont. I went on a playdate ("I'll show you mine if you show me yours") with little Michael down the block. When I told Mom about my experiment, I was greeted with a punishing silence.

In kindergarten, I became a kissin' cousin with my little cousin Wallace. When I told Mom how he kissed, she was silent. In first grade Bruce Bacon and I used to play underneath the porch; it was tight under there. When I told Mom we played post office, she was silent. In second grade

I played Sardines with some boys across the street. There was a tremendous amount of titillation because the person that found you crawled in with you—then bodies would accumulate, all bunched together. When I told Mom about Sardines, she was silent. In third grade there was a slumber party where everyone was running around undressed, jumping up and down on beds, kid stuff. Why I had a driving need to tell her about it, I'll never know. But when I told Mom about the party, she was silent. I don't remember all the incidences; I just remember a chain of confessions—a strange, unnatural, guilt-burdened impulse to confess.

Mom admitted once, "under the influence," that the only way she could control me was to make me feel guilty. In the emptiness that I remember, silence to this day terrifies me.

Early images I have of my mother are from photos in the family album, or of her walking through leaves in the fall, a gardenia in her red-brown hair. She had beautiful hair, combed up on either side, stylish—her own style—never too moneyed, like a Ralph Lauren woman long before Ralph Lauren.

She was very domestic, although she didn't appear to be; she was too skinny. I always felt I was going to harm her if I hugged her too hard. I didn't miss the hugging, engulfing mother until I saw Ethel Waters cradle Julie Harris in *The Member of the Wedding.* I would have loved a fat mother. I would have loved being held by someone bigger than I.

Taking care of a twelve-room house, two kids, and five acres (not that Mom was plowing away), began to take its toll. Deciding she needed a "live-in" housekeeper, Mom went—please tell me why—

to the Newtown Institution for the Alcoholic and brought back Lillian, the toothless wonder. One of the first things Mom did was get her a set of teeth. A frustrated drinker, Lillian was mentally deficient and sexually active. If a house painter was left alone with Lillian, we had to get another house painter.

She called Mom "Mommy." This was fascinating since she was older than my mother and four times as large. She also played the piano. Friends had lent us the most horrible, wonderful, old upright with some of the ivory missing. It resembled one of those cartoon pianos with smiling keys that were always jumping around. Lillian would play "Kitten on the Keys," while we danced around the picnic table in the dining room, filling our lives with this insane spirit. Nothing was tied down, including Lillian.

The morning was my favorite time. The kitchen was old and had settled on a slant, and Lillian never wore underpants. She'd sit on a stool next to the stove, flashing. I would always get down to breakfast first and sit at the formica table with my back to her so Tony had to sit opposite the flash. He could barely eat.

In some ways Lillian became my mom. With Lil, the crazy side, the intense side, was out in the open. She was with us about four years, until she finally drank herself useless. She'd sneak it. "Mommy, Mommy. I had too much to drink, Mommy." I can see her face to this day and I loved her.

But I had no idea the kind of stress Mom was under. Tony and I once asked her to join us while coloring in our frontier coloring book; she squatted down and colored a reddish skin on one of the pioneer ladies. When I said, "It's too red," she got up, ran into the kitchen, and started to cry, uncontrollably.

Drinking was not out of hand yet. It was around, but it wasn't running the house. We were aware of it on days like Thanksgiving, Christmas, big parties, evenings when my mother would curiously disappear. I'd find her in the car out in the garage, or in the bushes, hiding. I'd bring her back inside, but she didn't want to be there.

There was no external struggle that I can remember. The struggles with my mother were internal. Struggles against a powerful force, handed down from my grandfather at an early age. I had recurring witch dreams. One night I woke up, and there was a huge witch in front of me with a green, ugly face. I said, "Go away. GO AWAY!" That one never came back.

The legacy was so clearly passed on.

TWO

Mother love is a dangerous instrument.

—JOHN B. WATSON

My grandfather was the Gary Hart of Baltimore.

Born in Greenville, South Carolina, on January 9, 1878, his mother had a strong hold over him. Excessively religious, she was a strict disciplinarian, preoccupied with sin, sloth, dirt, and the dark.

Where his mother was proud, his father was profane. He loved his whiskey and was gone for weeks at a time, living in the backwoods with Indians and his two Cherokee "wives." When his son was thirteen, he left for good, making John B. even more dependent on his mother.

Big John hated school. At sixteen, when he entered Furman University as a day student, he couldn't wait to get out. But in his senior year, by what he called "some strange streak of luck," when a psychology professor threatened that any student handing in his final exam the wrong way would flunk the course, John B. turned in his test-paper backwards and had to stay another year. There is some conjecture that this early sabotage was caused by an ill mother, a reluctance to leave home, and a struggle with success.

After his mother died, he moved on to the University of Chicago, took his Ph.D. in psychology in 1903, then stayed on at the University, pioneering in animal psychology. Until then, research had been limited to studying trick horses as they pawed to four. Grandfather was the first to fashion hand-built mazes, labyrinths, problem boxes; the first to observe rats in the process of learning. Suitably impressed, the *Nation* reported the results of his findings. Superiors thought him both brilliant and tenacious, a "coming man" in the field of psychology.

Heady with success, it was obviously time for grandfather to turn in another testpaper backwards. So in 1904, John Broadus Watson fell in love with a student, my grandmother.

Her name was Mary Amelia Ickes. Born in Altoona, Pennsylvania, she was the baby sister of Harold Ickes (pronounced with a sneeze) who was famous for many things, not the least of which was being the first Secretary of the Interior who made people aware that there was a Secretary of the Interior. Becoming Administrator of Public Works during Roosevelt's administration, Great-uncle Harold battled private utilities and the press, and exhorted a hesitant America to get into the war.

There were seven little Ickeses. Although they lived near Ickesburg and had their own graveyard, grandmother's family was not well-to-do. Mary Ickes's mother died when she was six; her father died when she was sixteen. So the children were divided up, and Harold and Mary went to live with an aunt who owned a drugstore in Englewood.

Financially strapped, Harold struggled through the University of Chicago, while Mary went to Northwestern. Booted out, however, when boys sent a cold beer up to her room, she transferred to the University of Chicago, where she studied "introductory" psychology with the handsome young Dr. Watson—in a black-black-hair, brown-brown-eyes, mellifluous-voice, promising-future sort of way. Mary Ickes fell in love.

Although she was engaged at the time to a man named Al Something (the people in Mom's memories are all related), Mary daydreamed about the dashing professor and didn't do a "lick of work." All this culminated on examination day when she realized she knew none of the answers. She doodled in her exam book, then proceeded to write a love poem, an ode to John B. Watson, in Palmer-pen flourish. She was at "his black black hair, brown brown eyes" when she heard, "Time's up, pens down, close your booklets!" As he started up the aisle collecting the papers, she froze.

"Miss Ickes, your paper please."

"Oh, well. I . . ."

"What's that in your hand, Miss Ickes?"

He reached out his hand. Reluctantly, she gave it to him.

She had a way with words; all the Ickes' did. (Great-uncle Harold had such a flair, he spat out three volumes of *The Secret Diary of Harold L. Ickes* for Simon & Schuster, coming in at 2,092 pages.) So John B. Watson, flattered and fascinated, began surreptitiously to date his student, Mary Ickes, which was against the rules, society, and God.

Harold got wind of it and sent grandmother

back to Altoona. But when he found out they had already married under fictitious names, he gave a reception instead—although he considered his brother-in-law a "selfish, conceited cad." He wasn't far from wrong. Throughout the secret marriage, the bridegroom had continued to see one Vida Sutton, an old flame who had returned to town.

John B. Watson spent the summer of 1905 at Johns Hopkins in Baltimore continuing his studies, concluding that animals of all intelligence learn behavior by trial and error. That's what it says in the official biography. In actuality, he also spent the summer of 1905 becoming a "papa," far from the prying eyes of University of Chicago confreres. Since my mother's time of arrival was a tad short of a tabloid headline, Dr. Watson didn't want his beloved besmirched or himself beousted. So my mother was born in Baltimore on June 25th, or so they had written on her birth certificate in beautiful hand. She was actually born on June 18th, two weeks too soon (and celebrated the wrong birth date for 32 years).

I'd better clear up something immediately. My mother was born Mary Watson. My grandmother, as previously reported, was born Mary Ickes. So Mom was called Little Mary while her mother was called Big Mary. That worked for a while, until Mom got bigger than Big Mary, who was rather on the small side. So grandfather dubbed my mother "Polly." And that was the end of that. Then my grandmother thought Big Mary sounded like a gun moll. Since growing up in Chicago made her sensitive to that sort of thing, she preferred the corruption of "Rary." Rary stuck.

My uncle, Mom's little brother, was born John Watson. He became Little John to distinguish from Big John. When Little John grew up he shook the moniker, but "Big John" stuck. On Big John.

Moving forward, my father was born Paul Hartley. My brother was born Paul Hartley. That left us with one Paul, one Polly, and one Paulie. Every time someone called our house, three people answered. Paulie got fed up one day and changed his name to Tony. I'm not through.

I was also born a Mary—Mary Loretta Hartley. Dad decided I didn't look like a Mary Loretta (who does?), and I quickly became Mariette. "Ette," of course, coming from the diminutive. Why Dad decided that I deserved a diminutive, I'll never know. To avoid confusion, all monikers will now be used.

My mother is Polly.

My grandmother is Rary.

My grandfather is Big John.

My uncle is Little John.

My father is Paul.

My brother is Tony.

Meanwhile, back at the loop . . .

By 1908, Big John had built quite a future for himself. Wooed by a number of universities, he chose Johns Hopkins, where he was offered a full professorship and some of the finest experimental facilities in the United States. So when Mom was four, the family moved to a typical Maryland brownstone in Baltimore, not far from the old section of Johns Hopkins Hospital.

In 1913, in a series of sold-out lectures at Columbia, John B. Watson launched a hand grenade into psychological circles that lasted for decades.

Unveiling the term "behaviorism," he debunked most of the fundamental theories of his time. He felt that psychologists would make more progress if they ignored "consciousness." Since the concept could not be verified, it held psychology back from acceptance by the scientific community. "Consciousness" was as impossible to prove as the "soul."

Dr. Watson maintained that all behavior was reflex action—stimulus and response. To cry when you left someone you loved was a "conditioned emotional" reflex. Stimulus: the loved one left. Response: the lover cried. And the reflex could be changed.

Psychologists could become social engineers, guiding society "to ways in which the individual may be molded to fit the environment." They could encourage desirable tendencies while suppressing undesirable ones. Grandfather even went so far as to suggest that hardened criminals whose nervous systems were "irredeemably askew" should be "etherized."

Pragmatists, such as John Dewey, were attracted to grandfather's ideas. Behaviorism was a scientific approach to messy emotions. The controversy boiled over into *Life* and other popular magazines. Considered by some a seeker of truth, by others a seeker of spotlights, by 1917 John B. Watson was one of the most successful psychologists in America.

He then turned to the study of man. For years, he had been using Mom and Little John for his experiments. "A baby is more fun to the square inch than all the rats and frogs in creation." But no one had dared experiment with the human infant until Phipps Clinic offered Big John a laboratory where he could bring up children from birth under constant observation. He published his findings in *Psychology from the Standpoint of a Behaviorist* in 1919, making an enormous contribution to the studies of B. F. Skinner, Albert Ellis, and others.

My grandfather concluded that heredity was a minor factor in man's actions. He noted that fear, rage, and love were the driving forces, but reactions to these instincts were learned. Borrowing from Pavlov, he proposed that we use these natural tendencies to "recondition" and control behavior.

His most famous experiment was with "Little Albert." He introduced a white rat to a nine-month-old baby, who showed only curiosity. Then, to create fear, he struck a loud gong whenever the animal was near the child.

> "The infant jumped violently and fell forward burying his face in the mattress. He did not cry, however." The experiment was repeated. Little Albert began to whimper. The gong was struck over and over until "the instant the rat was shown the baby began to cry," and crawled "away so rapidly that he was caught with difficulty before he reached the edge of the mattress."

In subsequent experiments on "Little Albert," Grandfather used a rabbit, a dog, a fur coat, and cotton wool. The results proved that emotional reactions could be conditioned by external stimuli, by the abrupt sound of a gong. Although Grandfather admitted he had some qualms about conditioning a baby to fear an animal, he never got a chance to "recondition" his crawling experiment because the child was adopted. Today, there is a man called Albert walking these mean streets dodging cotton balls and quaking at the sight of Q-Tips.

Huxley shuddered. *Brave New World* was published twelve years later. Orwell followed with *1984*—the climactic sequence involved rats.

It was 1920, and Big John was at the top of the heap. Johns Hopkins, happy with his international reputation, voted him a salary increase; his book was doing well; Harvard was knocking on the door; and he was a sought-after lecturer. Bertrand Russell claimed that John B. Watson had made the greatest contribution to scientific psychology since Aristotle.

Time to turn in another testpaper backwards.

Ironically, while Grandfather was controlling the emotions of a nine-month-old, his were getting out of hand. This time the external stimulus was his young graduate-student assistant from Vassar. He should have hit that gong. He should have been hit with that gong.

Rary knew about Big John's affairs; she knew because Big John had told her. There was a certain Mrs. Esselin from Washington, famed for her red hair. There was that certain Miss Vida Sutton. Then, in the autumn of 1919, Rosalie Rayner arrived in Baltimore to study under Big John at Phipps Clinic. She came from a prominent and wealthy Jewish family—her uncle was Senator Rayner, chairman of the hearings on the *Titanic*.

Once again, Big John fell in love with a student. He was forty-two; Rosalie was nineteen and beautiful. She also had a beautiful car, a Stutz Bearcat, that attracted attention. Because of that car, a hefty section of Baltimore knew about the affair. Rosalie drove them to lunch in it, daily.

Rary got wind of "those two gadding about in that machine." Thinking this crush would go the way of the others, she befriended Rosalie, and invited his lab assistant and her parents to dinner. The families began to spend several evenings a week together, but while Rary was busy befriending, she was also rifling her husband's clothes. One day she found a love letter from Rosalie.

Rary went to New York to consult her brother, John Ickes, about what to do. While she was gone, Leslie Hohlman, a well-known psychiatrist from Phipps, stayed at the house. He and Big John used the twin beds in the master bedroom. And they talked. My mother lay in bed in the next room and overheard the entire conversation. That's when she found out that her father was in love with Rosalie, that they had been shuttling to New York on weekends, that he planned to send the family to Switzerland; and that, after two years, he could then get a no-muss, no-fuss divorce on the grounds of desertion, protecting his job at the university.

Mom heard every word and never forgot it. She was fourteen—only five years younger than Rosalie—and oblivious to any family tension. She had thought she was living in the "happiest, most wonderful family in the world." That night she wrote a letter to Rary warning her of Big John's scheme. Mom had final exams the next day. Pleading illness, she refused to go; she never returned to that school.

The next time the Watsons retired to the Rayner drawing room for coffee, Rary feigned a headache and said she needed to lie down. Instead, she headed straight for Rosalie's bedroom and her bureau, pawed hurriedly through the clothes, and struck gold: fourteen letters that John Broadus Watson had written in his infatuation.

Then she confronted Big John. Then she confronted the Rayners. Warning of the scandal that might ensue, she suggested Rosalie be sent on a grand tour of Europe until it blew over. Albert Rayner agreed, but Rosalie adamantly refused. Her father threatened to disinherit her. Rosalie still refused. My grandparents separated in July of 1920.

By the end of September, a copy of one of the love letters landed in the "in" tray of President Goodnow of Johns Hopkins, and Big John was promptly sacked. Hoping to keep Rosalie's name out of the papers, he readily agreed to the terms of the divorce. But on November 25th, when the hearings were reported on the front page of the *Baltimore Sun,* Rosalie was referred to as "R." Two days later, Rosalie was referred to as "Rosalie." Could "Rayner" be far behind?

That same September, Mom and Little John had been sent off to separate boarding schools. Mom was attending the now-defunct Low-Heywood in Stratford, Connecticut—making up her eighth-grade credits—when a schoolmate said at dinner, "Be sure and look on your bureau, Polly. There's something that will interest you." It was the first headline and the first love letter.

"To Rosalie mine," made most of the newspapers in America, complete with photos. Written in the vernacular of a smitten lab scientist, it went:

> "I have been an awful sinner, I know, and, in a way, so have you. Promise me your heart and body will still be mine. . . . Every cell I have is yours, individually and collectively. I can't be any more yours than if a surgical operation made us one. . . . I could kiss you for twenty-four hours and then find fault with the universe because the days are not longer." [I wish we could] "go to the North Pole where the days

and nights are six months long," [but I'll settle for a weekend in New York.] "Everything will be lovely and we ought to play safe. Still, play we will."

The divorce came through December 24, 1920, and John Broadus Watson married "his Rosalie" ten days later.

The following June, Mom left school for the last time: she barely completed ninth grade. Coming from a background steeped in academia, she harbored this fact like a shameful secret throughout her years; she even kept it from me. She had lost interest in school. She had lost interest in friends. For Mom, 1920 was the turning point. I think she lost interest in life.

Soon after the Baltimore scandal, the president of J. Walter Thompson, one of the most successful advertising agencies in the country, was intrigued by a man who proclaimed he could condition people to buy, sell, and salivate on cue. He invited Big John to join the firm.

Grandfather was fascinated with the psychology of advertising, what makes a buyer buy. Determined to learn, he spent two months selling Yuban in Macy's basement. Mom said, "He sold coffee like nobody ever heard of selling coffee. That good-looking thing with the white apron and the big white hat." He began to notice that items placed near the cash register sold briskly, that customers bought on "impulse." Thus, I have my grandfather to thank when I run the checkout gauntlet of Lifesavers, razor blades, and headlines proclaiming, "Human Bred with Giraffe Has Baby with 3-Foot Neck."

He planted the human animal under his microscope and went to town. Testing smokers blindfolded, he found that only two out of twenty could tell the difference between their brand and others. He coined the term "brand loyalty," and set out to break it. In doing so, he tripped upon "timed obsolescence." Automobiles were mechanically similar, he reasoned. Manufacturers should be encouraged to change design, give them style. And style is what makes everything obsolete before it's unuseable. If Kenmore added fins, we'd be buying a new washing machine every other year.

Testimonials by movie stars and sports figures had been used for years, but Big John thought bigger. He hired the Queen of Spain and the Queen of Romania to hawk Pond's cold cream and give the money to charity. Introduced as a man who had been a professor at Johns Hopkins "who will now give a talk on the care of the teeth," he made one of the first advertising broadcasts, sponsored by Pebeco. In a campaign for Johnson & Johnson's baby powder, he claimed that children should be powdered out of the womb—not just after their bath, but after each diaper change. The mother who used talcum powder was responsible and loving. The mother who didn't was uncaring.

He became vice president of J. Walter Thompson in three years.

But he missed academia terribly. Without a laboratory, he was once again reduced to reconditioning his own children. He and Rosalie had two more boys. Uncle Billy was born in 1921; Uncle Jimmy, two years later. At two and a half, Billy crowded in whenever Big John embraced Rosalie. Sent to Grandmother Rayner's for a month, Billy's strong attachment began to weaken, but Grandfather was determined to wipe out any residue. He reported on Subject "B" in his book, *Behaviorism:*

> When the parents visited the child, they clung together for a considerable time, to see if jealous behavior would occur. He merely ran up and hugged first one and then the other. This test was repeated for four days with the same results. The father, then seeing that the old situation failed to call it out, tried next attacking the mother, striking her on the body and head and shaking her from side to side. She, on her part, simulated crying, but fought back. The youngster stood this for a few minutes, then started in for his father tooth and nail. . . . He cried, kicked, tugged at his father's leg and struck with his hand. Next the father remained passive while the mother attacked him. She inadvertently punched below the belt, causing the father to double up in no simulated way. Nevertheless, the youngster started his attack on his father again. . . . By this time the youngster was genuinely disturbed and the experiment had to be discontinued. The next day, however, no jealous behavior was exhibited when mother and father embraced.

Though Billy and Jimmy adored each other, Big John continued to fixate on his fixation theory. Fearful my uncles would grow mutually dependent, he monitored them. They were not allowed to kiss or fight. Billy once asked if he could shake hands with Jimmy when he was about to be put to bed. Even though Rosalie bootlegged some affection, by the age of three, Jimmy had stomach pains.

As a psychologist, Big John decried the fact

"that there is so little individuality in the world. But, as an advertising man, I rejoice; my bread and butter depend on it." At $70,000 a year, tailor-made suits from Savile Row lined the closets of his beautiful maisonette on Fifth Avenue. In the summer of 1930, he fell in love with forty acres of property in Weston, Connecticut, and built an exquisite estate of fieldstone tucked into the rolling hills of Godfrey Road, just a hop and a skip from where I grew up; we used to have barbecues there.

Mom visited Whippoorwill Farm twice and came to adore Rosalie. They played tennis together, swam together, flirted with the same men. Rosalie loved parties; there were always a few friends from the theatrical world spending the weekend, actresses like Judith Anderson or Helen Menken—whose scandalous play, *The Captive*, landed the cast in night court.

Mom was in heaven; she longed to be an actress. She'd even left Low-Heywood when she was sixteen to attend acting school in Chicago. She'd only been there about a year, however, when she had met and married a handsome Texas law student named Gainer Jones, and moved to Houston.

But the marriage soon became hampered by jealousy. Friends thought it flattering that Gainer called her throughout the day, but Mom knew better. "He's checking up to see if I'm home. Aren't I . . . lucky." (Mom has a habit of delaying a word when she wants to say just the opposite. "He didn't let me out of his sight, which was . . . swell.")

But on those two trips to Weston—away from Gainer's scrutiny—Mom had a ball. She was the youngest in the crowd; the wives all hated her, and the men flocked around. Somewhere along the way, a fellow named Paul Hartley and his wife became a part of Big John's crowd. Although they'd just built the house at Charcoal Hill, it was common knowledge that their marriage was as rocky as the one in Houston. So Mom danced with this stranger named Paul Hartley, while his wife played the piano.

I once asked Mom if she liked him at all that first night. "No, but he liked me, or so he said. But he liked everybody, he was such a playboy. Besides, he was twelve years older, and it was common knowledge that he would never divorce his wife until his daughter was married."

After the glitter of Weston, Mom found it hard to return to Texas. She wanted out because she wanted babies, and Gainer was even jealous of that. He was also having an affair.

So at twenty-nine, thrilled by an invitation to live in Connecticut with Rosalie and Big John, Mom was about to leave Gainer when Big John called from New York. Rosalie was very ill, he said. "She's got the flu." But what was first diagnosed as intestinal flu turned out to be a deadly tropical disease. Rosalie died in agony the next day, June 19, 1936.

Mom fled Houston, rushing to New York to see Big John. "I felt so sorry for him. I don't know why I worried; he was . . . fine. And already involved with Rosalie's best friend, Judith Anderson." Finding it hard dealing with the number of women attending her father, Mom got her own apartment on East Fifty-something and snagged a job at Dorothy Gray Cosmetics, giving facials in their salon on Fifth Avenue. She ate at Big John's almost every night, then spent weekends with him in Connecticut, commuting into New York early

Monday mornings. She had a lot of dates, loved the freedom, but felt adrift. One particular Monday, Mom and Paul Hartley shared a train.

He said, "May I sit beside you?"

"Well, certainly."

"I guess you've heard I've separated?"

"Yes, I've heard."

"Well, I don't suppose you'd have dinner with me some night. I'm a pretty good cook. In fact, I think I'd make a pretty good husband."

After about six or seven dates, he called Mom one morning while she was on the road in some town in the South selling eyeliner, and asked her to marry him. "I want to call you tonight. Where will you be?"

"Greensboro."

That night on the train to Greensboro—curled up, feet aching—she drifted off. Swaying with the curve of the rails, Dad woke her up with a rose and a kiss.

True to his word, Dad waited until his daughter was married in 1938, got a divorce, and "filed his intentions" to marry the next day. The news that "Miss Mary Ickes Watson, daughter of John B. Watson, and niece of Secretary of the Interior Harold Ickes, became Mrs. Paul Hartley at a ceremony in her father's home . . ." made a number of newspapers, including the *New York Journal-American.*

Like the rats and "Little Albert," Mom and her brothers had grown up under a microscope, innocent receptacles of Grandfather's theories, conjectures, and absolutes. They also had the eyes of the world to contend with. And for a while—at least on the surface—they passed muster.

Mom doted on her father, although she admitted he was hard on her brother. Big John didn't like boys much; he preferred the company of women. He only spanked her once and not very hard, but he used to beat "the living daylights" out of his son. Mom always said Little John didn't seem to mind it; then in the same breath she would say, "Little John was the sickly one. Something was always wrong with his stomach."

Billy became a highly respected psychiatrist in New York, fulfilling his father's dream. Ironically, that same Billy, brought up with "minimal fixations," took an overdose of pills in his office in Manhattan but was stopped by Jimmy. His second suicide attempt while in his thirties was successful. Little John, brought up with "minimal fixations," became a deeply religious man but continued to have a queasy stomach and intolerable headaches. Taking about twenty aspirins a day, his stomach went; he died in his early fifties of bleeding ulcers. Uncle Jimmy also spent years with chronic stomach problems but, after intensive analysis, is alive and doing very well. My mother, brought up with "minimal fixations," attempted suicide over and over and over and over.

THREE

"Don't you know that drinking is a slow death?"

"So who's in a hurry?"

—ROBERT BENCHLEY'S RESPONSE TO F. SCOTT FITZGERALD

My son, Sean, got into advertising at the tender age of three when he was in bed watching a cartoon with Patrick, cradled in the crook of Patrick's arm. Pat looked down at his young son's face, bathed in the soft glow of the television screen, and was so overtaken by a wave of emotion that he said, "Oh Sean, I love you so much."

Without taking his eyes off the screen, Sean replied, "Thank you, PaineWebber."

Not surprising. Advertising's in his blood. My grandfather was in advertising; my husband was in advertising; even my father went into advertising.

Dad summed up his career, thencing himself through his Harvard reunion booklet:

> My first job after graduation was in the export-import business. This lasted two years. Thence a few years of skittering about including silver fox raising in New Hampshire. I ended up in the advertising business with N. W. Ayer & Son. Thence, to BBD&O in NY. Thence, to Newell-Emmett Company and Cunningham &

Walsh, after they absorbed the former. Thence, to retirement at sixty and into art and writing. I have painted off and on for many years, self-taught.

That's what it said in his *official biography*. In reality, after graduating in 1918, he married his first wife, hastily, and became a father, just as hastily.

He served his advertising apprenticeship at N. W. Ayer & Son in Philadelphia in the mid-twenties. Then had a brief stint as a cub with Batten, Barton, Durstine & Osborne in New York around 1930 before joining the small Madison Avenue firm of Newell-Emmett around 1934. The agency had its biggest account, Chesterfield, long before it was socially acceptable for women to smoke.

While consumers were adding halitosis, acidosis, athlete's feet, and B.O. to their list of concerns, Madison Avenue was replacing Wall Street in the minds of hotshot Ivy League grads. And the pay was excellent. A job with Young & Rubicam was instant status.

When we moved to Weston, Dad was still working for Newell-Emmett, which had been swallowed up in a spate of postwar advertising mergers by Cunningham & Walsh. Like a movie studio, an advertising agency was as good as its stable of stars. With Cunningham & Walsh, it was Texaco, Western Electric, Jaguar, the Yellow Pages, and Pepsi-Cola. Dad helped design the Pepsi script logo that was used for decades.

By now he was an account executive. I didn't know what that meant. Mom explained, "It means you have to kiss their ass. It means you have to drink with them and go on trips with them and travel back into New York after traveling from New York for dinner with them. It means you have to clean up after them, pamper them, change their diapers, and go to bed with them." From everything I know about advertising in the forties, she wasn't far from wrong. One industry definition was "Yes, sir. No, sir. Ulcer."

Returning once from a dinner with Pepsi executives, Mom was absolutely put out. "First they served us Pepsi-Cola for cocktails, then we had Pepsi-Cola for our wine drink, then we had ham basted in Pepsi-Cola. Well, I never!" (Mom would really say that, "Well, I never . . ." No one said, "Well, I never . . ." the way Mom did.) "It was the worst dinner I ever attended. They all sat around and . . . Well, I never . . ."

Dad had another account for Beech-Nut bacon with a man named Foote. Not Emerson Foote of Foote, Cone & Belding, but Simon Foote of Foote, Foote, Foote & Foote. At least that's what we called him. Fascinated by the long handles on advertising firms (Fred Allen once joked that Batten, Barton, Durstine & Osborne sounded like someone dragging a trunk down a short flight of stairs), we'd puff one cheek while hitting the "T"s, sending ourselves into gales of laughter with: phfft, phfft, phfft, and phfft. Simon Foote was always dragging Dad to Cuba with him. I asked Mom if they went fishing.

"Foote? He just goes drinking."

The suburbs continued to crawl outward along the train lines: Cos Cob, Riverside, away from New York at a faster pace. Advertising helped promote the image of the country gentleman. Americans went Anglo, re-creating half-Tudor houses and train stations all along the Eastern corridor. People dressed as if they were riding to hounds. Brooks Brothers had a run on brogues, Harris tweeds, and Wembley ties. Scarsdale resembled Stratford-on-Avon and Larchmont looked like the Cotswolds.

"Country" clubs sprang up: golf, yacht, tennis; everyone ate club sandwiches. Dad continued his love of guns and was a founding member of the Weston Gun Club, Mom learned tennis at the Weston Field Club, and Big John rode to hounds at the Weston Hunt Club.

Developers came in to quaint it up: village greens, stone cottages; every brook had its swan. And the station wagon was exactly that. A wagon that waited at the station. In the forties came the "woodie"—the wagon with side-wood paneling. I remember fifteen to twenty woodies lined up at the train station at 5:31 waiting for Dads. Each contained two children, one wife, and one dog. All of them in tweed.

Dad's drinking began a slow but steady escalation when he began the Westport-New York commute around 1946.

He started commuting the same year *The Hucksters* exploded onto the bestseller list. The talk of Madison Avenue and our dinner table, the book painted a greedy and manipulative picture of the industry. It concerned a dignified war widow, played in the movie by Deborah Kerr, huckstered into doing a testimonial for charity, shades of Big John and Pond's. The book sat on the bestseller lists for eighteen weeks while the romantic occupation took a dive.

Once a day, five days a week, Dad boarded the New York, New Haven, and Hartford. He learned to read a newspaper folded into quarters with the best of them, spending the next hour reading or dozing to the rhythms, while the conductors underlined the signs as they rolled past: "DARien! STAMford! GREENwich! MAmaroneck! LARCHmont! NEW Rochelle! GREAT Neck! Grannnnnnnd Cennntralll Staaaaaationn! Everybody off!" Debarking, he joined one of the tributaries that merged into the great hall of Grand Central Station. From there it was only a short block to Madison Avenue.

But he was born too late. He had missed the great days of the luxury railroad cars. The New York, New Haven, and Hartford had specialized in boiled Maine lobster and Cotuit oysters served in the splendor of mahogany and brass fittings. Earlier cars had indirect lighting and cooled air. By the time Dad started commuting, there was one meager fan that seldom worked attached to the front wall of each car.

When the Connecticut Turnpike opened in 1958, the car became king, and a generation of commuters was consigned to history. Maintenance cutbacks meant that the 5:15 became the 10:52, and commuters would arrive at that Friday night dinner party in time for Saturday's breakfast. Not a total loss. There was a good chance a lot of the partygoers would still be there. Drinking.

As I look back on it, I guess Dad was pretty high every time he came home from New York. Advertising men were not only famed for their martini lunch; they were also famed for infiltrating the bar car on the infamous 5:31, the commuter special, the traveling cocktail lounge. Events in the history of the iron horse had been transposed. Long Island farmers once stoned the first locomotives; now the only things stoned were the passengers.

So Dad would arrive home slightly primed, and

we'd be waiting at the station. We looked forward to having him come home from New York. My brother and I would get in our pajamas, climb into the car and sing, "Here comes my daddy now—hey pop, hey pop, hey pop." Mom would be all dressed up with that gardenia in her hair, waiting for their first drink together. Subtract the twenty minutes from the train to our house, and the cocktails would start after six. But you didn't know he was tight; he held it well. Mom was the one who didn't.

I think Mom started as a buddy drinker. I think a lot of women do. She drank with her first husband in Texas; she drank with Dad, with Big John, with the crowd. But Mom was not a good drinker, ever. Two drinks and she was over. She didn't know it, but she was.

Weston, at that time, was a hard-drinking community, and no one thought anything of it. Drinking was a part of living. Romanticized in advertising, books, and movies, getting blotto on the 5:31 was a major source of humor for *New Yorker* cartoons and Benchley briefs. "GREENwich! STAMford! SOBER UP for WESTport and SAUGAtuck!" The Algonquin Round Table of the thirties was under the table by the forties. Beer was for factory workers; wine was for dinner. The real creative artist drank martinis, manhattans, or scotch, neat.

When prohibition was over and you could buy "likker" that also tasted good, the social pendulum swung widely to the "wets." Drinking not only became acceptable; those who didn't were highly suspect. Teetotal could keep you off the party list. Especially in Weston.

For a while people drank nicely: a couple of cocktails before dinner, a little wine during, a smart liquor after. Nobody got drunk. That came later at the big weekend parties. Mom says she used to drink more at parties because they made her nervous; she thought she'd be more social. "God knows, I was social enough. I don't know why I thought I needed to get drunk. But people who didn't drink, for God's sake, were bores." She once described one of my father's many bosses: "I loved that guy; he was a good old drunk. His wife was a real alcoholic." "Good old drunk" was a sincere compliment. Trophies went to the sport who held it the most. Big John usually won. Since he loved his bourbon, he'd line his stomach with a pint of Nujol mineral oil before he went to a party. Others ate half a pound of butter.

There were a lot of artists, writers, and advertising men in Weston and Westport at that time: Robert Lawson, Hugh Lofting, Hardie Gramatky, James Daugherty, Wood Cowan, James Montgomery Flagg, Van Wyck Brooks, A. E. Hotchner, Martha Raye, Max Shulman, Johnny Held, and Fred and Ethel Mertz. (They had followed Lucy Ricardo when she moved to a television Westport in the late fifties.) I went to school with the daughter of "This is Douglas Edwards and the News"; the Lindberghs once lived on Long Lots Road.

Mom and Dad were in the thick of this—mixing with Big John's crowd, their own crowd. They loved to entertain, and Dad was an excellent cook. I loved to see him outside by the grill with his apron on, rustling up one of his "Hishity-hash and Hell-fire Stews." They were never alike and always delicious. He made great salads, prepared steaks and roast beef beautifully, and was the best lobster chef in the world. He would charcoal-broil them—lots of butter, lots of lemon. No matter how long they stayed on the grill, they were never overcooked—another important consideration when dealing with late trains. Smart hosts knew how to stretch the cocktail hour into three.

Tony and I used to sit at the top of the stairs at our house, listening as the parties got louder and louder and more and more raucous, everyone talking of Taft and Dewey. Mom and Dad had a lot of friends, mostly couples, mostly moneyed—the Vernums, the Snaiths. Bill Snaith was the head of Raymond Loewy, a huge industrial design firm that, among other things, redesigned the famous luxury train, the "Broadway Limited," and our Studebaker.

We were hardly rich, but we were hardly poor. That was what was so wonderful about Weston. It didn't matter whether you had a dime. If you were interesting, you were accepted. Your invitation to dinner was witty repartee. And what better way to ensure wit than by false courage? Two martinis before entrance, skip the hors d'oeuvres.

But there was no stability. Advertising men knew they could be fired if they didn't come up with the creative goods, toady to the client, or please the boss. It was common knowledge that an advertising career meant changing jobs every three or four years.

It has always fascinated me that those who need stability are the creative types, and those who live with instability are the creative types. Actors deal with it on a daily basis. I sometimes wonder if the average worker could bear to go job-hunting forty or fifty times a year for the rest of his life, facing personal rejection on looks, talent, personality, reputation—earned or otherwise.

But Dad was one of the luckier ones. For fifteen years he managed to hang on at Cunningham & Walsh. Until I was nine. Until the drinking got worse.

FOUR

"Are we there yet?"

—A YOUNG DAMSEL IN DISTRESS

I married my grandfather; I figured it out.

Patrick Boyriven is the only person I know who doesn't have to brake for a hot dog or go to the bathroom while driving from California to Connecticut. If my husband had his way, he would never eat or pee. Nor would we. The rest of us would be consigned to riding along, waiting to see who would break first, who would be the first to say, "Ahhhh, Dad."

When the children were small and their bladders were smaller, vacation driving was sheer hell. We'd all pile into the van: Patrick and I in front, Sean and Justine in back, Daisy the dog in the caboose. Marta and José, our long-ago housekeepers, would stand in the carport, waving. Then we'd perform a ritual called "Leaving the Driveway."

I have friends who've been known to bring books.

Just for the driveway.

Patrick would start up the van; I'd sort out the maps. He'd back out the driveway; I'd remember the sandwiches, "Oops!" Patrick would turn off the motor. I'd rush out of the van, past a waving Marta and José. If I leapt out, Justine invariably leapt out, "I will be right back," and shadowed me into the house. When we returned, Patrick would start the motor.

"What's wrong with your foot, Sean?"

"It's my new tennis shoes."

"Don't they fit?"

"They hurt, but I'll get over it."

Patrick would turn off the motor. I'd rush into the house past a waving Marta and José; Justine would follow. I'd clean Sean's room, then return with Justine and his other tennis shoes. Patrick would start the motor.

"Oops, forgot my curlers!" I'd get out; Justine would follow. Marta would be on automatic wave; José had returned to his gardening. Patrick would turn off the motor, then look at Sean's reflection in the rearview mirror, "Well, today we have our task cut off for us." (Patrick is French and has a tendency to lose control, mostly of his English, when he's upset.) I'd hem a skirt, then return with Justine.

At this point, Daisy would make a desperate break for freedom. I don't think this had anything to do with her Kal Kan; I think Daisy hated waiting. I'd get out; Patrick would turn off the motor. (Patrick didn't have to turn off the motor. Patrick turned off the motor to make a point.) When I'd return, Patrick would put the key in the ignition. The motor'd start, dripping with sarcasm. Marta would wave with renewed enthusiasm. Using the other arm.

We'd finally peel down the driveway, tear onto the freeway, while Patrick muttered "hass-ole" at every car between us and our destination. (I must admit there may be another side to this story. But that's Patrick's problem. Let Patrick write his own book.)

There we'd sit, hostages to Pat's prodigious bladder, feeling every bump, every pothole, egging Justine to ask every ten miles, "Are we there yet?" to soften him up. Bouncing along together, *pat*riarchal prisoners, watching the towns flicker by: Long Beach, Azuza, San Bernadino, Riverside. Once into the desert, our hopes for a gas station would dwindle as the towns no longer flickered; they rarely blinked. Hysperia. Victorville. Needles. Kingman.

I don't know why having to go to the bathroom turns sane people giddy, but within an hour, we'd begin to sing. We'd start with a subtle medley: "Moon River," "Cruising Down the River," "Climb every mountain, ford every streeeem." That wouldn't do it. Patrick would just ignore us—his foot glued to the accelerator. We'd try a new tack: "Those April showers, may come your way," ease into, "Raindrops keep falling on your head," then Sean would take it home with a spirited, "Baby, the rain must fall." That wouldn't do it. Patrick would feign indifference. Past Barstow, past Two Guns, past Flagstaff, Arizona, don't forget Winona . . .

If I felt Pat's lecture brewing, I'd signal the kids by breaking into something innocuous like "I loves you, Porgy." Then we'd sing a nice rendition of "Bess, you is my woman now—you is, you is." Past Albuquerque, past Wagon Mound, until the pain made us giddier; then we'd introduce the plaintive: "Let me go. Let me go. I gotta go, lover." Around Santa Fe I'd run out of hints and be forced to lay it on the line, "Hi diddle de dee, I really have to pee." That wouldn't do it, either.

So, on the same theory that mothers should lose

at all board games, marbles, and darts, I'd finally raise my hand and say, "Hey Pat, you're gonna kill me, but I'm serious; I've really gotta go." Call me Stella Dallas.

Pat would finally pull into a gas station; we'd all bail out of the side of the van and race for the bathrooms. We didn't race, actually, we waddled—in a sort of duck walk—legs crossed, knees clamped. Waddling to the back of the gas station, wrong side. Waddling to the right side, locked. Seeking the keeper of the key, little caring that the key usually shared a key chain with a small radiator.

The first stop would elicit only Gallic mutterings, what we call frog talk, as Pat drove down the exit ramp. But if it happened again within the next four hours—even though we might be traveling with my mother whose bladder is about as substantial as a colander—the lecture would start. Anyone moaning, fainting, or caught eating uncooked pasta was reminded that he would never have made it through the battle of Algiers. Patrick was in the battle of Algiers. Philosophically akin to Sean's karate instructor (see next chapter), Patrick's been preparing his children for the battle of Algiers since birth.

To Patrick, exercising natural functions only proves one thing: you're a sissy. People should be disciplined, tough. They should be able to survive for a week without having to cater to base bodily needs.

Once Patrick started his lecture, once one of us had the temerity to show our true colors—"Hey, Dad, I'm turning yellow"—it went on and on. He'd start in Colorado, "You Americans are so soft. How do you expect to get through the Third World War? If there was a Third World War on your premises, there is no way that you could win it." And I'd say—while barreling captively down the Kansas interstate—"I don't understand, Pat. How can not peeing be practice for the Third World War? Hell, even in the French resistance, I'll bet they peed in the trenches."

Years later, when Pat and I had to pack up the family and move everything from West to East to do *The Morning Program,* he offered to drive the van cross country. Fine. He also offered to take the whole family along to save on airfare, but to a man we said, "Uh-uh." We took a pass. Let someone else cross his legs cross country.

When I was a child some of my happiest memories involved our vacations. We summered twice in New Hampshire at Little Squam Lake where Dad had raised silver foxes. That first year, when I was eight, Mom taught me how to swim. She had very strong hands that guided me, very lovingly. She was less afraid of touching in the water. She was also wonderful when I was sick. Anything else, the relationship was muddy, but she wasn't afraid of mothering when I was sick.

But Dad was always protective, a tiger father, with a wonderful voice and a broken nose, broken while boxing at Harvard. Mom thought he looked like Paul Lucas. I thought he looked like F. Scott Fitzgerald. He preferred Hemingway—the artist, the boxer, the hunter, the gun collector. I think, in many ways, Hemingway was his god. In later years, Dad grew a beard, asking us if he looked like him.

I loved him in his red-and-black wool shirt, his pipe, and his baggy pants. I loved the romance about him, the masculinity, the hair on his arms, the hair on his hands. More than anything, I loved watching him draw, watching those hands. Dad was a pretty prolific painter. He wrote a book on how to paint, had it endorsed by some friends—a galaxy of successful commercial artists that included Albert Dorne, Everett Shinn, Stevan Dohanos, and Norman Rockwell—then sold it to Harper & Row.

Just before the second summer, Margaret Brister wrote an article about the book for Westport's *Town Crier,* with a terrific picture of Dad—sketch pad in one hand, cat in the other.

> There is undeniably something contagious in the artistic atmosphere that dominates the life of Westport. About a year ago I was discussing this very topic with a group of friends, and . . . expressed a frustrated yen to paint but how, I wanted to know, would I ever begin. . . .
>
> The answer was swift and to the point, and it came from pretty Polly Hartley: "You just wait until Paul's book comes out! It'll tell you everything you want and need to know—and I mean everything!"
>
> Twelve months later . . . "Paul's book" came to me in the mail. . . . It is called appropriately, *How to Paint.* . . .
>
> "How to Find Spare Time" would not be remiss as a biographical title for the author. For Paul Hartley is a busy advertising executive five days a week and an artist, gardener, and much-sought after party guest on weekends, with no visible time for writing.
>
> Decidedly visible and an unbeatable asset in Mr. Hartley's crowded life are his three beautiful red-heads—his wife, Polly, eight-year-old daughter, Mariette, and seven-year-old son, Tony. With a friendly brown poodle named

"Pi," a lustrous black cat as yet unnamed, and good-natured "Lil" as major domo of the household, the Hartleys live in high-geared, happy contentment in their sprawling white home on the Weston road.

Mr. Hartley, an amiable, handsome man of vigorous energy and exuberant wit, has had an unusually checkered and adventurous career. At various times he has been a farm-hand, professional cook, prize fighter, sailor, insurance salesman, professional artist—and even a hobo.

His art, outside of his training at Harvard, has been self-taught. He has sold several portraits, and many paintings in his own established style and theme—that of rugged agricultural Americana based largely on farm subjects of his native Ozarks.

The indefatigable Mr. Hartley believes that everyone has the urge for self-expression, and that painting is by far the most relaxing and engaging of avocations. To use his own picturesque words, "Painting is violently and pleasantly habit-forming." On second thought so is knowing Paul Hartley.

Contrary to Margaret Brister's glowing assessment, Dad was in rough shape. That second summer at Little Squam Lake—when I was about nine—is burned into my memory.

Dad was too shaky to drive, so Mom drove us up. We all piled into the Studebaker—including Pi, our chocolate-brown poodle, given to us by composer Richard "The Hills Are Alive" Rodgers who lived over on Hull Farms Road—and for the next 300 miles, the backseat unnerved the front seat with "I Spy," reading Burma-Shave signs all the way to Lottie D. Fletcher's Cabins.

We owed our Studebaker to Bill Snaith and Dad's loyalty. Our second Studebaker—in the early fifties—was beautiful, but having that '46 Studebaker was like having a brother named "Mervyn" that you had to defend on the playground. Designed by Bill's firm, it was nicknamed the "coming or going" car, because the trunk looked like the hood and the hood looked like the trunk and all four fenders looked the same.

The first time we pulled into a gas station, the attendant asked, "Which way ya headed?" When Tony and I chorused, "Little Squam Lake!" the attendant said, "Coulda fooled me."

The second time we pulled into a gas station and the attendant asked, "Which way ya headed?" Tony and I began to catch on. Every gas station attendant from Mashapaug to East Holderness joked, "Which way ya headed?" then would laugh heartily, tickled by his *mal mot.*

We had only been at Little Squam Lake a day or so when "Foote, Foote, Foote himself" called Dad and told him to come back to New York immediately. No more than that, no reason why, so we put Dad on a train and continued our vacation.

It rained Monday, Tuesday, Wednesday, Thursday, Friday, Saturday, and Sunday.

Poor Mom. What does a mother do alone on a lake with two exuberant kids, one exuberant dog, all with the energy of an Electrolux, stuck inside a ten-by-twelve cabin with woodburning stove and plaid pullout? She watches her darlings dress up and put on shows, that's what. And, boy, did we put on shows: camp shows, magic shows, musicals, jamborees. We put on matinees, evening performances, twilight double headers, revivals, revived our revivals. Mom oohed and aahed until she was oooohed out. She laughed at nine-year-old humor, and the more she laughed the more the nine-year-old repeated the performance. All those years, I thought she loved it. She later admitted she was ready to run screaming into the arms of Lottie D. Fletcher. If there had been a Lottie D. Fletcher.

We went swimming in the rain, getting scratched when we'd dive under Pi as he dogpaddled across the pond. We picked blueberries in the rain; then Mom cooked blueberry pancakes while we put on the early show.

"Mom, look at me!"

"Ooh, yes, Mariette. That's wonderful."

"Mom, look at me!"

"Aah, yes, Tony. That's grand."

Snug in our cabin, rain on the roof. All was right with our world.

But when Dad arrived in New York, Foote advised him he was withdrawing his account. When a major client leaves an agency, account executives take the heat. Dad was summoned into John B. Cunningham's office and fired. Why he lost the account nobody seems to know. Mom suspected drinking, but as she says, "They all drank."

And so, on a hot summer day, Dad took his last commute from Manhattan to Westport, arriving home to an empty house, while Mom continued to ooh and aah in our small little cabin—sensing he'd been fired but keeping it from us—determined not to spoil our vacation.

Years later, however, while watching the movie *On Golden Pond* I looked at the shape of the lake, the color of the water and said, "God, I know that water; I know those rocks." It brought on such a strain of sadness. It turned out to be Little Squam Lake.

FIVE

"Jake, for God's sake! Get your eye on the ball and your hands out of your pants."

—BLEACHER EXHORTATION FROM A SIX-YEAR-OLD SOCCER PLAYER'S MOTHER

Justine took up everything when she was little: gymnastics, ballet, acting, tennis, tap. She wore her tap shoes everywhere, even to church, clicking down the aisle at Easter.

Sean took up soccer, then karate. The day of his first lesson I was halfway out the door—on my way to Justine's glassblowing class—when I looked back fondly at my son. There he was decked out in white lounging pajamas, all of five, in a group of twelve. After they'd done a couple of combat exercises, the instructor—kind of a stud, kind of a Chuck Norris—had ordered the dinky dozen to do twenty push-ups; then lined them up and said:

"Okay, good work. Who's tired? Anybody tired?" He went to the first boy. "You tired?"

"No, sir."

He went to the second boy, "You tired?"

"No, sir."

He went to the third boy, "You tired?"

"No, sir."

He arrived at Sean, "You tired?"

"Yah, I really am."

Chuck Norris pounced with glee, "Hey, you're not tired! In fact, none of you are tired! Twenty more push-ups!" The whole class groaned, got down on the mats, and pumped their collective elbows while he paced, "In combat, warriors must never show the enemy they're fatigued; that's the first sign of defeat. Got it? Now, who's tired? You tired?"

"No, sir."

"You tired?"

"No, sir."

"You tired?"

Now I had spent an inordinate amount of time teaching Sean to be honest about his feelings. Unfortunately, all my work was paying off. I winced as Sean repeated:

"Yah, I really am."

Chuck Norris was dumbfounded. "What would you have done in the middle of Nam, boy? Walk up to the enemy and say, 'I'm tired?' You're not tired. In fact, none of you are tired. Twenty more push-ups." The whole class groaned, got down on the mats, and did twenty more push-ups.

"Now, who's tired? You tired?"

"No, sir."

"You tired?"

"No, sir."

"You tired?"

Eleven heads whiplashed Sean's way, their eyes like slits.

I broke into a coughing spasm to get his attention. I waved my arms; I fanned my face. I stood there helplessly mouthing dictums from the doorway—"Just say no"—but he answered:

"Yah, I really am."

Chuck Norris was incredulous. "Do you know

what you're doing to the rest of your troop here, Boyriven?"

Sean didn't answer.

"You're really that tired?"

Sean didn't answer.

"Well, if you're so tired, make like a cockroach."

Sean didn't move.

"You know what a cockroach is?"

That's when I knew he was doomed. No self-respecting kid in the middle of affluent Los Angeles knew what a cockroach was, and I had failed to teach him. Sean shook his head.

"Lie down on your back."

Sean did.

"Raise your hands and feet in the air."

Sean did.

That's the way I left him. I left my only begotten son with his hands and feet in the air, practicing to be a cockroach for when he grew up.

Most of my childhood centered around practicing. I loved to practice; I lived to practice. The more compulsive, the better. I practiced diving at the Weston Field Club. I practiced swimming, I practiced ice-skating. I wanted to be an Olympic star—and genuinely thought I would be—because when the pond was frozen, I would race and beat all the men. (I realized later that it was usually on Sunday afternoon when all the fathers were drunk and wearing hockey skates. I was sober and wearing figure skates, so I could get a good edge and race in a straight line.)

I started piano lessons at six, taking them from a man named George Hendricks, who had tobacco stains all over his fingers. No one warned me that I'd have to practice by myself, so I lost interest fast. Mom got fed up, accused me of not practicing, and threatened me with "no more lessons." That did it. I became Emile Zola's cause in *J'Accuse.* Mariette Dreyfus. It became life-and-death that I prove to Mom she was wrong. I'd crawl out of bed at three in the morning, sneak down to the piano, light a candle, and compose silently, writing down the notes. I felt like Mozart working to pay the rent.

Then I took up the cello; Tony took up the tuba. Once a week, we'd stand at the bus stop on the Newtown Turnpike. Me with my cello; Tony with his tuba. I'd watch this little yellow school bus jauntily bouncing along, then it would get a glimpse of Tony and me at the next stop and do a squealing-brake take. How do you get two kids, a cello, and a tuba on a school bus without taking up seventeen seats?

No one warned me that I'd have to practice by myself, so I lost interest fast. Then one day, Mom accused me of not practicing. I began to practice that cello two-to-four hours a night, compulsively. Until the night I was practicing in celebrated cello pose: my legs spread-eagle, wrapped around that cello, when Dad walked by and observed casually, "Isn't that stretching a good thing too far?" I got so embarrassed, I stopped playing. If I'd known it was an old risqué joke, I'd probably still be playing the cello. I wouldn't be making a silly ass of myself on morning programs; I'd be making a respectable ass of myself at Carnegie Hall.

Shortly after that, Mom pulled Faxon Green and me out of school and took us to Westport to see *The Red Shoes.* I walked right out of that Main Street movie house and went into ballet. I was taught by a man named George Voladine who had a dance studio on Wilton Road and presented his troupe to the community once a year in a "Ballet Miniature." He used to carry a ruler with him, threatening to hit me on the knees if I didn't *plier* right. For a budding martyr like me, he was perfect.

I begged Mom to buy me red shoes and she did. Thank God we didn't live near a train. Remember what happened to the girl with the red shoes? When she puts them on, she can't stop dancing—obsessively, compulsively dancing—until she dances right in front of a train. Tragedy is enormously attractive when you're eight.

When I came out of a movie theater, I was the leading lady until I washed. After seeing *For Whom the Bell Tolls,* I was Ingrid Bergman and my hair was very short. It stayed short until the following Saturday when I saw Barbara Stanwyck in *Cattle Queen of Montana.* Then I had gray at the temples. I looked a little one-dimensional after *Snow White.* I wanted to dance like Moira Shearer, sing like Rosa Ponselle, dance with Gene Kelly, and live in sin with Gary Cooper.

I always wanted to be Ingrid Bergman, even with the Senate shaking their collective finger; besides, she was a quarter-inch taller than I was. So was Kay Kendall. Oh, but the one I really wanted to be was Deborah Kerr. She always kept loveliness about her. I never felt her career had any compulsion, nothing strident; it just happened, gently. She sat in her perfectly appointed English estate reading *Swann's Way* until Hollywood called with an offer that she reluctantly agreed to, gently. Little did I know that my life would cross paths with Miss Kerr, or various parts of her, over and over again.

Mostly, I wanted to be Karen of the red shoes. I did ballet concerts with Nadia Westmore, who was little and Italian and wore tutus, and always played the princess who was saved by the handsome prince. I was big and a Wasp and always played the caveman. There was Nadia, on her little toes—peep, peep, peep; then I'd enter—boom, boom, boom. I wore my red shoes and hated her a lot.

Then one day, Mom accused me of not practicing. So I went out and found a stick, nailed it between two tree trunks, and practiced on my ballet bar in the middle of winter. I'd *plier* and *pas du seul* for hours, while fantasizing my reentry into the kitchen, hobbling on frozen bleeding stumps. Martyrdom was/is my specialty.

When I was about eleven, Mom took me to see a touring production of *Jack and the Beanstalk* starring children my age, fourth-fifth graders, at the Bedford Elementary School. It was incredible. I turned toward her and whispered, "I have to do this." She winced—it was a fourteen-mile drive to rehearsals every three days—but went along. So I joined Claire Oleson's Silver Nutmeg Theatre Company, leading off with the part of the Cook in her White Barn production of *Alice in Wonderland.*

The rehearsals were rugged and lasted for weeks, but that didn't bother me because this time I was practicing *with* people, not sitting up alone at night like Mozart, watching tapers drip. I was in heaven.

The production was beautifully designed by one of the men from the Famous Artists School. They had built a gingerbread cottage on rollers to be used for the entrance of the Cook and the Duchess with the Pig. The house would be wheeled out by an unseen stagehand to center stage while the Duchess with the Pig and I walked along behind it, hiding until our entrance. Then I'd burst through the front door, clanking all of my pots and pans, throw them down, scream and yell, followed by the Duchess with the Pig. A wonderful rowdy debut.

Opening night went beautifully. Right up to the moment when they pushed out the gingerbread cottage. I couldn't move. Standing beside me was one of the Famous Artists, a man named Dave Poor.

I said, "I can't move."

"But you have to. I have to wheel out the house."

I said, "I can't move."

Poor Dave Poor. He just stood there, a little paralyzed himself. Then, without warning, he pushed out the house, giving me a simultaneous nudge that sent me reeling onstage behind it. There was no going back. As the house went rumbling on stage, I had to rumble with it. It reached center stage and came to an ominous halt. The audience gave the gingerbread cottage an entrance round, then waited. I looked everywhere for an exit. Twenty yards of open air stage right; twenty yards of open air stage left. And the wings were filled with a mob of motioning fists—stagehands, cast members, Claire Oleson. The Duchess gave another nudge, I plunged through that center stage door and . . .

When I saw that audience, when I felt that darkness, there was a feeling of being home. I still have that feeling in churches. There was a feeling of never, ever, wanting to leave.

And, on top of that, I had something new to practice.

I'd do my lines in fields, away from the house, so no one could hear me. I'd walk through the woods and declaim on rock fences. Then one day, Mom accused me of not practicing. I stormed into the woods, stood on a rock fence and worked my lines for hours. When I finally thought I had been sacrificial enough, I looked down and found myself covered with ants.

I always wanted to play Alice; I never did. Judy Scottwood played Alice. When we went on tour to schools throughout Connecticut, I was promoted from Cook to Caterpillar. You know the one in Disney's version: "Whoooo arrre yoooooou???" I sat on a mushroom playing with a balloon that represented a dew drop. One night, my scene newly over, I was still sitting on my mushroom, holding my balloon, when someone handed me another balloon. Before I knew it, *Alice in Wonderland* became a play about balloons. The more the audience laughed, the higher I tossed the balloon. It was during the trial scene, so everyone was supposed to be watching Judy Scottwood. They weren't.

As I came offstage, delighted by my comedic skills, Claire Oleson greeted me with, "Don't you ever do that again!" There followed a ten-minute lecture on the ethics of "upstaging." Attention can be easily, too easily, diverted from the main action on stage with one small motion and has been one of the leading causes of homicide backstage. I was sorry to hear that because I'd had a wonderful time. But I never did it again. There have been times, however, in my theatrical life when I longed for balloons.

I always wanted to play the princess in Thurber's *Many Moons;* I never did. Emily Something (I am my mother's daughter) played the princess. I was now twelve and the biggest, so I had to play the king.

I always wanted to play the first fairy in *A Midsummer Night's Dream* because he was a girl; I never did. I played the King of the Fairies.

I always wanted to play Kate in *Kiss Me Kate;* I never did. I played Old Vincentio, the eighty-nine-year-old bald guy with no teeth. For the first twenty minutes, my parents didn't know who I was. "For sooth, for sooth. No tooth, no tooth."

By seventh grade, I finally got the lead. The lead *boy* doll in *Rackety Packety House.* All the characters were dolls, so all the furniture was oversized, built taller than we were. One day I jumped off this very, very high table onto a needle that went halfway into my foot. I went through the entire performance with that needle in my foot. All that martyr practice had finally paid off.

I became one of the young stars, albeit tall, which meant that I continued playing all the men, all the kings, all the cavemen, tall trees, and bad fairies. After three years, I finally rebelled and said I would no longer play a man. So they let me play women—wicked mothers, wicked witches, ugly hags, women cavemen.

I learned a tremendous amount during those years. I learned poise; I learned I could be outrageous and people would laugh; I learned to love writing. I even learned to love Shakespeare. But it took me three long years to learn to speak up—unlike Sean who admitted he was tired, unlike Justine.

Justine has always had the wisdom to say no and wait for a better shot. When she was nine, performing with the Boy's Harbor Theater Company in New York, she decided to audition for *The Wiz.* I tried to discourage her. There aren't a lot of parts in a black show for blond, blue-eyed, Waspy kids. But she unleashed an argument from which there is no conceivable parental rebuttal: "But I want to."

She came home furious. "You know what I'm playing?"

"What?"

"A brick."

"A brick?"

"Yah, a brick. And backup to the scarecrow."

"Are you going to do it?"

"Are you kidding! A brick and backup to the scarecrow? I've worked in this theater company for two years, I deserve better. A brick and backup to the scarecrow! Would you?"

Hell, yes. I'd have played the mortar.

That's why I've always wanted my own show. I wouldn't have to worry about stealing attention. I could play all the girl parts, and I wouldn't have to wear those terrible tights anymore.

SIX

"How were you able to get here with the bridge out?"

"I flew."

—COUNT YORGA'S REPLY TO MY INQUIRY

My early relationships with men were less than successful. When I was five, I fell madly in love with Keith Basso. His father, Hamilton Basso, would later write *The View from Pompey's Head,* but I didn't care; I loved his kid. It was your standard basic passion. I loved him one day, hated him the next. Loved, hated; loved, hated. We went on a school picnic once to Compo Beach. We were sitting around having a wonderful time when Keith came up to me and looked into my eyes. As I looked down into his, he said:

"Mariette."

"Yes, Keith?"

"Would you carry my fish for me?"

"Oh, Keith, could I?"

I carried his dead fish all day long. Showing it to everyone.

It didn't get better.

When I was studying at the White Barn with Claire Oleson, Sam Jaffe (later to be known as Doctor Zorba on *Ben Casey)* and his wife, Bettye Ackerman (later to be known as Doctor Graham), starred in a production of *Noah.* I played one of the passengers on the ark, complete with bear costume. Obviously, I had to walk up the gangplank with the other bear when the rains came, but I wasn't interested in the other bear; I was interested in the lion, a guy named Ed Doctorow (later to be known as E.L.).

He was about twenty-two, Mr. Joe Cool, and had no idea I was madly in love with him. The two of us were crawling around the stage one night—in full animal regalia—when he asked me if I'd like to meet him outside during intermission.

After my sophisticated, "Gee, sure," we sat on this little white balcony and tried to talk. I say tried to talk because I couldn't answer him; I was absolutely tongue-tied. He had his lion head under his arm; I had my bear head under my arm.

"So." He said.

It was one of those beautiful summer nights in Connecticut, and I couldn't take my eyes off the moon. I gazed at the moon; I stared at the moon. Thank God there was a moon to look at. Then he moved a little closer.

"So," he said, "so. What's your name?"

I said, "Mariette Hartley."

He moved a little closer. "So," he said. "Where do you live?"

I said, "About five miles down this road." (I wasn't about to tell him I rode my bike there.)

"So," he said. "You been acting for a long time?"

"Yes."

"You're cute."

"Thank you."

He moved a little closer. "How old are you?"

"Oh, please don't ask me that. Everytime somebody asks me that it ruins everything."

"You can't be that old, and you can't be that young. C'mon, how old?"

"Twelve."

The lion moved away.

I've always had trouble like that. I had the height of a college student and the sophistication of a preschooler.

Reel life was worse.

In the years to come, I played victims, tomboys, plain passive sisters, but "naive" continued to be my strong suit. This was especially apparent when I played Cynthia in *The Return of Count Yorga* who got it in the end—or the neck—while the Santa Ana winds swirled around her. I had to stand there while a man with darting eyes and darting cape breathed heavily down on me and say, "How were you able to get here with the bridge out?" I had to lie in bed as he entered my room, fangs drooling, and say, "Oh, hello." I had to sit on the other end of a mansion-length table while Count Yorga looked at me as so much *marrons glacés* and say, "I wanted to call my mother, but I couldn't find a phone."

I was always romantically misfiring. After I fell in love with a 100-year-old man on *Twilight Zone,* I moved on to *Star Trek* and became the first human to dally with Spock. Though the affair was brief—he had fallen in love with me on a four-day pass from his time zone—I taught him to eat meat. Before me, Spock was a vegetarian.

Then one day my manager, Arlene Dayton, said, "You're doing *The Incredible Hulk.*"

I said, "No, I'm not."

She said, "You don't understand. It's a great

part and you'll win an Emmy for it. You're doing *The Incredible Hulk,* honey."

So I played the bride of *The Incredible Hulk.* I was a doctor, the only woman who got to watch David metamorphosize into the Hulk. It happened when we were sleeping together. All of a sudden his pajamas started ripping in the chest area, he began to turn green, his eyes began to twirl and he let out this huge manly roar. I did what any woman would do. I shook him and said, "David, it's me, Carol. I have to get a tissue sample."

(Actually, the episode was sensitively written and directed by Ken Johnson. Bill Bixby, Ken, and I became friends. And I did win an Emmy for it.)

I was on *The Dating Game.* Twice.

Tom Selleck was once Bachelor #2, but not when I did it. When I did it, I took Bachelor #2 and got the orthodontist with halitosis.

There's a predatal agreement before you go on the show that if you don't want to go out with the guy, you can take the gift instead. I didn't know how to do that. I mean, if you take one look at somebody coming round the partition and get nauseous, you can't say, "I'd rather take the hairdryer." So I took a deep breath and chose Bachelor #2. The first couple won a flight to Moscow; the second went to Spain. I went to Scottsdale, Arizona, with the orthodontist.

The second time I did *The Dating Game*—I don't remember if it was because I needed money, a hairdryer, or my career was dead—I ended up with a surfer who couldn't talk. I heard something pathetic in his voice and glommed on. I heard lost soul, I heard social misfit, I heard major neurotic with advanced psychosis. I sat there on that commercial break, patting my feet to the theme music, and thought, "This guy's for me."

But my earliest relationship, the love of my life, was my dad.

He had dash. And, in the beginning, exuberance. He was the best storyteller. He'd tell wonderful Canuck stories; then the two of us would laugh and his gold teeth would show. And he loved cats. We always had cats everywhere. In and out, mostly in.

He hated Beethoven and Mozart. He called it "Tweedle-dee-dee" music, "piccolo people." But he enjoyed Debussy and Ravel, and Marian Anderson was the love of his life. He used to whistle "Tenderly" through his teeth. It wasn't a whistle, really; it was like a simmering tea kettle. As if a whistle could mutter. It drove Tony and me crazy.

He also loved guns. When I was about ten, he taught me in the backyard with tin cans; I practiced for hours becoming an ace shot. Some of the guns were displayed on an open leather gun rack in my brother's room, basically hunting rifles. One night I was talking to Tony about homework, idly going up the rack of guns, putting my finger on each trigger with my hand over the barrel, talking, "click," talking, "click," talking, "click." For some reason, I didn't put my hand in front of the last barrel—the one that didn't go "click," the one that went "BLAM," right through the wall, a hole the size of a plate.

One day when I was about twelve and doing the dishes, Dad came up behind me and whispered: "Mariette, with legs like that you'll never get a cab in New York. What cab driver's going to stop?"

So he offered to teach me how to whistle. I turned around and was dumb enough to say, "Oh gee, Dad, would you?"

I practiced for a full winter. Outside. In the snow. I shoved my fingers in the sides of my mouth, spat a lot and got very cold. Spring arrived, my fingers thawed, and I, by God, could whistle.

Dad decided to put it to the test. I was to take the commuter train to New York, get out at Grand Central, whistle down a cab, ride around the block, get out at Grand Central, and take the commuter train back to Westport. That was it.

The next morning I waved good-bye to my father from the train—all decked out in my patent-leather shoes, my drooping white socks, my hand-me-down gray suit with somebody else's initials on the left side, my little tam, my white gloves, and my patent-leather purse. One hour later, I was in Grand Central Station.

As I climbed the steps to Forty-second and Madison, I was shaking. I took my right glove off, tentatively put my fingers in my mouth, and whistled. Two cabs stopped. Honest to God, this is a true story. Two cab drivers began to threaten each other. Two middle fingers took to the air. And I figured I'd better get into the first cab quick. I hopped in, still shaking, started putting my glove back on, and the cabbie turned around with this big cigar and said, "Where to, young lady?"

"I'm just going around the block."

" 'Round the block?"

"Yes."

A Brooklyn shrug. "Sure, sure. 'Round the block."

And as we went around the block, I finally got

up my courage. "Ah, excuse me. I know this is gonna sound dumb but . . . Well, did ya hear the whistle?"

He turned around, took the cigar out of his mouth, and said, "Whaddya mean, lady? I seen the legs."

It was almost the end of an inferiority complex. Well, not quite.

Dad was out of work, off and on, for about four years. There were two strikes against him. He was fifty-three, and the GIs returning from Europe had flooded the market. Thankfully, *How to Paint* was somewhat successful, for he sold another, *How to Paint Better,* to Harper & Row around 1950.

Then one day Dad came home with another idea. He'd write a book and call it *How to Beautify Your Home with Color.* He eventually sold that to McGraw-Hill in 1952. In it, he maintained that "each individual prefers one of the two great tribes of color—those with a warm cast or those with a cool cast." It was fascinating, but it didn't bring in much money.

That summer he got a job selling advertising for *Playbill.* Although it paid pretty well, once again he took on his boss; he'd ride with Dad on the morning train, return with him at night, come over every Saturday or Sunday. That lasted for about six months. Then the tide finally turned. It was 1953, I was about twelve and still studying at the White Barn, when Dad began working for Al Dorne at the Famous Artists School in Westport.

A small, determined, stocky ex-fighter with John L. Lewis eyebrows, Al Dorne was kind and everyone liked him. He was president of the Society of Illustrators and was well-known for his

Frigidaire campaign during the war years. Dorne had joined with Fred Ludekens, a *Saturday Evening Post* regular known for his Western artwork, to found a home-study school. The faculty was made up of successful illustrators including Norman Rockwell, Jon Whitcomb, Peter Helck, Harold von Schmidt, as well as illustrators that were the backbone of the *Saturday Evening Post:* Ben Stahl, Robert Fawcett, and Stevan Dohanos. Dorne had good reason to dub it the Famous Artists School.

They originally set up shop in an old mill on the Post Road. By the time Dad joined them, they were on the Saugatuck River in Westport in a two-story building that rested on a landfill called Cape Dorne.

Each member of the faculty created one course, using his own material, philosophy, techniques. When a student's lesson was received, the drawing was covered with tracing paper by a skilled illustrator who made marginal notes, then drew his suggested corrections dealing with composition, perspective, light, and shadow.

They developed a test to weed out people who weren't capable of enjoying the course. Not to be confused with another school's Bambi-like head, "If you can draw this picture . . . ," the Famous Artists test included a number of rights and wrongs about design and composition. Then a separate page might have a faint outline of a figure, "Use your ability to portray how the wrinkles and folds would fall."

These were first-rate artists who were wise enough to know that artistic talent couldn't always be reduced to a textbook. One story told over and over was about the New Jersey woman who did not do the intended lesson but sent them a large-framed triptych of the golden gates of heaven. Dorne thought it "a magnificent primitive," and instructed them to "send the lady back her money and tell her never to take a lesson again."

To those at the school, Dad seemed a sort of Frank Buck type, high-powered, an ex-advertising executive from Madison Avenue. He was a very popular man, a big party guy. People were drawn to the way he looked; he was deeply attractive, very creative, and knew everybody. And he was finally doing what he'd always wanted to do—living, breathing, and talking art.

He liked to go out to lunch with Dong Kingman, the internationally famed watercolorist. To hear them talk, Main Street wasn't Main Street with the drugstore on the right; it was described in terms of color and light, in terms of sketching. That old ramshackle building wasn't a place where they made embalming fluid; it was picturesque, a natural exercise in cross-hatching.

Things were going a lot better for Dad.

SEVEN

"She's a weed! She's a weed."

"I think she's pretty."

—A PANSY'S REBUTTAL TO A
TIGER LILY'S DISMISSAL OF
DISNEY'S ALICE

Eva Le Gallienne lived about a mile down the road from our house, just past Cobb's Mill. Everyone in Weston was aware of our highly acclaimed and slightly notorious neighbor. In the summer of 1954, word got around that she was teaching a course at Lucille Lortel's White Barn Theatre to young professionals coming in from New York. The class would meet once a week, concentrating on "scenes from Shakespeare, Ibsen, and Chekhov."

Claire Oleson set up an audition for Harley Patterson and me. Harley was another one who always played the prince, usually to Emily Something's princess. I was prettier than Emily but she was shorter, so she and Harley made a better couple.

Harley and I rehearsed for weeks, sequestered in my bedroom. Oh joy of joys, something to practice. We chose the scene from *Twelfth Night,* where Viola says, "Make me a willow cabin at your gate." I always wanted to play Viola but Harley won, so I studied Olivia. Why I wanted to play Viola, why I wanted to play the part of any woman playing a man after playing all those men, I'll never know. Maybe I figured I'd have it knocked.

When the day came for our audition, we got up on that little stage, said a meek hello to a darkened house, and sat—nay, anchored ourselves to the chairs. Timidly I began: "Give me my veil: come throw it o'er my face"; rose midscene to a saucy crescendo: "In his bosom! In what chapter of his bosom?"; itemized my beauty: "item, two lips, indifferent red; item, two grey eyes, with lids to them; item, one neck, one chin, and so forth"; while Harley 'tis-ed and alas-ed and 'twill-ed and hallooed the name of Olivia to the reverberate hills. I reverberated back: "What ho, Malvolio!" Since there was no Malvolio, it was the end of our scene. Three weeks' work exhausted in three minutes.

There was a nervous lull. Then a small woman in lavender and violet swept up the aisle from the back of the house. Slow motion, fast motion, one of those moments never forgotten. It was almost as if there were a light around her. She told Harley she was welcome to take the class, but had a great deal of work to do. Then she turned to me, "You, on the other hand, have great promise and must continue." Well, there went the knees. Someone of her stature, having that kind of faith in an awkward kid from a three-minute audition, could not have given me a more lasting gift. Those words still ring inside me, even when I'm feeling low.

She warned us, however, "I'll be sticking you both in a corner. Since this class is primarily for professionals, I doubt if you'll get very good parts or very much attention."

We didn't care; we were elated, "We'll play henchmen. We'll scrub floors."

* * *

She was known as Miss LeG to some; E. Le G. to others. The first day, she sat at a little table, the class facing her in a semi-circle; I was so intimidated. All these older people, big-time professionals from New York; they had to be about twenty-one, twenty-two. Peter Falk had worked there. Now, there was Steve Press, Roy Bacon. Tony Carbone was her favorite; he was very talented, kind of Brandoesque. As she went around the circle, each read expertly; then she'd assign him a part. We were to work on a scene the whole summer, perform it for our peers; then, if it passed muster, perform it for the public. She called everybody by his last name: Mr. Press, Mr. Carbone. All very European, very respectful, very wonderful.

We read all morning. I kept wondering what part I was going to play, mentally reneging on my offer of henchman. I lost some hope when she got to Harley; she didn't get much of a part. Then, just as it was my turn, we went downstairs for a break. I gave a few shy "hellos," but no one paid much attention. All these professionals chattering earnestly, long-standing members of the club. Harley and I clung to each other, concentrating on our Orange Crush. After the break, Miss LeG said, "All right. Now we're going to be doing the balcony scene from *Romeo and Juliet.* Mr. Bacon, you'll play Romeo; Miss Hartley, you'll play Juliet."

"What ho, Malvolio!" For two glorious months someone would be paying attention to me.

LeG believed that only through acting can one learn to act. It required constant study. The harder the conditions, the better—which, of course, was right up this particular martyr's alley.

So I practiced. I took to the woods and I practiced. I stood on rock fences and practiced. I declaimed to the trees, to the squirrels, to the crows. Mom swore if she heard, "O, swear not by the moon, the inconstant moon," one more time, she'd move into Mo Percy's garage. Dad cued me, Tony cued me. Breakfast, lunch, dinner. "O Romeo, Romeo. Wherefore art thou, Romeo?" turned into an equally passionate, "Oh, Mariette, Mariette. Therefore, go now, Mariette."

I liked anything repetitive. "Fain would I dwell on form, fain, fain deny." "It is nor hand, nor foot, nor arm, nor face . . ." Tony saw me coming and locked his door. Dad was deeply sorry he had kiboshed the cello.

I had just turned fourteen, the same age as Juliet, but I was very nervous, didn't understand the verse, and didn't know how to say it. Halfway through the course, I went up to LeG and asked her to help me privately. People were aghast. "You can't ask a woman like that to tutor you privately. That's an incredible imposition." But she said, "Of course."

Sometimes she tutored me in a tiny gazebo in the back of the theater, sometimes at her house. I went as often as I could, cutting through the woods. It was a long hilly walk, over rock fences, through the crisp ground pine.

She had bought a tiny house in Weston in 1926 that sat on about ten rocky acres of woodland. She later built another house on the property, called it "Toscairn" and continued to add wings with every job—each bay window, each fireplace, represented a play.

Her study was magical. There were books from floor to ceiling with one shelf devoted to the works of her father, the poet, Richard Le Gallienne. Large windows behind her desk let in the rose garden. Known as the Blue Room because of the faded Italian blue walls, it contained favorite pieces of furniture, leftovers from Civic Rep productions: Hedda's armchair, the sofa from *Camille,* the spinet from *Dear Jane,* and an old Victorian ottoman that had found itself typecast in anything by Chekhov or Ibsen. On her desk was Juliet's dagger, L'Aiglon's riding crop, and Masha's snuffbox; on the wall a poster of Bernhardt. Even Phoebe, the pig-in-residence, was a living prop from *Alice in Wonderland.*

When LeG was fifteen, she became obsessed with the idea of obtaining a copy of Sarah Bernhardt's *Memoires,* but the book was out of print. She spotted a copy in a friend's library, borrowed it, and laboriously copied the 800 pages, French word for French word, in her own hand. A benefactor had it bound into two volumes of blue and gold. It now sat on her shelf with an inscription from Bernhardt.

I loved listening to her speak verse. She had a kind of Gielgud voice, very covered, very cellolike. There was a tone in it, a maternal vibration, a blanket covering me with warmth.

She taught me it was not enough to know Shakespeare's lines. "You have to breathe them, live them, absorb them, then speak them as if they're your own." She taught me to bring out the music without losing the meaning. I didn't know how to breathe. I had to learn vocal technique, develop my rib cage, choreograph each breath.

I literally sat at her feet while she told me stories about *Peter Pan, Alice in Wonderland,* the days of the Civic Rep. She had started in 1926 to provide theatergoers with popular-priced classics similar to those in large cities in Europe. "Libraries of Living Plays." The company took over the Fourteenth Street Theatre, an old burlesque house in New York, charged thirty-five cents to $1.50

tops for a first season that included *Three Sisters, Cradle Song, John Gabriel Borkman, The Master Builder,* and *Twelfth Night.* By the end of the fifth year, after adding four productions per year, thirty plays were rotating in repertory. One of them, Susan Glaspell's *Alison's House,* won a Pulitzer Prize. LeG also started a free school known as the Apprentice Group, whose graduates included John Garfield, Burgess Meredith, and Howard da Silva.

I couldn't hear enough about the 1933 production of *Alice in Wonderland.* Faithful to Tenniel's illustrations, LeG had designed a system of trolley platforms to keep the play flowing, uninterrupted by scene changes or blackouts. Characters came to Alice as figments of her imagination. She used marionettes over seven feet tall for the Walrus and the Carpenter and one-foot-high oyster puppets that danced in Tenniel boots. Josephine Hutchinson played Alice; Burgess Meredith, the Dormouse; Joseph Schildkraut, the Queen of Hearts; and Julie Harris, the White Rabbit.

I was in love with her, there is no question. "You have a need for heroes, don't you?" she once asked. She was around fifty-five, short—but never seemed short—with wispy grayish brown hair, a tiny nose, and translucent skin that she powdered. She had gotten a great deal of her grace from fencing. She dressed beautifully. She always wore cashmere sweaters of lavender or periwinkle blue, four-gored tweed skirts, and those Joyce shoes with the wedged heel that made her leap up, bouncing when she walked. And she could read in seven languages.

She was my spirit mother. She taught me about life, about risk. To have a teacher like that in those formative years when no one in the world seems to understand. . . . When parents seem like alien beings. . . .

Summer ended and the time came for me to present the balcony scene in front of the others. I stepped out on that balcony—in reality *up* on that balcony, it was a box—and heard Roy's, "But, soft! What light through yonder window breaks?" My practicing paid off: "O Romeo, Romeo!" By the time I arrived at the words, "My bounty is as boundless as the sea. My love as deep; the more I give to thee," there was nobody in the world but him and nobody in the world but me. Magic happened. "And all my fortunes at thy foot I'll lay. And follow thee, my lord, throughout the world." I heard the nurse call "Madam"; I felt the urgency. "Good night, good night! Parting is such sweet sorrow. . . ."

It was the most extraordinary experience I'd ever had, and LeG was smart enough to know it. She bounded up the steps, "Well, you did it, ducks!" Then just as quickly began to prepare me for the inevitable disillusionment. "Of course, we couldn't hear you. Now you're going to really have to work because that magic doesn't come to you all the time. You have to develop a technique to make it seem as though it happens all the time." Bernhardt described the moment as *"Dieu était là."* God was there. But Bernhardt had something it would take me years to achieve, enough technique to fall back on when God was out for coffee.

Miss LeG knew about that. She had had the same experience when she played Juliet at fifteen. "I started the scene and remembered nothing until I 'woke up' with the tears pouring down my face, and, shaking with emotion, fled into a corner . . ." She called it a mysterious power.

Duse had experienced it, playing Juliet at fourteen. "Ah, grace! The state of grace!"

Another of Le Gallienne's protégés had experienced it. In 1937, preparing to play the part of Hamlet, she was casting about for an Ophelia. A year earlier, a young girl had been sent by her parents from Wisconsin to audition for her. Though LeG found her audition clumsy and monotonous, she also recognized an "inner truth" and brought the girl back to try out. She got the part. One day during a dress rehearsal the company was electrified as "the sacred fire struck." Young Uta Hagen was transformed into Ophelia, into a region that Miss LeG once wrote she would not "set foot in again for many years. Novices are sometimes favored with this sort of revelation, but it is only after years of discipline and prayer that it occurs with any frequency, and only the most spiritually evolved can hope to summon it at will."

LeG agreed with Stanislavsky. It takes about twenty years before an actor begins to "know anything about acting." So for Uta, for me, for all those she guided, the work began. She gave me a full scholarship to study with her the following summer, concentrating on Shakespeare, and her own brilliant translations of Ibsen and Chekhov.

Whenever I saw LeG work, I knew how to do it. I watched me through her. She assigned me the part of Hilda Wangel in *The Master Builder*. While directing me one day, she had the Master Builder above me, upstaging me, forcing me to act with my back. I remember how she used her back; an entire mood would emanate from the way her muscles moved. True acting comes from inside. Things happen to backs when things happen inside.

I became little LeG. I followed her, I copied

her. I'd sit at her knee while she regaled me with stories about Eleonora Duse. I had a particular fascination, of course, with Duse's spells of exhaustion brought on by tuberculosis—her strong will, silent pain, wonderfully severe hemorrhages. I envisioned her delicately coughing little flecks of blood into her lace handkerchief, sacrificially ravaging her lungs in an effort to send her art to the higher reaches of the back balcony.

LeG taught me that an actor may be in full command of external show, but if he's unable to feel the emotions, the audience won't be moved. Conversely, he may feel the emotions, but if he can't project them, the audience still won't be moved. She taught me about the harmony in the movements of humans when they're unaware of being watched; that self-consciousness destroys this harmony, breaks up the symmetry, making movements awkward, clumsy, meaningless. Duse could sit in a chair, motionless, and hold an audience spellbound with the intensity of her thoughts.

Most importantly, she taught me that while some actors exploit the self, her aim was the elimination of it.

She was living proof. In 1931 she left off working in her garden to light a recalcitrant water heater. Unfortunately someone had left the valve open, and odorless propane gas was circulating freely throughout the basement. As she descended the basement stairs, she struck a match on the side wall, causing a deafening explosion. The whole cellar became a mass of liquid fire. Her hair charred, her hands severely burned, she was on the critical list for a week. After a series of operations, both hands remained thick, clumsy, and disfigured. Having lost the middle joint on the little finger of her right hand, she could no longer bend it.

She developed elaborate hand makeup for the stage—shading them, highlighting them, giving them contour. She studied them by the hour, finding positions that looked best, positions that were less obtrusive, until she overcame her self-consciousness, until the movement of her hands became second nature. Then she never dealt with them again.

Before they were burned, no one ever thought of her hands as beautiful. She felt "they were large strong hands, like those of a worker." After the fire she began to receive letters from artists, sculptors, painters, photographers, each requesting a few minutes of her time, to mold, photograph, portray, etch . . . her beautiful hands.

EIGHT

All those threads pulling us back to another world, another time.

—FROM "THE STORYTELLER"
BY JANE YOLEN

During the years I was growing up, I was trying very hard to be a regular person. It wasn't easy because I didn't feel like a regular person, being this tall when I was twelve. I pushed; I desperately wanted to be popular. I was almost hoarse by nine in the morning saying hello to everybody in the school hallways: "Hello, Sandra. Hello, Faxon. Hello, Paul. Hello, Pat. Hello, Jane."

And skipping eighth grade didn't help.

In belated compensation, seven years after Montessori, I was skipped from seventh to ninth. Although Bruce and Keith had skipped earlier, I left a lot of friends behind. As bad ideas go, it was about the worst.

To say that I was emotionally unready is to raise understatement to a fine art. The difference between a seventh and ninth-grader is staggering—puberty is a quick-change artist. There was only one thing positive: I was no longer towering over everybody, and I could finally get away from Johnny Ekkleberry at the dances.

There I was the first day of ninth grade at Horace C. Hurlbutt Junior School, thirteen years old, pre-prepubescent in my poodle skirt and cat collar, not knowing anyone in my class, and the first thing I noticed, natch, were these cardigan-draped chests coming toward me during class change. Out front of the pack, so to speak, was Pat Shurick, who would have made Jayne Mansfield blush. I literally bumped into her at the corner of the building. I was going in, she was going out, and I glanced off her chest. Then I got a load of her lips. My father would have been furious; she wore lipstick.

Chalk it up to self-defense or unbridled awe, but Pat Shurick became my friend. She was like Pinky Tuscadero, Fonzie's girlfriend, but *Happy Days* it wasn't. She was the kind of girl who wore bras and a cinched-in waist, and when we'd go to school dances, she and Hank Schacte would dance and neck while Julie London sang "Cry Me a River." Since Hank Schacte was the only person I ever wanted to dance with, I'd call my mother and say, "Mom, this is a disgusting party. Please, pick me up."

The "hello, hellos" were all part of the same thing. I was afraid to talk. I wasn't afraid to be funny, but I was afraid to talk. As far as I was concerned, I was big, I was ugly, and no matter how much other people said it wasn't so, nothing convinced me.

Horace Lanute didn't help.

Horace Lanute (rhymes with cute) was my humiliator. As I'd walk down the hall—"Hello, Faxon. Hello, Marcia. Hello, Pat"—Horace would jump from the lockers and yell, "HEY THERE, HEIFER!" I swear he lived in that locker; I swear he never went home. (He probably still doesn't, because he's a fireman in Westport.) He would jump out with his flattop and say, "HEY HEIF-AHH! Here comes HEIFAH HARTLEY!" I thought I was going to be hoarse by 8:45, but it was Horace who was hoarse saying, "Here comes Heifer Hartley" in the hallway.

Dinner conversation those first few months centered around Dad's new idea and my desperation. He was going to write a book titled *How to Be Liked—Better,* basing it on questionnaires sent out to thousands of people. After discussing it with genuine enthusiasm, Mom asked:

"What happened at school today, honey?"

"Oh, Mom, all these new kids, I don't know any of them. I only know one kid and he's in the Projectionists Club."

"Just concentrate on your work and the people will come to you."

But Dad was doing better. Famous Artists was turning from a small operation to a big one. They added a cartoon course, assembling an outstanding faculty: Rube Goldberg, Al Capp, Milt Caniff. Eventually in the late sixties they added the Famous Painters School, headed by Ben Shahn; the Famous Writers School, headed by Bennett Cerf and Rod Serling; and in 1964, the Famous Photographers School, headed by Richard Avedon and Alfred Eisenstaedt. Somebody was doing something right.

That fall of '54, when we all moved over to Staples High School in Westport for tenth grade, Jane Yolen became a friend. It was obvious Jane would be a writer; she was very articulate and spoke four languages: English, Spanish, Double Dutch, and Pig Latin. Although Marcia Cassedy went to another school, we continued to be pals because she was tall, lived down the road from me, and had two false teeth in front. She used to take them out when she wanted to impress, sticking her tongue through the empty space.

Most of my friends were pretty bright. I think I unconsciously hoped if they could talk enough, it would rub off. Schoolwork was still a struggle, and the struggle prodded me to push even harder for popularity.

"Hello, Faxon. Hello, Lynne. Hello, Horace."

"HEY THERE, HEIFAH!"

Then one night Dad came home with another idea. He'd write a book called *How to Choose a Hobby*. After discussing it with genuine enthusiasm, Mom asked:

"What happened at school today, honey?"

"Oh, Mom, there's this cute guy in Glee Club. All the girls kept egging me on to ask him to the Bounty Ball. Then Melissa Yowl pushed me across the gym and I almost bumped into him."

"What'd he say?"

"He said, 'Hi.' "

"What'd you say?"

"I said, 'Would you like to come to the Bounty Ball with me?' "

"What'd he say?"

"Oh, Mom, he was wonderful. He said, 'Sure.' "

So I started dating my first real beau, Alexander Wolfgang Mack. Sandy Mack. He was a junior; I was a sophomore. He was a terrific pianist, sang, had his own band called "The King's Men," and I became a piano widow at fourteen. I also became Happy Hartley, the class clown.

Four years earlier, I had learned that I could become acceptable by being funny. I had picked up this insight at—dare I say it?—Girl Scout Camp. Now, you don't go to Girl Scout Camp if you're ten and cool; you go to a place like Camp Winona. But I didn't have a lot of choice. Dad had said, "It's either 4-H or Girl Scouts." Fortunately Margery ter Weele's mother was a Girl Scout leader and had taught me to make sailboat napkins, so I knew all about Girl Scouts.

I absolutely hated it. It was the first time I'd ever been away from home, except for overnights at Faxon's, and even though I was only two hours away, it seemed like forever.

You know what happens to open cabins at night? Bugs. And scary people that turn into shadows that turn into scary people. Every cabin had a name; ours was Sleepy Hollow. We would be greeted with "Sleepy Hollow, time to wake up!" while the moon was still out; then have to forage through the woods to find kindling for our morning fire. We didn't even have a lake to swim in, just a pool. We'd walk around with bloodshot eyes and hair that smelled like Clorox.

I wrote home fairly regularly, about twelve times a day. Pretty much the same thoughts—"I want to come home."

Dad wrote back, "Hang in there, we'll be up in a week. If you still want to come home, we'll bring you back." He ended the letter with, "Remember, you're a Hartley."

Now I didn't have a clue to what that meant, but it sure sounded good. "Remember, you're a Hartley." So I slapped mosquitos and remembered I was a Hartley. I coughed up chlorine, I braided lanyards. Midway into my sentence they had Acquaintance Day—the halfway mark before parole. All of our camp counselors had names like "Hoot Owl" and "Mickey Mouse." Tenderfoots were told to delegate one from each cabin to make up a story as to how they came by them; I was chosen. When they arrived at the steps of Sleepy Hollow, I began the Infamous Improv of Troop 402.

"One day on the reservation of the Okeechobee, a girl baby with a Mohawk was born . . ."

I know now, from first-hand experience, that ten-year-olds are not exactly a tough audience and have been known to break into hysterical laughter over the hyphenate "poo-poo." But I didn't know it then and it changed my life. Every one of them, including the counselors, laughed hysterically. When Mom arrived the next day, I just glared at her. "What are you doing here? Geez!"

So I turned funny and walked down the halls: "Hello, Lenore. Hello, Melissa. Hello, Faxon. Hello, Lynne. Hello, Horace."

"HEY THERE, HEIFAH!"

Then one night Dad came home with another idea. He would write a book called *How to Get a Divorce.* After discussing it with genuine enthusiasm, Mom asked:

"What happened at school today, honey?"

"They're filming *Man in the Gray Flannel Suit* with Gregory Peck on Main Street."

"You're kidding!"

"Yah, it's gonna preview in Westport," chimed Tony.

"Who told you that?"

"Horace Lanute. He says a woman from Weston was on *Strike It Rich.* Her kids have polio."

"Horace Lanute lives in his locker; how would Horace Lanute know?"

"She's just angry because Horace Lanute calls her 'heifer.' "

Mom was alarmed, "I thought you said you were getting more popular in school?"

"I am. But Horace Lanute does not a high school make. Geez."

The conversation turned to Canada. Tony and I were doing odd jobs, trying to save enough money to help pay for a trip we'd been planning for over a year, a trip with Mom and Dad to Jasper in Quebec.

I baby-sat as much as I could. I used to sit for Amy Vanderbilt over on Valley Forge Road. The first time I went, I expected her to talk the way she wrote, introducing me to everyone. "Miss Hartley, this is Mona, my personal maid. She's going to look after you while you are here, so call upon her if you need anything." She would then turn to Mona and say, "Miss Hartley will spend the evening with us and will be in the North Room." But she never did, she just said "Hi." And there was nothing in her refrigerator.

Dinner conversations also included the Army-McCarthy hearings. We'd jump off the bus and break for the house, snapping on the TV, or go down the road and watch at Big John's. It was fascinating. We loved watching the rages of the committee, "Point of order, Mr. Speaker!" and the contempt from the accused, "I am not and have never been . . ." For four years we'd been hearing that movies, television, and radio were loaded with subversives, Commies, and pinkos. They even had a red hunt in Norwalk, the next town over. Highly suspicious of those who took the "Fifth"—all those people sneaking around like Boris and Natasha with bombs in their hands—I vowed I'd be like Dorothy Parker, I'd keep it in perspective. When she was asked if she ever conspired to overthrow the government of the United States, she said, "I can't even get my dog to stay down. Do I look like someone who could overthrow the government?"

It was a time of social awakenings. I remember going down to Newport News with Betty Snaith and the boys and seeing "for whites only" signs. I remember that Tony Duke was ostracized for letting his "Fresh-Air" kids from Harlem swim in a Weston stream; I remember seeing the tenements in New York. I fought for the downtrodden, the underdog, and spent most of my high school years begging.

"What's going on at school, honey?"

"Faxon and I are going to be at the Weston Center, Saturday. We're selling poppies for Poppy Day."

"I thought you did that last Saturday."

"No. Last Saturday we were selling Peanuts for Polio."

"Is that when I saw you with Susan Grondona?"

"No. That's when Susan Grondona and I were collecting for Easter Seals. Oh, Dad, she really makes me uncomfortable."

"Why?"

"She's so neat."

"You're neat, too."

"I don't feel neat. My slip's always showing, my sweaters have nubs, and I can never find my kilt pin. I'll bet Susan Grondona saves all her kilt pins in a little box that says, 'Kilt pins.' "

Not long after that, Dad came home with another idea. He'd start a correspondence course for beginners, to teach people how to paint. In essence, a kindergarten course for painters. A "prequel" to the "How to Paint" course at Famous Artists.

"It'll be great. Anybody can do it." He formed

a banner in the air. " 'The Hartley Course for the Beginning Hobbyist: If you can paint an apple, you can paint anything.' Whaddya think?"

As usual, Mom was supportive, "I think it's a heck of a good idea. But would you do it through Famous Artists?"

"Oh, no, no, no. On my own. I can finally be my own boss. It's not at all like the Famous Artist course. That one's more advanced."

"Could we live off it?"

"Sure. I could sell the course for what . . . at least $39.95."

"It's a great idea, Dad."

"Maybe I can get Al Dorne to write the twelfth course, the summary."

Mom got cautious, "I wouldn't tell Al Dorne about it yet, Paul. I wouldn't tell anybody."

That night Dad sat at the picnic table outlining the twelve courses, step by step. By the end of two weeks, he had a number of pages.

Then Dad, who wasn't the best sizer-up of people, told an officer at Famous Artists about his idea over a couple of drinks. Then the officer told Al Dorne, and Al Dorne was furious and called Dad in.

So in the summer of 1955—just before we were to leave for Canada—Dad was fired from Famous Artists. Not necessarily for drinking, as I thought then, but indirectly for drinking, possibly for not showing good judgment.

Mom drove us up to Quebec; Dad promised to join us later. She was determined that Tony and I have a good time, and we did. I had my first champagne, fell in love with a French ski instructor, and went waterskiing. On talent night, I went as a Can-Can girl and loved it, Tony went as a flapper and hated it. I won the contest, but I'll never forget Mom coming out on stage as Maurice Chevalier and singing, "Every little breeze seems to whisper Louise." She went to meet the airplane that arrived once a day—to see if Dad was on it—but he never was.

After Canada, dinner conversations began to center around Mom.

"Maybe I should go into real estate, whaddya think?"

"You'd love it, Mom. You've always had a feeling for houses."

"Maybe not."

"Why?"

"My math's so bad, I'll never pass the exam."

"You can do it."

"Yah."

"Besides we can't afford it. It costs money to get the real-estate license."

So in the spring of '56, Dad stayed home and Mom went to work, selling clothes for Bootsy Beach at the Separate Shop in Westport. It was one of those toasty shops, filled with women's finery: Glen of Michigan, Shetland sweaters, silk blouses. When Mom learned she could sell anything, her self-esteem started to rise.

I worked upstairs during that summer in my pedal-pushers. It was a very pleasant time for the two of us, good camaraderie. During Christmas break, I did all the wrapping, took care of the stock. For some reason I began to dress like Dad in his red-and-black wool shirt, his baggy pants. I'd go down to the Separate Shop dressed like my dad in his old clothes.

"Tell your Dad about the fashion show, honey."

"The Separate Shop's putting on a fashion show

at halftime for the Writers and Artists basketball game."

"Oh? Who's playing this year?"

"Will Yolen, Rod Serling, Parke Cummings, and A.E. Hotchner for the writers. Steve Dohanos, Eric Gurney, Bob Fawcett, and Milt Green for the artists."

"That's great," said Dad.

A few nights later, he had another idea. He'd start the "Hartley Course in Oil Painting" and teach art at home. We were all excited. We moved the piano against one wall, the picnic table against another, and turned the dining room into a studio. His excitement lasted a month, as did the course. When I try to remember what it was that fell through, all I can think of is—*he* did.

Dad never brought home a paycheck again.

NINE

You got a fast car.
But is it fast enough so we can fly away?
We leave tonight or live and die this way.

—TRACY CHAPMAN

It all turned to hell.

Throughout my early years, Dad had been a periodic drinker—weekends, nights. Sometimes when he felt it was getting out of hand, he'd even stop drinking for three weeks to a month. But it got to be fairly steady after he was fired from Famous Artists. We tried tossing his bottles in the river. That was going to be the answer.

Tony was the scapegoat more than I. At some of the high school football games, they'd reserve a special section in the stands for fathers of Staples squad members. Tony was playing; I was cheerleading. Dad would show up reeling drunk. When he had that *look,* we knew we couldn't communicate.

Tony also got the brunt of it at dinner.

"Did you mow the lawn today, Tony?"

"Yes."

"Did you pound down the mole hills? You're gonna kill the mower. Did you pound down the mole hills like I told you to?"

Mom would leap in. "Betty Snaith was in the

shop today. She says Marilyn Monroe was televised on *Person to Person* from Milt Greene's. Everyone was talking about it. There must've been fifty kids standing on rock fences over on Fanton Hill Road to get a look."

Tony'd "Va-va-va-voom."

"Oh, va-va-va-voom," I'd scoff.

"Anyway, we should thank our lucky stars because I sold her two dresses. I just don't know how we're going to live if I don't do well on commissions."

Tony and I would stare at our plates.

"I've got an idea," Dad would say. "Let's write a cookbook. We'll call it *How to Cook Without a Book*."

Mom would look at him; Dad would look down, then mumble, "Did you polish the car, Tony? Did you polish the car like I told you to?"

That spring of 1955, Dad started to paint these kind of schizophrenic, manic-depressive oils. He'd line them up outside, like an art show. God, they were awful. Some were filled with somber colors; others were filled with swirls. One had this horrible eye made of violent purple.

And the big parties were getting worse. There was always booze wherever we went: picnics, restaurants, the Field Club, the Gun Club. I brought kids home who would understand. They'd see my Dad with a buzz on and say, "Oh hello, Mr. Hartley." Dad never had a click-off period; Mom did. Dad would just get rubbery, kind of lush and easy.

When Mom's drinking got worse, every dinner was a week long. It would start off friendly enough, especially if Mom had had a good day of commissions:

"What happened at school today, honey?"

"I got the lead in this year's musical. I'm doing everything—acting, singing, dancing, writing, producing."

"I don't know how you do it. You work so gol' darn hard."

Dad would join in. "Who else is in it?"

"Tom Winkopp, Eddie Jarman."

"Eddie Jarman?"

"He did magic tricks in the Bedford Talent Show, remember? He didn't win because the judges sat behind him and saw how he did them."

"I'm in it."

"Are you, Tony?"

"Yah, I'm in the boy's chorus line."

"Faxon's in the girl's. She's going to sing a duet with Alan Green."

"This dressing could use more lemon, don't you think?"

Mom would go to the kitchen for more lemon, but we knew better. She'd go to the kitchen for a drink; we could hear her opening the bottle. Then she'd return, we'd change our faces, and Tony'd interrupt the silence.

"Mariette made the papers."

"What papers?"

"Today's *Town Crier*."

"Wanna hear it?"

"Sure! You get the paper, I'll get more carrots."

I'd race hell-bent for the paper—racing to beat the alcohol, racing to keep the connection. Maybe she wasn't too far gone yet, maybe if I made her laugh, maybe if I made her feel good. Because on the second drink we could hear the click. I'd look at Tony; he'd look at me; Dad would concentrate on his plate. "Say bye-bye."

Each time Mom would return there'd be a decided change. Her posture would be a little sloppier; her speech would be a little slurred. Mom cared about her appearance. She always looked soft, feminine; I can still see her fingernails, long and Revlon red. Her pride, her dignity, compounded the horror when she drank. The click was when the lipstick started to smear, and the mascara started to run. Tony and I'd just sit there, watching the decay.

I'd return with the paper and read with some urgency, hoping for a sober response before it was too late: " 'Three young stars are rising from the ranks of Staples High School. The effervescent Mariette . . .' "

Tony'd laugh, "Effervescent."

I'd counter "Yes, effervescent."

"What's it mean?"

"Got me."

We'd all laugh, except for Mom. Her eyes would look right through us. Because we weren't us anymore, although we made the mistake of thinking we were.

She'd go back in the kitchen.

"Mom, you want to hear this!"

"Just be a minute!"

" 'The effervescent Mariette,' " I'd shout, " 'interviewed amongst her dolls yesterday, revealed her plans for a theatrical career. This beautiful redheaded "doll," '—shut up, Tony—'has studied drama for seven years . . .' "

Dad would beam, "That's my girl."

"Mom, can you hear this?"

"I'm listening!"

" 'Sitting on a blue bedspread with a striped ruffle, Mariette told of her love for stuffed animals and dolls! A shelf across one wall of her room contains her collection, which must exceed twenty-five!' "

Mom would return.

" 'Her father, Paul Hartley, has written three books on how to paint and is now writing a Beginners Art Course.' Listen to this, Mom, listen. 'Mrs. Hartley is manager and saleswoman at the Separate Shop.' " I'd look over to Mom; there'd be a slight smile. "Did you hear that, Mom? 'Mrs. Hartley is manager and saleswoman at the Separate Shop'?"

"Does it say she wouldn't have to be if her darling husband had a job?"

"Actually no, Mom. It doesn't say that."

"Well, it should."

Dad would put down his fork, "Did you paint the fence today, Tony? Did you paint the fence like I told you to?"

It was very hard for Mom to admit the real rage. During this time, her basic mood was anger—anger that she was working, anger that Dad was jobless. She was making forty bucks a week, and Dad was drinking a lot of her money away. She was tired, but the only time she let it out was after the third drink. Dad became the leech, the drunkard, the man who forced her to work.

I kept trying to figure out what was against Dad, what was against us. Ordinarily, Mom had a way of speaking that was almost resigned, but when she began drinking it became a stream of vitriol. I don't think Tony and I were the targets, but the shotgun splattered.

The conversation would take an abrupt turn.

"Big John was over yesterday. He's amazed you're still out of a job. I said, 'Daddy, Paul's trying.' I didn't know what to tell him."

"There's nothing to tell."

"I don't know how you can sit around all day, Paul."

"I'm not sitting around; I'm painting."

"Um-hm, well, to each his own theory that you want to buy. I'm so proud of Daddy; they're gonna honor him in New York this fall."

Dad would get bolder, "I'm surprised they're not naming him Father-of-the-Year."

"He was a good father!"

"I don't think Billy's particularly happy, Polly."

"That's not fair, Paul. I love my kids, but I don't believe in kissing them all over the place, I just don't. Dad's right; he just went a little overboard. I argued with him all the time about that. He loves to argue. People get wild, but they come back for advice; he gives awful good advice."

"Oh, admit it, Polly. He has a lot of crackpot theories."

"Well, at least he has some, Paul. At least he's made something of himself. Unlike some people I know. He may have gotten fired, but he didn't quit. He marched right into Madison Avenue and look what he's accomplished. That beautiful, big old house."

"Dad's trying, Mom."

"I'm going to get a job, Polly; I'm going to have a job before the week is out."

"You do that."

It was high dudgeon all night. She'd leave a room, the door would slam, we'd wait. We knew another entrance was forthcoming, another tirade.

Dad would just sit there, muttering: "Oh, damn. Oh, goddamn. Oh, God."

It got so that every night we'd sit down to dinner and it would start. Like the Chinese water torture, the same thing all over again—the same arguments, the same accusations, the same door slams. Then we'd wake up the next day with so many questions that we didn't dare ask. There was a fragility in the house, a feeling of walking on eggs. We could never criticize.

And since Mom had blackouts, she never remembered. I'd wake the next morning, and it was, "Hi, how are you? Is everything fine?" It was chilling. I wanted to ask, "Did you know I found you in the bushes?" But I didn't know how to say it so she wouldn't feel ashamed. When you wake up and everything's business as usual, it tests your sanity. You can't ask, "Do you remember last night? Do you remember the pain you caused Dad, you caused Tony, you caused me? I really don't want to go through a night like that again."

I started drinking with Sandy when I was fourteen; we'd go to his house or across the state line. He was a much better drinker than I. I was more like my mother. I didn't know where I was, what I was doing, or who he was.

We were also making love.

It didn't have much to do with sex; it had a lot to do with needing to be held. But I was not ready for sex at fourteen; it had so many other implications. Everything got to be too close, too tight, so I'd pull away. I remember once throwing rocks at him on the football field. The only way I could deal with the pressures was to hit out at him.

Drinking made me a lot more free sexually; the restrictions were off. I was a compulsive, compliant "good girl" by day and a "bad girl" at night. I know now I wasn't a bad kid. I didn't know it then.

I felt like a hypocrite. Standing there in the choir of the Norfield Congregational Church, singing solos. By now, I was a very popular kid.

I was an honor student; I had accumulated a stack of yearbook credits: "Most Popular, Best Disposition, Best Personality," and ironically, the "Good Citizenship" medal. I was a cheerleader, standing at the games in front of the bleachers, in front of everybody, knowing that I was evil, knowing they could all see it. I wasn't wearing a megaphone; I was wearing Hester's "A." I think that was the reason for the compulsion; I was afraid they would see the other side, the dark side. Even though I knew someday Sandy and I would get married, I felt like a whore.

I once confided in Marcia Cassedy. Not the smartest move, I picked a staunch Catholic. I should have picked a short atheist. She told me if I had sex again, if I didn't ask for forgiveness, I'd go to hell. (Marcia Cassedy is now a psychotherapist living in Palos Verdes.)

I felt strange. I remember coming into Mom's room one morning, "Mom, I keep thinking in the past tense. I keep thinking about this girl that was."

About six months ago I dreamt I was on a sandy beach with the sun beating down, permeating my body. Then a shadow came between me and the sun. It was a huge bird, like an eagle, but dangerous, like a griffin—wings spread, coming toward me. It landed on my stomach. It had talons, red, bloody talons, that ripped open my skin, split open my stomach. I tried to get away from it. I ran through a wood toward a small cabin, threw open the door, and looked behind. It hadn't followed me; I was away from it. So I slammed the door shut. When I turned, it was standing next to me. I hadn't seen it come in. But it was there.

TEN

Loving has much more to do with the capacity of the giver than . . . the deservedness of the receiver.

—FROM *DAILY AFFIRMATIONS: FOR ADULT CHILDREN OF ALCOHOLICS*

When Justine was two she loved shoes, only shoes. She preferred nudity to clothes. Surrounded by a mob of contentious two-year-olds, she blew out the candles for her second birthday wearing only cowboy boots and a one-gallon hat. For her third, she wore nothing but her birthday suit and fins. She had no shame. What she had was a shoe fetish. She'd scuffle through the house (while the rest of us chorused "These Boots Were Made for Walking") in anything she could find: galoshes, sequined pumps, beach thongs, bowling shoes, and mules.

Our daughter had a serious problem, and it was getting worse. She'd lie in wait at the front door, taking any shoes that walked in. On party nights, she went through eight or ten pair an hour—reeling all over the house. We kept warning her not to mix them, but she wouldn't listen—a wedgie here, a wing tip there and she'd fall flat on her face. She started out like any kid, your basic booties with bunny ears. But soon the neighbors were talking; she walked on a tilt.

We thought of professional help. There was a sanatorium in Napa Valley. But I gotta tell ya, it was heartbreaking—all those two-year-olds walking in sling-back heels—pitching forward with every step. But there was another alternative. Shoe-enders. They could take her from a size 12 to size 10 gradually.

One day when I was in the living room relaxing with Pat, and Justine was in her bedroom playing with her little friend, Justin, a sound began to emanate from the bedroom. A sound that got louder and louder. A sound that sets every mother's teeth on edge. The sound of silence. I went and knocked on the door. "Honey?" Nothing. "Justine?" Nothing. I knocked again. "Justine, is everything okay?"

Then I heard her four-year-old soprano, "Oh-yes-yes-yes, Mummy, oh-yes-yes-yes. We're-fine, we're-fine, everything's-fine."

"Oh. Okay. Well, call if you need me."

I went back to the living room, picked up my newspaper, but couldn't concentrate. So I went back in and tried the bedroom door. The bedroom door was locked.

"Hey guys, what are you doing in there? Justine. Justine?" Nary a peep. "Justine, why's the door locked?"

A small voice wavered, "Because we're playing Charlie's Angels."

"Oh. Okay."

I returned to the living room, closed a curtain on the afternoon sun, sat down next to Pat, and picked up my newspaper. Pat asked idly, "What are they doing?"

I said, "They're playing Charlie's Angels."

I put down the newspaper. We looked deeply into each other's eyes and broke for the hallway.

"Justine, open the door! Justine? Justine! What are you doing?"

"We're playing Charlie's Angels."

"How do you play Charlie's Angels?"

"Well, first we touch tummies, then we touch tushies, and if that doesn't work we go out and ride bicycles."

Pat's voice got lower, "Justine, I want you to open the door this minute."

The door slowly opened. There stood Justine and Justin in their original skins, buck naked.

Pat turned to me, the voice of reassurance, "It's okay, darling. She still has her shoes on."

I called my mother "Polly" from the age of four or five; the parental line was never drawn. She wanted children very badly but clearly did not know how to play the part of mother; she was much more comfortable with "friend." And we were friends. We were really pals. She had a terrific spirit and, thank God, was never perfect. There were a lot of mothers in Weston who seemed to be. Since I continued to chafe at perfection, I couldn't wait to get home. The two of us could giggle and laugh about the goofiest things. Humor off the side pocket.

On a practical level, Mom was always there for me. The message was: "I will drive you; I will take you; I will do for you; I will be there for you." But that's when it got mucked up. As a pal, Mom never talked about boundaries. I knew I had them but was never sure what they were until my actions were met with silence. Then I saw her as Mom the Judger, not Mom the Nurturer.

My mother has said that if I came up to hug her, she would hug me "up to a point." That was always stressed. Here was a woman who had never been caressed as a child, who had been taught that it was harmful to touch too long. So I kept saying to myself, I must need too much. If I can't be satisfied "up to a point," I'm unfillable, a bottomless pit. Because my mother, whom I love and judge my whole life by, says I am. I made a decision on my worth by how much Mom gave.

So I grew up being very ashamed of big feelings. On stage they're acceptable, so theater was my savior. But there's a trap with acting: you become someone else. Since I had long thought being anybody else was preferable, I became a chameleon. I learned to please.

Those evenings when I was twelve, thirteen—and Mom was in her cups—we'd sit by the fire in the book-lined living room and have our "fireside chats."

We'd talk a lot, but it was more like mutual confessions—confessions between a child and an adult. She would confess to me, then I would confess to her. She'd laugh and say, "Is that so?" I'd think she understood. Then she'd mention it two or three nights later at dinner when she was drunk—not only in front of me, but in front of everybody. Like Charlie Brown and the football, I kept getting sucked in because she'd sit there, listening so attentively, then laugh and say, "Is that so?"

I gave my mother enormous power. She was my high priestess, the one who was supposed to make everything okay. In my dreams I was like the "sorcerer's apprentice," pouring paint in the well outside my bedroom window. "This is yellow, Mother. Do you like it?" There would be no answer, so I'd misconstrue the silence as displeasure and run back and get another. "This is red.

Do you like it?" There still would be no answer. "This is blue; this is brown; this is green." I was frenetic—to please, to please, to please. Then I'd listen closely to the silence. "I can't hear you, Mom. Let's start again. This is yellow, Mother. Do you like it?"

It wasn't Mom's fault; she had no training. The only strictures she had were those of Big John. And dealing with sexuality in our children is like running a sack race through a minefield.

As I was telling Mom my secrets, she was telling me hers. But hers were hard for a twelve-year-old to handle. Men were to be scorned and never trusted, she'd say, then follow with an in-depth graphic report about her sexual relationship with Dad. The more she drank, the more in-depth it was. Ultimately, what came out was that Dad was the most incredible lover. It seemed very important for Mom to keep telling me that. There was no one better in the world; no one had taught her so much; no one had taught her the things he taught her. The things she now told me.

I was curiously fascinated. It was like watching a snake devouring a mongoose. There was a part of me that was repulsed, that knew I wasn't supposed to be hearing this, that didn't want to hear it, and a part of me that was seduced.

Those fireside chats were full of anger, loathing, and depression. It took years before I realized that her battle with Dad, his drinking, his ineffectuality, his depression, was real. But she fought him with passivity, with innuendo, with asides. She didn't feel she would be listened to if she simply said, "I wish you wouldn't drink." Since I always took Dad's side, she was entreating me to be *her* ally, to know she was beleaguered. But she wasn't convincing me; she was convincing herself.

So this twelve-year-old who was taller than she, and certainly appeared to be an adult, became her confidante, her ally, her best friend. And I was good at it. But I was in way over my head and priorities got turned upside down. We couldn't talk about feelings, we couldn't talk about affection, we couldn't talk about touching, but we could talk about sex. Big John's influence was keenly felt. (Years later, when I was crossing a congested boulevard in Los Angeles, I took Mom's hand, but she pulled it away. "Don't. People will think we're lesbians.")

My parents wanted it both ways. Mom could talk about sex, Dad could lace his conversation with sexual innuendo, but I didn't dare. Because what I had to say would have deeply upset them. I wouldn't have been talking about sex in the abstract.

You don't think as a kid. You don't think you can get pregnant; you don't think you can die. I lived in monthly terror, convinced that I was pregnant. There I was singing at the Norfield Congregational Church, "What a friend we have in Jesus," with thoughts of, "Oh my God, what if I'm pregnant?" Every month, I'd watch the calendar. Two or three days late for my period would send me into a frenzy. That's when I'd get down on my knees and say, "I'll never do it again. I'll never do it again. I promise." I'd get my period, breathe easier, then find myself a week later doing it again.

Then there came a month when two or three days turned into four or five, one week turned into two, and terror. How could I have a baby? I was fifteen years old, I was a cheerleader, an honor student. That happened to the other girls, the shady ones, the ones that were whispered about, the wrong kind of girls.

The day that I had to tell my mother I was sleeping with Sandy was one of the blackest of my life.

I was in desperate need of affection and approval and felt the only way I could get it was to die and have people standing over the stretcher as I was being wheeled out, saying, "Oh, she was such a terrific kid." In my head, I was still a "was."

It was a razor when I was fifteen. I never really thought I was going to die. It was a razor in the upstairs bathroom. Then I walked down the steps, walked through the dining room past the picnic table to where Mom was standing by the fireplace, and said, "Look. I think I'm pregnant."

"What!"

The wounds were superficial, enough blood to be frightening, enough blood "to . . . get attention." I don't remember much else, except I wasn't pregnant and that "I got her"—not in a punitive sense—but that I saw her eyes for the first time in a while. She really looked at me. And she didn't know what to say.

She called Sandy. I can still see us sitting in the living room, still see Sandy sitting in the chair, telling my mother we were lovers, had been lovers for quite a long time. I'm sure she was staggered, but she did her best to hide it. When Mom talks about those times now, she opens with, "Some things are hard for a mother to take." Oh, how I wish she'd said that then.

Knowing we would continue, she took me to the doctor to be fitted for a diaphragm the next day. For her age and that era, it was a gutsy thing to do. The only problem was that that trip to the doctor's office, that examination, made everything real, made everything seedier. My guilt and shame went unaddressed. And shame corrodes.

Then one day, just before my high school graduation, Dad came home with the news that the Tates wanted to sell the house. He was exuberant, "We'll buy it." Mom snapped, "Don't be silly." They wrangled all night, doors slammed, Mom went upstairs and wept. But reality won out, the Tates sold the place, and we moved into the "little house" on Cavalry Road. I always tripped on the name of the street. It came out "Calvary."

We went from our marvelous house filled with sun, space, the fireplaces, the piano, the stream in the back, to a two-room—not two-bedroom—two-*room* house on Cavalry Road. It was the guest house to a bigger house, with a tiny kitchen, and a screened-in porch that was our extra room. Not much help in a Connecticut winter, but it was all Mom could afford.

Everything fell apart.

Mom went off to work. We'd go off to school. We didn't know what Dad did all day; Mom thinks he took to his bed. He had given up ideas about writing, about painting. Mom would come home from work, and he'd have his apron on, cooking. I'd hate it for him; I'd get home from school and see him in that kitchen in that apron, and my stomach would go. When Mom was sober during the day, she was fine; she worked. But after two drinks, she would come at him.

"Oh sure, uh-huh, drinking again. I work all day at forty bucks a week, come home, and dinner isn't even ready. Who's setting the table? Where are the kids?"

"On the porch doing their homework."

"So I suppose I have to set the table."

"I'll set it."

"Paul, it's six o'clock. When are we going to eat?"

"I'm sorry."

"Hell, it doesn't matter. Even though I'm the one that's working, it's just . . . fine."

We'd sit down to eat.

"What happened in school today, honey?"

"We worked on favors for our Senior Prom."

"What's the theme?"

"Pink Champagne. We had purple and pink streamers all over the place. We had to work 'til five."

"That's wonderful, baby. I'm glad someone else in this family works 'til five."

"I'm going to get a job, Polly."

"When, Paul?"

"Soon."

"Sure, right. You do that."

"Did you trim the hedges, Tony? Did you trim the hedges like I asked you to?"

Someone once asked Mom in an interview about my early angers or rebellions, and she said, "Mariette was never angry. I never had trouble with those kids; I never screamed at them. When they went to bed, they went to bed. When they dressed for school, they dressed for school."

The interviewer pursued it, "But Mariette said in one article that she didn't know how to be angry."

"Well, I don't remember much anger with the kids."

"That's what she's saying: she didn't know how to be angry."

"But I think that shows there was a good relationship all the way around."

"So she never rebelled as a teenager?"

"She really was sweet sixteen. We always seemed to have a good time together."

"I think she feels she pushed a lot down. She didn't know how to get to her anger."

"Oh, well . . . what was there to get angry about?"

ELEVEN

A relationship involving violence is incredibly focused attention—there's a heat to it that's almost erotic.

—FROM RUSSELL BANKS'S *AFFLICTION*

I was twenty-six before I knew what anger was. Like Dad, I kept turning it on myself. I did everything not to get angry, including marrying a husband who beat me up.

There are various kinds of suicide.

When I told Miss Le Gallienne I'd been accepted at Carnegie Tech, she took me into a little cubbyhole downstairs in the White Barn and cautioned, "Duse used to say, 'I am the enemy of mothers.' Don't go to school, act." Her words kept echoing in me. I was only sixteen and didn't particularly want to go to college, but my parents felt it was important.

So in the fall of 1957, I got a full scholarship to study drama at Carnegie Tech in Pittsburgh, but ended up majoring in Paramedics 101. It was the school for *Harold and Maude*. Our principal occupation was to keep each other from jumping off the top of Moorwood Gardens. My roommate and I shared the corridor with Greta who had a lot of trouble with self-image. She had so much trouble that every week she attempted some kind of suicide. We'd come up the elevator from a date and see this pool of blood and say, "Oh boy, Greta's done it again." The next week we'd hear the sirens and, "Oh boy, Greta's tried something else." It got to the point where I'd get off the elevator, see her door slightly ajar, and think I saw feet swinging.

One of my best friends was Barbara Colby. She wore red, red lipstick, had these great black eyes, and I thought, "Maybe that's the way to look, black eyes, black hair." I thought it was dramatic, severe. I wore my hair pulled back; my sweaters were black, my skirts were black, everything I wore was black—except for my White Briar pipe. I was so tough, Mom walked right past me at the Westport train station when I came home for a visit. She didn't know who I was, either.

I continued to have a difficult time with my studies. As in high school, I got good grades; but it took me longer than anyone else on the corridor to do my homework. I've always wondered if I didn't have some kind of learning disability. Swaddled in scholastic inferiority, I had test problems, organizational problems. I suspect it wasn't a fluke that I did so well in Montessori but had to struggle in regular school.

Carnegie Tech had a deserved reputation for putting out top-notch actors, but I was bored. I'd been acting since I was ten and most of the acting students in my class were beginners. For our first lesson our acting teacher, Mary Morris, got up on stage—we were in the audience—and proceeded to demonstrate stage right and stage left: "All right, class, now this is the sofer. The sofer's stage right. And this . . . this is the chair."

Even so, Mary Morris was wonderful. And old.

God, she was old. O'Neill originally wrote *Desire Under the Elms* for her, that's how old. She wasn't blind, actually, but close. We were terrified she was going to fall off the stage when she was doing *The Corn Is Green.* We sat in the front row with bated breath while she neared the edge of the stage, oooooohing and aaaaaaahing, hoping she could hear us and take warning.

So the day Mary Morris told me that "geniuses, like you, should not stay in drama school," I decided to leave. I suspect Mary Morris said that to a lot of people, but I took it seriously.

Charlie Moore, one of the teachers, came up to me and said, "So, you're leaving, huh?"

"Yes, Charlie, I can't take it anymore."

"So, what you gonna do, kid?" He kind of sounded like Humphrey Bogart. "So, what you gonna do? Where you gonna go?"

"I don't know. Maybe Hollywood."

"Why?"

"I don't know, I just thought I could make some money out there."

"You're never going to work. You're too tall. You'll do nothing but Westerns."

Despite Charlie's predictions, I left Pittsburgh and Greta dangling.

But I didn't go to Hollywood. With the help of LeG, I auditioned for John Houseman and was given a scholarship to study with his theater group at the American Shakespeare Festival the summer of 1958 in Stratford, Connecticut. Started only four years earlier, the festival had grown quickly. Only the summer before, *The Merchant of Venice* had opened to rave reviews for Morris Carnovsky's Shylock and Kate Hepburn's Portia.

When Inga Swenson had to take a leave of

absence from *A Winter's Tale,* I went on for her as Perdita. It was my first professional job, it was Shakespeare, and I was terrified. My back started to act up; I had spasms offstage. Every night Mom had to bring me home from Stratford and help me upstairs to bed. But it gave me my Equity card.

This was around five years after the McCarthy hearings, and quite a few of the festival actors had been blacklisted, including Morris Carnovsky and Hiram Sherman. Will Geer had taken the Fifth, thumbing his nose at the committee. There was still enormous passion in their opinions. People, with their careers intact, were loathed for naming names.

John Houseman and I had a distant but cordial relationship. I used to baby-sit his kids, Sebastian and Michael. But I was always impressed with his moral integrity. While in rehearsal for *Winter's Tale,* pickets appeared outside demanding the firing of our "Red" production stage manager, Bernie Gersten, who had recently been called before HUAC's hearings in New York. Houseman refused to fire Bernie or pay him off to pacify Equity. Some trustees resigned, funding was lost, the future of ASF was uncertain, and Houseman was held responsible.

That winter, when I was eighteen and still studying with Houseman, Big John died of cirrhosis of the liver in Connecticut. That same winter I met Tom Something.

From the day we met, he never let me out of his sight.

He was older than I; an attractive man who could cut a smooth figure, but his age showed in his bottom jaw.

I wish I could say I didn't know he'd been in prison, I wish I could clearly explain the insanity of my behavior, but I knew things were a little on the shady side. He dismissed it as petty larceny, so I didn't take it seriously. Give the guy a chance, right?

After only a few days, he started to badger me to marry him. A continual litany:

"Will you marry me?"

"Will you marry me?"

"Will you marry me?"

"Will you marry me? I'm dying of cancer."

He tossed me that one as we were boarding a bus. He said he'd just left the doctor; he had a brain tumor and would I marry him and make his last months happy. He told me not to worry about medical bills; he had a lot of money. I pitied him; I told myself he was dying of cancer. I married him a month later, in the spring of '59.

I seem to be incapable of fully reentering the mind of that very young, very immature girl. When I try to understand her motivations, I get nowhere. I had no knack for handling people; I was gullible, unsophisticated. I had such a compulsive need to be honest, it never occurred to me that others might not.

When Mom came to New York to meet Tom, she didn't like him on sight. But I was so headstrong, she was afraid of speaking up. I found out years later that she went home on the infamous 5:31 and made a beeline for a drink in the club car. She was crying when a friend came over to her:

"What's the matter, Polly?"

"I've just met the man Mariette's going to marry and he's way too old for her and—oh, I don't know—he's kind of a smooth-talking son of a bitch."

But Dad liked him. I wanted to scream, "Don't buy it, for God's sake, don't let me marry this man!" But I didn't know how to stop the momentum.

We didn't have a public wedding, but Mom had announcements engraved. She also gave me an exquisite bracelet of small pearls and diamonds, one made especially for Rosalie.

I was making around $250 a week at the Shakespeare Festival—not bad for those days—and I'd saved up. So Tom went down to deposit my money, his money, and our marriage checks into my account; he bought us a new Morris Minor car; and we set out for the Delray Beach Hotel in Florida for our honeymoon. The first night we stopped at a hotel in Nag's Head along the North Carolina coast. Checking out the next morning, Tom complained to the room clerk that there was no heat in our room; he refused to pay the bill. There was no heat in Georgia either. There were flies in the coffee, hair in the food, bugs in the bed, any excuse to avoid paying. After we continued to wend our humiliating way down the coast, I was relieved to see the Delray Beach Hotel. Tom wasn't. It was located next to a bridge with a bell that dinged every time the bridge opened, reminding him of meal calls in prison, so we had to move.

When we got back to New York, I had literally fifty cents in my pea jacket. When Mom asked Tom where we were going to live, he gave her an address on Park Avenue; then we moved into a sleazy hotel on First Avenue by the Italian open-air market. There were rats in the closet, bugs in the bed. That's when I learned that all my checks had bounced because Tom had never put the money in my account. He had used it to buy the car; he had even pawned Rosalie's bracelet.

It didn't take me long to learn he was a pathological liar, a con man in every sense of the word. He was charming, ingratiating; he could sell porkrinds to a kibbutz. After Dad wised up, he called Tom a onetime salesman. He could sell anything in the world . . . one time.

And where was I? I really can't tell you. I can only say he used to wake me up at three in the morning with, "I want spaghetti al dente," and I'd get up and make it. I had packed those colors, that pleasing palette, and marched right into the adult world. "This is green, Tom, do you want green?"

I married him out of pity and stayed out of fear.

I made the devil's own bargain with my brains when I married Tom. I told myself it was because he was dying. That wasn't the reason. I think I wanted to become moral for my parents. I had taken it for granted that Sandy and I were going to get married—we went together all through high school—but when the subject came up, he said he had to go to college, he had plans.

I went nuts in college, proposing to everyone I met. My idol was the siren of Carnegie Tech, a girl who never wore makeup, never wore a bra, and was pure nymphet. There was something very attractive about that—blatant sex, no guilt. But I had guilt. So I tried to legitimize my life by marrying Tom. Now I'd be able to go to bed with somebody with a license. In some muddleheaded way, I thought that would make everybody happy. It would make Polly and Paul happy; it would make a dying man happy.

I don't remember the first beating; I just remember they got pretty rugged.

Tom was a master at making me believe I had asked for it. It didn't take much. I was riddled with feelings of worthlessness and guilt; someone finally cared enough to beat some sense into me, cared enough to give me boundaries. I remember having delusions of martyrdom while being beaten against the kitchen door, "This is right, this is right, this is right." It felt deserved.

He was always there; he never left. It was consuming, flattering. The words were "I will be there for you, I will drive you, I will do for you, I will be you" and underneath were the beatings. Not at a dinner table with innuendo and silence, but up front—a good whack to the head. I knew who the enemy was; the conflict was out in the open. Anger had been so convoluted in that Weston house—ricocheting off walls—it was refreshing to have it come straight at me. I didn't have to sift through silence. On top of that, I could caretake. I could save his life. What a bonanza.

I was never alone. Never out of his sight. So I had little outside contact with others. They asked me to play a small part in *The Merry Wives of Windsor* and understudy Inga Swenson's Juliet at Stratford, but Tom wouldn't let me go unless he was part of it. So I talked someone into letting him have a backstage job.

Tom's jealousy had no logical litmus. It would kick up because I'd be talking to someone, or thinking a thought he wasn't a part of. I'd be on the phone; he'd find an old letter. Then he found my diaries. The year before, I had written about my first summer at Stratford; I had a crush on John Colicos. I had also written about Earle Hyman, describing the way he walked. Tom ranted for hours, then called Mom up and told her that I had slept with "niggers." He had plenty of proof, he said, pictures, letters.

I kept quiet about the beatings for a long time out of some misguided sense of shame, but one night in the car on the way to Stratford, he grew violent and I began to fight back. He was a strong man, who had been beaten himself as a kid. Somehow I managed to push him out of the car and drove to Weston. When Mom opened the door, she almost fainted. I had no idea how bad I looked, but there was blood all over the place. Dad told Tom the next time he did that, he'd kill the "bastard."

That November, I went on a thirteen-week, thirteen-city tour playing Helena in *A Midsummer Night's Dream* with Will Geer and Bert Lahr, and Perdita in *A Winter's Tale.* Tom wouldn't let me go unless he went, too, so I got him a job. But it was hard to keep the beatings a secret while on tour. When we lived above Ellen Geer, she said, "Are you all right? I keep hearing these sounds. They're deafening."

I don't find it hard to understand why a woman imprisoned in her own home loses touch with reality, why she stays in a marriage when she is being beaten. I don't find Hedda Nussbaum's staying unfathomable. When you come into a relationship with that amount of self-hate, hitting becomes a form of touch—a warped form of affection. But when I learned I was pregnant, just before leaving Chicago for L.A., I had to think twice about bringing a child into that atmosphere. At first, I was thrilled; I'd always wanted children. But I was brought back to reality when I called Mom and she said, "You're not going to keep it, are you?" I knew she was right. I didn't want to know, but I knew.

On Christmas Eve, Tom and I entered a shabby house on a Tijuana back street. I was standing next to this open-wire heater about to crawl up on the kitchen table for the abortion, when my slip caught on fire. I suffered no loss of dignity. I had none to lose.

In the spring of 1961, when I was back in Chicago doing *Saint Joan* for CBS's first repertory workshop, I chopped off most of my hair, then spent three days in the library copying all the minutes of Joan of Arc's trial down by hand. I was surprised how much Shaw had taken from the actual trial, almost verbatim. Tom picked me up at the library one day. Furious over God knows what, he threatened to kill me. The choice was another beating or bailing out of the car. I bailed out, landing on a curb in Chicago.

When the tour ended in L.A., Tom wanted to stay there. I was nervous about going west; I'd never had to hustle and didn't know how. But Tom won out. We took a room in one of those transient hotels in the center of Los Angeles; I dug out a résumé, and set out to get a job with no hair and no wardrobe—practically living in a checkered dress and a black bolero sweater.

The beatings escalated. Each new beating had had a residual effect, building the fear, compounding the terror.

One of the worst nights was in L.A. Tom and I were standing in line to see *Summer and Smoke* at a movie house on the corner of Sunset and La Brea. I recognized a friend ahead of us and went up to exchange greetings. When I rejoined Tom, he was on the boil.

"You slept with that guy, right?"

"He's just a friend. I knew him from school."

"You slept with him. You fucking slept with him."

"I didn't sleep with him."

He landed a good whack. I kicked off my high heels and ran; he chased me. I ran around the corner and hid behind a car in a parking lot. I must have stooped behind that car for two hours. It was cold and I was terrified. I had a genuine fear that night that he would find me and kill me. I was beginning to believe it was just a matter of time.

Even though it was night, the streets were well-lit on Sunset. I didn't know where to go, how to get there, had no money. I finally came out and stood on the street corner, barefoot and shivering, hoping I could flag a patrol car. That's when I noticed the man tending the newspaper stand across the street. I don't know if he had been watching me all this time, but I must have looked pretty disheveled. He walked across Sunset, carrying a stack of newspapers, "Here, luv, you need these more than I do." Then he placed the whole stack under my feet. I'll never forget his kindness.

Eventually, a police car pulled up but, no, they couldn't help. They were apologetic but there were rules, "We have to see blood." Although they did drive me home. There was no place else to go.

TWELVE

Things are always darkest before the dawn.

—DIAMOND JIM

Just before Justine's sixth Halloween, I was transporting her, along with her latest lothario, Matt, in car pool.

Matthew asked innocently: "Justine, what are you going to be for Halloween?"

"I'm going to be Wonder Woman."

"You can't be Wonder Woman."

"Why not?"

"Because you don't have those things." He cupped his hands in front of him.

Eager to help, eager to save my daughter's fragile femininity—her fragile femininity was fine, but I was projecting—I countered:

"You mean bracelets, Matthew?"

"Nooooooo, you know, those things." His voice rose with frustration, "Those things, *things!*"

Justine was defiant, "What things, *things!*"

"You know. Ropes."

Well, as my husband, Patrick, can tell you, I don't have any ropes either.

I also didn't have any hair when Sam Peckinpah

interviewed me for the part of Elsa in *Ride the High Country.* I had just finished *Saint Joan* and was still married to Tom.

Walking into Metro was like walking into Oz—going up those steps, going through that turnstile, asking for Mr. Peckinpah's office. Tilted back in his chair, his cowboy hat on, his boots propped on his desk, he had me read the love scene between Elsa and Heck Longtree. There was a pause, then he said, "I think you're wonderful."

About a week later, I was called in for my first screen test. Sam took me into the deeper recesses of MGM where there was a dusty, old costume shop with reams and reams of Western costumes. He found a dusty, old tailor and had me try on a dress. When I came out from behind the racks, the tailor looked at Sam:

"Whaddya think?"

Sam thought for a while, then whispered something. I thought he didn't like the dress; it wasn't the dress. The tailor escorted me back into the racks, had me take off the dress, then inserted pads in the front. Not shoulder pads, pads. You know, ropes. We reemerged for Sam's approval.

"Whaddya think?"

Sam observed the handiwork, thought for a while, then whispered something. I followed the tailor back into the racks, took off the dress; the tailor added more padding. We went back out.

"Whaddya think?"

Sam sighed. The tailor took me back into the racks.

Sam crimped his nose. Sam bid two aces.

By the time Sam and his confederate were finished, I was built like Jane Russell in *The Outlaw.* I could barely walk for fear of pitching forward.

The next thing we had to deal with was my St.

Joan hair, or lack thereof. When they told me I would be wearing Deborah Kerr's wig from *Quo Vadis?* I was beside myself. But when they plopped it on, I didn't look like Deborah Kerr in *Quo Vadis?;* I looked like Van Johnson in drag.

I did my screen test toting ninety-nine bales of cotton, while wearing a red fright wig. Unlike Judy Garland who is transformed in *A Star Is Born* from Esther Blodgett to Vicki Lester, I went from Mariette Hartley to Harpo Marx. With ropes.

About four days later, they told me I had the part. That was when Sam said, "I don't like that wig; I think it's shit." A man after my own mouth. So in the script he had Heck say, "You know, the way you do your hair looks real nice," and Elsa respond, "Pa had me cut it short."

Now considered a classic, *Ride the High Country* opened in the summer of 1962. Actually, it never opened. It sort of sneaked into a few theaters, unheralded, tacked onto the bottom of a double bill. The top attraction was an Italian import called *The Tartars,* starring Richard Thorpe, Victor Mature, and Folco Lulli. The film's only claim was a generally undocumented appearance by Orson Welles. Although MGM gave *Ride* a whisper campaign, its quiet virtues slowly gained it a cult following.

Released as *Guns in the Afternoon*—a more sock-'em title—the picture opened to tremendous acclaim in Sweden, France, and England, and five years later was Metro's highest-grossing picture in Europe. On this side of the Atlantic, you were lucky if you caught it at a drive-in.

The critics were almost unanimous in their praise. "That Hollywood can't tell the gold from the dross has seldom been so plainly demonstrated," grumbled *Newsweek. Time* called it "a minor *chef d'oeuvre* among Westerns," citing "a rare honesty of script, performance, and theme . . . Actors McCrea and Scott give the action strength and substance . . ."

For me, it was an auspicious debut. The critics were enthusiastic, predicting a rapid rise to stardom. My future as an actress, they said, was assured. Oh, ho ho ho and fiddle dee dee. Although one reviewer noted that my figure was only adequate. He should have seen it before Sam got hold of it.

We started shooting around November. We rehearsed in L.A. for four days, then were bussed up to Inyo National Forest near Mammoth Lakes in the High Sierras.

The story is simple.

Steve Judd (Joel McCrea), an aging lawman, has been hired by a banker to transport gold from Coarsegold, a mining camp on the crest of the High Sierras, back down to Hornitos. Since there's only one trail in, the four-day trip is dangerous; six miners have been killed. The bank president admits thematically that he expected a younger man. McCrea: "Well, I used to be. We all used to be."

The movie is tightly focused and filled with lovely touches: McCrea jerking a string off his frayed cuffs before the job interview, surreptitiously taking out specs to read the bank contract.

He runs across an old trail buddy, Gil Westrum (Randolph Scott), now a sharpshooter in a sideshow. Scott and his new sidekick, Heck Longtree (Ronald Starr) sign on to accompany McCrea. McCrea wants to do an honest job; Scott and Starr want the gold.

En route, they stay the night at the ranch of Joshua Knudsen (R. G. Armstrong), where his daughter, Elsa, "a plain but appealing girl" is mucking out the barn wearing pants, hat, gun boots, and no hair.

The dinner scene is one of my favorites. Pa Knudsen says grace while Elsa glances surreptitiously at Heck; Heck at Elsa. "Bless us, oh Lord, and these thy guests and forgive them the mercenary desires which brought them here. Amen."

Scott is polite. "I thank you for entering a plea on our behalf, Mr. Ka-nudsen, but what's this about mercenary desires?"

"You're on your way to Coarsegold, ain'tcha? . . . Well, them that travel there do so for one reason only—to traffic in gold . . ."

McCrea explains, "We're not trafficking, sir. Merely transporting."

Knudsen: " 'Into the land of trouble and anguish come the old lions . . .' Isaiah, Chapter 31."

Scott changes the tenor, "You cook a lovely hamhock, Miss Ka-nudsen, just lovely." He looks at McCrea: "Appetite, Chapter One."

The following morning, Elsa runs away and joins them on the trail. She's "what you might call engaged to Billy Hammond (James Drury)," a miner up at the strike. Entering Coarsegold, they discover a tiny Sodom and Gomorrah tucked into the slopes, a tent city of stray dogs, snow and mud. Mostly mud.

If the town is a cesspool, the Hammond camp is a sty. Her fiancé has a pack of four unwashed brothers, a litter of Hammonds. As Elsa enters their camp on horseback, one brother drools, "Looks like a warm one," expecting to share in the marital bliss. They look like Larry, Darryl, Darryl, and Darryl with handguns.

When Elsa is married at Kate's Place, the local brothel, "I now pronounce you man and wife" cracks like a starting gun, and the Hammond brothers are all over her. Dancing, kissing, mauling. Peckinpah's quick cuts build to a frenzy. Heck and McCrea get Elsa out by force and set off the next morning to return her to her father.

McCrea catches Scott and Heck attempting to sneak off with the gold shortly before the Hammond brothers attack. In the showdown, McCrea is done in by his failing eyesight. Scott and Heck bow to McCrea's integrity and return the gold to the bank.

Most of Sam's work dealt with misfits, outsiders, loners. His characters were not epic heroes, but men who measured each other by their values instead of their biceps. A Western is a perfect canvas for moral conflicts. *Ride the High Country* was a small story, but it had stature when played against the immense scenic tableau.

The producer, Richard Lyons, and MGM head Sol Siegel had given Sam a free hand to rewrite the Bill Roberts/N.B. Stone, Jr. script and cut the picture. Siegel, however, left the studio just as they were beginning to dub, and Joe Vogel took over. Vogel reputedly slept through most of the screening, hated the picture, and released it as a second feature.

He thought the movie distasteful, especially the brothel scene. There was an unruliness about it, a kind of threatening anarchy. But Sam wanted the audience to see Coarsegold through Elsa's eyes, and through Elsa's eyes it was terrifying.

It was a fascinating movie—philosophically, psychologically. And I was perfect for the part of Elsa. She drifts; she doesn't know who she is.

Because of that, she destroys everybody around her—the innocent leading them to the slaughter. She had no identity; I had no identity. I was led from one scene to the other. I didn't have the first clue about movie acting. I never saw dailies because they were sent down to Los Angeles. The other actors were way beyond me.

When I asked Joel McCrea what advice he could give me, he said, "Ah, I think you're doing pretty good."

"But don't you have any suggestions? I'll take anything."

"Well, always read the scene before the one you do; then stick in your stomach and go on."

I watched the day they shot Joel's death scene. Throughout the movie, there's an understated affection between Scott and McCrea. I looked up at the tears streaming down Randy's face when he looked down at Joel and said, "So long, partner." I was awestruck. I had never seen that kind of acting. In theater, you can fake it. How do you get to that place where you can do that without shame, without fear, in front of a camera? It took me another twenty-five years.

For a man known primarily for Westerns, what better name than Sam Peckinpah. I fell in love with him; he had such charisma. He was kind of a wizened curmudgeon with a terrific sense of the West. Growing up on the side of a mountain, he lived it, breathed it.

We had a wonderful relationship, a tender connection. He would gently cajole me into a performance, humor me. Shooting the violence of the wedding scene was tough because I saw my two years with Tom flash in front of me. But I learned I could use my life. I could get quiet, internal; I didn't have to yell to the balcony. I knew how to play it, and Sam knew I knew. He made me feel comfortable showing those feelings; I felt safe with him. Now I see my terror in Elsa's eyes when I view the movie.

It wasn't until the ground was pulled out from under him that Sam got tough with me. We were just about to shoot the mining camp scene in Coarsegold when we got the news that snow was coming. They told Sam to come home; they couldn't find an alternate location. He pleaded with them not to leave all that beautiful scenery. "God, don't make me use fake snow in Vasquez Rocks." But MGM pulled the plug.

It was snowing the next morning as the trucks and buses pulled out of camp, heading for L.A. Five miles down the road it was totally clear—blue skies, beautiful weather. Sam was livid. He generally started to drink about eight or nine in the morning—most all of them did—but not this hard, and not tequila. He was sitting behind me, like a demon, taunting. I don't remember the words, just the tone. It was "Miss Innocence" and "Miss Naive." A vitriolic barrage that frightened me. But our affection and respect survived it.

I didn't see much of Sam after that. But when he died just after Christmas in 1984, his memorial service was unexpectedly wrenching.

I was sitting next to Jason Robards, whom I had never met before. Jimmy Coburn spoke. So did Kris Kristofferson, so did Ali MacGraw. When it was my turn, I said a few words, ending with a line from *Ride.* Then they screened excerpts from some of his films.

When they played a scene from *The Wild Bunch,* Jason cracked. They had played that same theme at Jason's wedding, when Sam had been his best man.

Then they screened the scene from *Ride the High Country.* It was the last scene, brilliantly conceived, when Joel's life is blasted away by the Hammond brothers. Lucien Ballard, the cinematographer, kept the camera stationary and Joel died simply, passing out of the frame. Left in the frame were the majestic Sierra Nevada Mountains. This stegosaurus, this man filled with the West, one of the last living cowboys, died leaving a permanent monument behind him. As had Sam.

That's when I broke. Jason took my hand.

There were a lot of transients in the family of the theater to whom I became strongly attached, then never saw again.

My husband, Tom, was jealous of Sam throughout the shooting of the movie, convinced we were having an affair. Dick Lyons, the producer, had restricted him from the set. Peckinpah had, too. After I left for Connecticut that Christmas, Tom called Sam and threatened him with a gun. It scared the hell out of Sam, and I don't blame him.

Coming home one night after a day of working on *Ride,* I knew I was going to be beaten. I was working with a terrific gal named Jenie Jackson (Kate in Kate's Place) who had a pair of the most enormous breasts I had ever seen in my life. They weren't freaky, they were beautiful. But she insisted on pushing them into these triangular bras she had designed herself. I'm sure Sam wanted it that way.

She also had a big heart. She was an ex-showgirl, and went with a guy named Diamond Jim who wore diamonds everywhere. There was a sweetness about their relationship; he was a show guy, too. Anyway, that night I walked off the lot feeling doomed, knowing I was going to end up in Laurel Canyon with Tom, knowing he was going to accuse me of something because he always found something to accuse me of. As I walked down MGM's Main Street, Diamond Jim caught up to me, and I said: "I know what's going to happen, and I'm scared."

It was one of the rare times I could actually talk about what was going on. And he listened as we walked, and listened some more, then turned to me and said one of the most profound things I'd ever heard: "Things are always darkest before the dawn."

It landed like a ton of bricks. How did I know it was a screaming cliché?

He was right; it got darker. But boy, I'll tell you, at some point, the dawn came. I don't know quite when, but the dawn came. And it keeps on coming.

THIRTEEN

Life looks so beautiful, especially here in Africa. Sometimes you forget how cruel it really is.

—RUTH, THE MISSION GIRL

When I went home for Christmas to the Little House on Cavalry Road in 1961, Dad was drinking heavily, but I needed him; I needed my dad. I had filed for divorce and was afraid of Tom's violence. When we arrived back in Los Angeles, Tom met us at the airport, enraged. How he knew which day, which plane, I'll never know, but he backed off when he saw my father.

With every beating, I had gotten better at fighting back, or running, or losing Tom. The day I knew it was over, that I didn't need him, that I could live alone and survive, was the day I took a walk down Kirkwood Avenue by the Laurel Canyon Mountain Ridge. I felt alone, free, liberated, and I breathed in and out deeply. Then I caught Tom, out of the corner of my eye, following me. He had no reason to; I wasn't with anyone. There was only the silence and the air. That's when I realized in a kind of thundering truth, that he was jealous of the air I breathed. I walked faster; he walked faster. I jumped a small ravine and taunted him to follow, knowing that he was terrified of heights. He didn't follow; he fled. At first I felt pity, then rage, but mostly a sense of victory. I knew I could get away, really get away for the first time.

Dad and I stayed at the Strathmore Arms, a funny little hotel in Westwood Village. I had just finished *Ride* and was to begin rehearsals for an eight-week stint as Isabella in *Measure for Measure.* Having left ASF, John Houseman had formed a theater group at UCLA. Dad went with me to every rehearsal, every performance; he didn't let me out of his sight. Nor did Tom. He sat in the front row of the audience every night, wearing a bright-pink shirt.

He always seemed to know where we were. Dad and I would go to a restaurant; he'd be in the next booth. We'd drive to my agent; he'd be in the outer office. I spent my waking hours looking over my shoulder, peering into shadows. I knew better than to be caught out alone.

Within weeks, however, my move to L.A. looked like a blessing. California had awakened in Dad new possibilities, new dreams for the dreamer. The clincher came when he was offered a job. So Mom began to pack up the house, a van would bring the furniture, and Dad would fly out to drive Mom back in the tiny Nash Metropolitan. Then they'd look for a place of their own.

In the interim, Dad and I found a little beach house on the Pacific Coast Highway, overlooking the ocean at Pacific Palisades—sort of a cable car wedged into the side of a hill, owned by one of those looney beach ladies. We thought it was terrific. It was like living in a diner: you could stand at one end and see every room.

Mom arrived from Connecticut and pronounced it, ". . . lovely." The truth is she hated it on sight.

She had good reason. For the sake of privacy, I had taken the "unfinished" basement and one wall was nothing but mud. Since muck was still oozing out of it from a recent mudslide, I went to rehearsals smelling like wet clay. Eventually, I gave in, moved back upstairs, and slept in the living room. A couple of weeks later, Dad's job fell through.

Meanwhile, Tom was still dogging us. He'd come by the beach house, heckling, badgering—first from the street level, then from the beach—swearing up at us. It made us all jumpy. Mother pronounced him ". . . charming" and the house ". . . the same."

It was such a bizarre time.

Thanks to Sam, I had one of the last of the seven-year contracts with MGM. To fulfill my commitment, I was offered *Come Fly With Me* with Hugh O'Brian and Dolores Hart. It was the usual fare: a trio of husband-hungry airline "hostesses" mix it up with a pilot, a jewel thief, and a Texas millionaire on a trans-Atlantic flight. I was the one from the Midwest who falls for Karl Malden. Obviously, this was a little before Gloria Steinem went into action. Obviously, this was a little before Dolores Hart went into the convent.

Okay, so it was fluff, but I had a good part. More important, it was to be filmed in Paris, Vienna, and London. I was not only thrilled, I was ecstatic. Since MGM would pay for a companion, Dad urged Mom to go with me. So we went to a shop in Beverly Hills and had a ball buying clothes. I filled out forms, got my shots, got my passport photos, got my checkup with the insurance doctor. Producers want to be sure you won't cough or keel over in the middle of a shoot, and if you do, they want to get paid for it.

For two weeks, I rehearsed. First with Dolores—I liked her a lot—then with Karl, whom I adored. Then one day, in the middle of a publicity shoot, there was an emergency call from Metro's insurance doctor, a Dr. Wolfan. They told me to get over to his office right away, somewhere in Hancock Park. He greeted me with a stunner.

"You have hepatitis."

"What!" It made no sense at all. "Is it infectious?"

"Not this type."

"Then I can still do the movie."

He looked away.

"But I feel fine! Please I've got to do this movie. I've rehearsed; I love the people I'm working with. Sick or not, I'll finish the shoot, I promise. I won't get you into trouble. Can't you just sign the forms?"

He sat there, shuffling through his notes, never looking up; but something told me that he was receptive, that he was contemplating options, so I kept right on talking. I told him about all the money spent on clothes, luggage. Money that we didn't have. Money that should have been spent on basics, something frivolous like rent. I was deep into the second verse before he cut in.

"When do you start?"

"Two weeks."

"That's not much time," he hesitated, "but there might be a way."

He said there was a machine available, an artificial kidney machine, that had been used in the trenches of Korea to detox the blood. He said he couldn't promise—it was new—but it might hasten the healing process, might make me well by the time I had to leave. It sounded horrific, but I said, "I'll do anything." Then he called Peter Shaw, the new head of Metro, advising him there was a "little" problem. Shaw agreed to wait.

So for the next two weeks, Mom would come with me as I went back and forth to his office. I'd lie down, he'd put a needle in my arm, take out a pint and a half of blood. Then I'd watch this machine cleanse it and pump the blood back into my arm. About an hour to take it out, an hour to put it back. It was like something out of Buck Rogers, but Wolfan wielded the pen that would sign my insurance clearance. If he'd asked me to leave my kidneys for collateral, I probably would have.

By the end of the first week, I felt miserable. I still drove Mom to the treatments, but she'd have to drive me home; I could barely move. I started to feel suspicious; so did Mom and Dad. Then we'd have long discussions into the night, second-guessing ourselves. This was the movie doctor, right? Employed by a major motion-picture company, he couldn't possibly be a quack. Besides—Wolfan kept reassuring me—it was the hepatitis that was making me sick.

By the end of the second week, I felt worse. And Peter Shaw was getting impatient.

"We need Wolfan's clearance, Mariette."

"One more day, I know I'll feel better."

"We've got a lot of money riding on this."

"Please, one more day."

I could hear his reluctance. "Okay. One more day."

One more day turned into two, three. I called Shaw, then he called me.

"Sorry to have to tell you this, but we've offered Lois Nettleton your part."

That same day, in desperation, I went to Doctor

Blanc, the resident doctor at Metro, and had him retest me. But when I called for the results, he mumbled something about the decision having already been made. "It's too late, get some rest."

I was devastated; I was also very sick. No longer afraid I would lose the movie, I went to a local doctor—a young man in Pacific Palisades—who confirmed our deeply denied suspicions. He was amazed.

"You never had hepatitis. And if you had, this certainly wasn't the way to treat it."

About a month after the diagnosis, Dr. Wolfan committed suicide, leaving me with a cartload of questions. Why had he committed suicide? Why had he diagnosed hepatitis? Why had he prescribed such a bizarre treatment? When I ran into Dr. Blanc at a cocktail party about seven years later, he said he didn't know either, but he knew I didn't have hepatitis. He found out too late; his hands were tied. The studio was in crisis; everyone's hands were tied.

MGM had enough problems. They didn't need a lawsuit.

It was the end of an era, the end of the studio star system. Production costs were increasing, stars wanted percentage deals, and television wasn't about to go away. Like some of the other great Hollywood studios, Metro became a distribution-packaging firm for independent producers. The few productions originated by the studio were aimed for television: *The Man from U.N.C.L.E.*, *Rawhide*, *Dr. Kildare.*

When Dore Schary resigned in 1956 and Louis B. Mayer died in 1957, the MGM stock company headed for the history books. The second generation of Metro "stars," Greer Garson, Walter Pidgeon, Ava Gardner, Myrna Loy, had long ago drifted off. So had the third: Pier Angeli, Ann Blyth, John Ericson, Dewey Martin.

When the system limped into the sixties, we of the fourth generation—aka "We of the Never-Never"—were also limping. Richard Chamberlain was under contract, along with Joan Staley—Peckinpah kept telling me that if I didn't behave, he had her warming up in the bull pen—along with the entire cast of *Where the Boys Are.* Connie Francis, Yvette Mimieux, George Hamilton, Paula Prentiss, Jim Hutton, and Dolores Hart. I missed being a Fort Lauderdale cutie by one year.

Everything began to disintegrate. Chunks of Metro's back lot were divvied up and sold off as prime real estate. In the infamous MGM auction, costumes, sets, and other memorabilia went with the wind along with *Gone With the Wind.* Sadly, I watched them bulldoze the soundstages. The day after I finished shooting *Skyjacked* on Soundstage 8, Soundstage 8 was skyjacked. By the middle of the sixties, MGM had pruned its ranks with a chain saw. The stock company was down to one contract player, Chad Everett.

If I had done *Come Fly With Me,* I would have fulfilled my commitment and been on my way. But I hadn't done *Come Fly With Me,* hadn't fulfilled my commitment, and MGM was feverishly completing all commitments. So, in the autumn of 1962, they loaned me out to an independent producer named Al Zimbalist for a jungle movie. From "high country" to "low country" in one short year.

But I set a record.

In 1953, Clayton Moore had the dubious distinction of starring in *Jungle Drums of Africa.* Shot by Republic, all sixty-six episodes, it was reputedly the dullest of all the jungle movies that had gone before. Luckily, Clayton Moore went on to "Lone Ranger" fame. With one less word in the title, and sixty-five fewer episodes, *Drums of Africa* beat out the Republic dud by a jungle mile, becoming the all-time snore champ. And I had the dubious distinction of starring in it.

So, they loaned me out for a movie called *Drums of Africa.* For a jungle movie. To rid themselves of my commitment and of leftover jungle footage from *King Solomon's Mines* which was burning a hole in the MGM vault.

King Solomon's Mines. What a classy movie. Produced by MGM in 1950, it starred Stewart Granger and Deborah Kerr. Tough white hunter tangles with cool lovely lady until they "suddenly realize their hatred has given way to love." Shot in Kenya, Tanganyika, and the Belgian Congo, the film was visually stunning, with Oscars all around: cinematography, art direction, editing. Rare shots of tribal dances, especially those of the majestic, aristocratic almost seven-feet-tall Watusi, graced the high-gloss monthlies.

In order to have a film that panoramic, they'd had to overshoot. Miles and miles of leftover footage were gathering dust in the catacombs of MGM. There was so much excess film of high quality that MGM used it over and over: *Tarzan, the Ape Man, Trader Horn,* even the remake of *King Solomon's Mines* in 1977.

The prime user, however, was Al Zimbalist. Even before *Drums,* he had ransacked *King Solomon's Mines* for the 1959 adventure, *Watusi.* George Montgomery and Taina Elg "suddenly realize that their hatred has given way to love." He seemed to suffer no lack of footage. Or, shame, for that matter.

Al Zimbalist. I'll never forget him. He always wore a visored hat and carried hard candy, offering it to everybody, including the animals. I still don't know if he was related to the producer of *King Solomon's Mines*—a guy named Sam Zimbalist—but I have my suspicions.

Now an average movie might use five or six minutes of stock footage: PLANE TAKES OFF; AERIAL VIEW OF MANHATTAN; PLANE LANDS. Hopefully, MIDDLE SHOT OF CROWD WAITING AT GATE would be new footage. A B-movie might use more. I figure for *Drums* they shot about eight minutes of new film. The rest was borrowed from *King Solomon's Mines.*

True to the vagaries of Hollywood, Edgar Rice Burroughs never set foot in Africa. Neither did Al Zimbalist. Neither did we. Most of the filming was done on an MGM soundstage, back lot, or the Disney Ranch. When you're shooting a movie in a week, there's not much time to travel. That's right, one week. It was one of the longest shortest weeks of my life. I promise. One. Week. Even if it was two weeks, it was a week. They also couldn't afford to rent the elephant at night.

I thought you'd never ask.

Their main concern was to "tie in" the look of the two movies. One way was easy: duplicating the sepia tones. *Solomon* was kind of brown. *Drums* became kind of brown. But they also had to duplicate hundreds of natives, hundreds of animals. Not so easy.

First they hired a native from central casting to "tie in" all the natives. The closest this guy'd been to the jungle was Tarzana on a Saturday night.

Then they raided Jungleland. They hired one zebra, one antelope, one hippo, and two hyenas who were so scared they could hardly laugh. They just clung to each other and shook. I don't think they hired the crocodile; I think he was stock footage, because the same crocodile entered the same water the same way about eight times.

Next they hired the elephant to "tie in" the herds. When cutting the movie, they'd insert an establishing shot from *King Solomon's Mines:* a large herd of elephants lumbering away from the camera on the African veldt. Then they'd "cut to" new footage: a middle shot of the elephant from Jungleland at the tail end of the herd. Just kept marching him through. With makeup.

They got an elephant that was so punch-drunk—I swear on the grave of my movie career—he could not get his ears up. Honest. They had to use rubber ears. At six o'clock in the morning, they were mounting rubber ears on this sagging old elephant.

Then they hired the rest of the cast. Lloyd Bochner was the tough white hunter, David. I played the cool lady, Ruth. Torin Thatcher played my kindly father figure with the perennial pipe. Hari Rhodes played the native, Kasongo, and set back the civil rights movement by two years. And Frankie Avalon—who'd probably prefer to go nameless—played Bochner's young associate, Brian. Frankie's job was to sort of hang around, singing to birds in the jungle à la Snow White—something called "The River Love." I'm not kidding.

Frankie and I were about twenty-two. I felt older than I do now. I don't know how Frankie felt. I could guess.

For the purpose of matching prints, we were dressed exactly like the cast of *King.* All those years I'd been such a dedicated fan of Deborah

Kerr's. I somehow knew, after this movie, it would not be reciprocal. The closest I was ever going to get to Deborah Kerr were her khaki culottes. Bochner was also swathed in khaki, topped by Stewart Granger's white hunting hat with the leopard-skin band. In fact, most of us wore hats, thus obscuring faces.

The way to tell if you're seeing footage from *King* rather than *Drums* is the "more than five" test. If there's more than five of anything, you're watching *King Solomon's Mines*. *Drums* is what they call an "under five" movie: under five actors, under five elephants, under five trees, and under five minutes. I call it Uncle Ben's.

The script was filled with authenticity—references to Mombasa, Tambuto, Ambuta—with the story taking place at the close of the nineteenth century. (There was no choice. They were closing the nineteenth century in *King*, too.) David né Bochner comes to Equatorial East Africa to engineer a railroad, along with his young associate, Brian. They meet Ruth née Hartley, working at a mission, what else? David is forward, curt, blunt, outspoken. In other words, manfully sexy. Ruth is affronted, cold, crisp, aloof. In other words, interested but dares not show it.

In other words:

BOCHNER: "Tell me, how do you come to be working at a mission of all places?"

HARTLEY: "Why shouldn't I?"

BOCHNER: "Rather *dull* for a pretty girl like you."

HARTLEY: "Why should it be any duller for a pretty girl than a plain one?"

In other words, I wish we'd had other words.

Bochner goes off on jungle adventures, along with his young associate, Brian. Ruth stays home by the fire surrounded by animal wall mounts and Torin Thatcher, puffing wisely on his pipe. Meanwhile, the jungle drums are heating up, happily obliterating parts of the dialogue. When Bochner returns, Ruth is thrilled but dares not show it. "Suddenly realizing that their hatred has given way to love," they kiss, but Bochner, regrettably, has to leave. Ruth is then captured by a white-slave trader and tied up.

> CUT TO: Establishing shot from *King Solomon's Mines.* Five hundred chanting, leaping Watusi wildly out of control.
>
> CUT TO: Middle shot. Devious slave trader moving menacingly toward Ruth.

Mustering all my masochism, I got to say: "Go on, hit me. Show us how brave you are. What kind of a mother gave life to a monster like you?"

But that's so much Shakespeare to what Torin Thatcher had to ask Lloyd Bochner while protecting my honor in another part of the forest. I love that name, Torin Thatcher. Anyway, Torin asked: "How long have you ever stayed faithful to one woman?"

To which Bochner replied: "Sixteen and a half days."

To which Torin said: "At least you're honest."

At that, Lloyd got angry. I don't know if it was at that, or the fact that he had to say "Sixteen and a half days" with a straight face. "If you were a younger man, I'd knock you from here to Mombasa."

To which the drums escalate, repulsed by the whole scene.

Ruth somehow escapes, eventually saving Bochner, along with his young associate, Brian, who has also been captured. Brian then turns into Frankie Avalon and sings "The River Love" accompanied by a harmonica as the credits roll and Stewart Granger and Deborah Kerr—hats on, backs to camera—walk off into the jungle whilst animals cavort. Then everyone groans and crawls out of the theater.

The movie was shot at breakneck speed. We hadn't even finished Day Two when they were gearing up for the love scene. Visually complicated, the movie tied in a long shot of Deborah Kerr's double, bathing in a gigantic river basin. It's a magnificent establishing shot: lush African wilderness, rushing water, the towering Murchison Falls. Then they would come in tight on me, humming, scrubbing, preparing for my lover.

The original love scene with Kerr and Granger had been a nightmare to film. Since their camp was at the foot of the falls, they spent nearly two hours every morning crawling up to the top. Then they worked on the love scene in 140-degree heat. There had been other dangers: amoebic dysentery, malaria, wandering snakes. During one war dance the Watusi got so worked up, they began throwing things. Seven spears were pulled out of a camera case. I honestly would have preferred the spears, the snakes, and the dysentery.

But I was no fool; I knew we wouldn't be winging to South Africa. I knew we'd use a green set. In Hollywood parlance, a green set is anything with lakes, trees, or rocks that are fake, plastered, or potted. You've seen them a hundred times, where Hoss and Little Joe camp for the night. Right next to the papier-mâché boulder. I was a pro; I was used to a green set. Though I did wonder how they were going to suggest the size of the Upper Congo on Soundstage 12.

Humming, singing—frankly, a little excited—I prepared in my dressing room, while they set up the pool. I'd been humming and singing all of three minutes when someone knocked on my door.

"We're ready, Mariette!"

Doubling my pace, I slathered on body makeup, while the seamstress pinned me into my nudie bathing suit. Two minutes later, another knock.

"Mariette?"

"I'm coming!" Geez!

I threw on my terry-cloth robe and hurried out of the dressing room.

"Okay, I'm ready!"

I looked around the soundstage. Nothing much had changed. No pool, no green set. No Murchison Falls. The only person standing there was Al Zimbalist.

"Al? Where's my green set?"

"Here it is, honey."

He handed me a bucket—one galvanized pailful of water—then ushered me in front of a cyclorama of blue sky rolled down from the ceiling and flapping in the wind. It wasn't supposed to be flapping. We weren't talking clouds, just blue sky. He had me take off my terry-cloth robe—while the grips looked down from the gridiron drooling, Lord knows why—then sat me on an apple box and secured my pail. Humming and singing and splashing as I bathed, I now had to pretend that this one pail of water between my legs was the entire river basin of the Upper Congo. Want to talk about acting?

Forty mortifying minutes later, we were shooting the next scene. As I sat on the low limb of a tree, virginally covered, shaking out my tresses, Lloyd Bochner entered with his little cravat, looking very much like George Sanders, sounding very much like George Sanders—pipe in mouth, lockjaw—and we had this wonderful conversation:

> HARTLEY: "By this time tomorrow you'll be gone."
>
> BOCHNER: "I have to go. You know that."

Typical movie structure: the climax, the insoluble problem, until the denouement, twenty minutes away. Not in this movie. There was a short pause before he said, "But I could come back."

Then we kissed. Until we were interrupted by a baby elephant. My next line was: "Oh, a baby elephant. How cute. His mother must be somewhere near." In the final version, the editors cut to stock footage of a mother elephant in such a trumpeting rage, it would have sent "tough white hunter," "his pipe," and "dear Ruth" up the first cardboard tree.

Someone finally put us out of our misery by yelling, "Cut! That's a print!" Then Lloyd and I climbed off our limb and tripped down to my mother and father, who were standing there, proudly looking on. Lloyd turned to my father and said through his pipe, "Well, Mr. Hartley. How does it feel to see your daughter kissed by a star?"

We began filming my scenes with Bochner's young associate, Brian. My turn in the hole with Frankie.

Literally. When the star is shorter than the love interest, the star stands on high ground; the love interest stands in a trench. I'm about five foot nine; Frankie Avalon's about five foot six. I got the trench.

Then.

The best part.

The real key to enjoying this movie at five A.M. on Yuma's flagship station is to realize that we, the actors, never knew what we were looking at. We had to guess. Snakes, hippos, vultures, rain forests. All of that footage would be spliced in later. If I reeled back in horror—the back of my hand placed delicately over my lips—in reality I was in mortal terror of the EXIT sign on Soundstage 12 in Culver City. In the movie, they'd insert vultures eating a gazelle on the plains of the Kalahari.

We'd look ahead with rapt interest. The original star-crossed lovers. Make that cross-eyed. Frankie looking slightly to the left; I looking slightly to the right. Both looking myopically into the middle distance.

We begged Al Zimbalist to tell us what it was we weren't seeing. Sometimes he would. When he knew. Most of the time he just offered us candy. He certainly didn't know on Day Four, when cameras were rolling and Frankie and I were standing by the lone potted tree, looking out over camera cables.

Frankie had to say, "This country needs people like you, Ruth."

And I had to say a line that would make blowing out two hundred candles a piece of cake.

"Does it? Does it, Brian? Or do we just fool ourselves into thinking other people need us because we need to be needed?"

At that point, I screamed, he froze. We had been directed to recoil in horror, but that's not why I screamed and he froze. What we were supposed to be seeing was a cobra eating a mongoose. What Frankie and I were *really* seeing—and no one warned us, thank you very much—was a stagehand being eaten by a fire hose. Honest to God, the guy had to be 350 pounds, struggling with a flat, writhing fire hose, simulating a cobra eating a mongoose.

I looked down at Frankie; he looked up at me. We were all we had. And I had to say, "Sometimes it's good to see things like that."

Honest, that was my next line. It's on record, preserved on film.

"Sometimes it's good to see things like that."

Drums of Africa. The high point in my career. Howard Thompson wrote in the *New York Times:* "Stay with it, Miss Hartley, Africa or elsewhere."

I almost didn't.

FOURTEEN

That's all you said is jes to "swallah" it, Mister Dillon. You didn't say nothin' about chewin' it a'-tall.

—CHESTER GOODE

Although my daughter knew the melodies to *Evita* and *Chipmunk Rock* by the time she was five, she's never been able to tell a joke. I, in my time, have been accused of missing a setup, but even when Justine embroiders the setup, it barely matches the punch line. It barely belongs in the same day.

She also sings a lot. When it comes to lyrics, she knows all the syllables. She has a hard time, however, with the total word. We used to do a jazz riff, "Oobla dee oobla dough, oobla bo bo bo," each concocting her own refrain. Justine's best went: "There once was a *dog,* who had a new *shoe,* who went to a *farm,* and even tell *you.*" She had the same respect for commercial compositions. For years, I thought the lyrics of "Beat It" were: "Domicide fuckit, domicide fuck. It doesn't matter, who's in the trunk."

So when it came to comedy, we called her "La Bomba." Try as she might, Justine could not tell a joke. And God knows she tried.

Sean would tell one:

"Say 'Wow' at the end of each sentence, okay?" He'd say a line, take a long pause, we'd say "Wow." When he got to the end, "Wow" was the punch line. Good joke; well told.

Justine would be salivating, palms itchy, knowing that when it came to equal time, I out-Solomoned Solomon. You could see her mind ticking, gag-writing in block letters as she went.

"I got one! Say 'Boy' at the end of each sentence, okay? Okay, guys?"

No one said much.

"Just say 'Boy' at the end of each sentence, okay?"

One "okay" fell to the floor. That's all it took.

"There once was a girl . . ." She took a long pause, we did our part.

"Boy."

"Not yet!"

She had no knack for knock-knocks:

"Okay, I got one. Ready? Ready, guys?"

"Knock, knock."

"Who's there?"

"Boo. Hoo."

Sean could barely hide his disgust. Hide it, hell, he flaunted it. "Geez, Justine, just say 'Boo.' "

Okay, Henny Youngman she wasn't.

Okay, Beulah Bondi she wasn't either.

I'm not sure but this inability might have something to do with spatial concepts. That and logic. Justine had a rough time with both:

I'd be away; I'd say, "I've missed you."

She'd say, "Why? Where was I?"

She'd ask: "How was your meeting?"

I'd say, "Real nice."

She'd say, "Was I there?"

Whatever the reason, her inability to do stand-up sent Sean into deep depression.

"You're angry because she hogs center stage, right?"

"That's not the reason."

"You're angry because she blows your best material, right?"

"That's not the reason."

"What is the reason? Because she's alive?"

"You're getting warm."

When a friend arrived from New York, we went out for sushi, and were eagerly sharing the events of the past few months. Then Sean told a joke:

"What is the fastest animal in the world?"

"I don't know. What?"

"A cow dropped out of a helicopter."

Justine's eyes lit up: IITTTTTT'S JOKE-TELLING TIME!

"I got one, okay? Okay, guys?"

Pat groaned. Even I, Perfect Mother, tried to put her off: "Please, Justine. We just want to talk."

"Just one, okay? Okay?"

"What can it hurt?" said the friend.

Sean groaned. Justine let fly:

"Why did the frog cross the road?"

"I don't know. Why?"

"To get to the watermelon."

My friend laughed heartily, even though she didn't get it. I could tell she didn't get it because I sat there watching her laugh with a dry mouth. But Justine was in Borscht Belt Heaven. It went on all night.

Pat had a theory: "Maybe it's West Coast humor."

I had a theory: "It's the way she tells them."

My friend had a theory: "Why did the friend leave town?"

Oh, how I wish Justine had been on that Paramount soundstage when I shot *Gunsmoke* for CBS.

Charlie Moore was right; I went Western. I did four *Gunsmokes,* four *Virginians,* one *Cimarron Strip,* and four *Bonanzas,* even playing an Indian squaw. The day I was finally able to wear a skirt without fringe, I was very self-conscious.

I was the romantic interest on all four *Bonanzas;* I went through the whole Cartwright family—one brother at a time. Then I took on Ben. Unfortunately, there wasn't enough room on the Ponderosa, let alone the marquee, so I died a lot. When you're involved with the lead on episodic television, you're either going to die or leave town. Marrying Bill Bixby on *The Incredible Hulk* didn't help. Hell, I was coughing at the wedding. My expectations were significantly reduced, however, on *Ben Casey, Dr. Kildare,* and *Marcus Welby, M.D.;* I walked *in* terminal.

So when Lorne Greene and I seriously talked marriage on *Bonanza,* the writers came down with premarital jitters and hustled me on the first northbound stage to San Francisco. Some time later, the producers passed on a letter they'd received:

> Dear Lorne:
>
> I've watched your show for years, I've never missed a week. I've raised seven children according to the Ponderosa morality, the way Ben Cartwright raised his boys. I just have one question. When you almost married that girl last week, didn't you know she was that terrible Indian squaw you met the year before?

But my first shot out of the box was *Gunsmoke.* What a way to start. On the air for twenty years,

Gunsmoke was not a television show so much as an institution blessed with talent: James Arness (Matt Dillon), Dennis Weaver (Chester), Amanda Blake (Miss Kitty), Milburn Stone (Doc Adams), Ken Curtis, Burt Reynolds, and a series of guest writers, directors, and stars that included Sam Peckinpah and Robert Redford.

I did a story called "Cotter's Girl" that involved a dying old drunk who begs Marshal Dillon to get his "little girl, Clarey," living out on the trail, to his sister in Harrisburg. The "little girl" turns out to be twenty-year-old me, sitting in a tree, wearing sackcloth blouse, subsisting on "sweet clover, prairie chickens, fish. Sometimes I eat 'em cooked." I was a Western Eliza Doolittle who falls head over heals for Dillon, holding him à la Heimlich while riding tandem back to Dodge. Arness stands six-foot-six. His horse was as wide as he was tall; I was sore for two weeks.

The good folks of Dodge City set out to civilize this bumpkin before they put her on the stage for Harrisburg. Chester, a guy with a gimp leg, teaches her how to curtsy; Miss Kitty, a saloonkeeper who's been chasing after the marshal for twenty years, teaches her how to catch a man; while Doc Adams sits around saying nothing, chuckling wisely. At the sign of a perfect curtsy, Clarey is deemed civilized and put on the 9:03.

It was a lovely Kathleen Hite script. The first woman writer on CBS radio, Hite specialized in Westerns, and wrote about five hundred of them. She was terrific with dialogue. Take this exchange between Clarey and Matt when she walks into his jail, giving him a rib-cracking hug.

"Hey, Dillon."

"Now, Clarey, just hold on."

"I can't wait for huggin' ya."

"Yah, but just hold on now."

"You don't like me any better than you did, do you, Dillon?"

"I do, Clarey. And you're learnin' real well, too. But . . . well, you see, all this business of runnin' around huggin' a man just every time you feel like it—you've got to cut that out."

"You mean, I'm s'posed to let him hug first?"

"Yah, that's the idea."

"Well, what if he don't hug?"

But the bedrocks of Dodge City were better known for their giggling than their gunslinging. The cast had worked together for so long they were like four kids in a sandbox. When one of them started laughing, they all did.

Things were going fine until we got to the last scene of the day. It had to be about four-thirty in the afternoon because Dad and Mom—still protecting me from Tom—had arrived to watch a little of the shoot before they drove me over to *Antigone* at UCLA where I had an eight o'clock curtain.

Chester, Matt, and I took our positions for the master shot. We were sitting at a table in the town restaurant: checkered tablecloth, a few cowpokes at adjoining tables. I was in the center, Chester to my right, Matt to my left. For some reason, there were more observers than usual.

" 'Cotter's Girl,' Scene Twenty-one; Take One!"

Silence on the set; cameras rolled. The scene started inauspiciously. Since it was "Clarey's" first time in a restaurant, I followed Chester's lead. When he tucked his napkin under his chin like a bib, I did the same. Matt—stern parent, deep voice—put his napkin pointedly on his lap. Then

Joe the cook set plates in front of us containing huge T-bone steaks with roasted potatoes. No one moved.

> CLAREY: Why we waitin'?
> DILLON: You can start anytime.
> CHESTER: You see, it's customary for the lady to begin eatin' first.

Easy stuff, nice writing. Heck, we'll be out of here by five. Or, would have been, if I hadn't faithfully followed the next stage direction. I grabbed this huge greasy steak with one hand, sank my teeth into it, tore off a wad, and started chewing.

There was a slight pause. Chester and I waited for Jimmy to say his next line but, for some reason, he was staring into his plate. I looked at Chester; Chester looked away. Finally, Jimmy said his line, slightly strangulated:

"Clarey, you really should start eating with a knife and fork."

"Why'd I do that?" Since my mouth still contained the left flank of a cow, the words couldn't quite escape, getting chewed along with everything else. I had grease all over my hands, all over my mouth and could now see that Jimmy was stifling a laugh the size of Alaska. Chester's next line didn't help.

"Well, like I say, it's customary. And I'll tell you another thing, it'll sure help keep your hands a lot cleaner." At that point, Marshal Dillon wet his chair.

That's when I understood why there were more observers than usual; they'd read the script. They were the only ones who had read the script. Jimmy had a tendency to ingest the dialogue, paying scant attention to the stage directions. So, the first time I jammed that steak in my mouth, he was gone. All it took to make matters worse was my wiping grease off my mouth with the back of my hand. Gone again. Took them ten minutes to "de-levitate" the set, while Jimmy reassured everyone, "Okay, I'm fine, now. I'm just fine." Being tired didn't help.

" 'Cotter's Girl,' Scene Twenty-one; Take Two!"

He put on his stern Matt Dillon face, squared his shoulders, checked his boots, and got very serious. "Clarey, it's kinda like the dress we bought. It just looks better."

"Better" burst out of his mouth in a whoosh that infected Chester, infected the next table, infected the camera crew. I hadn't seen a laugh that big since I did a show aptly called *Breaking Point.* On that one, all I had to do was open a door and face Jack Warden. For some mystifying reason, every time I opened the door, Jack would grin, I would grin, then we'd howl. It got worse with each take. It was one of those long build-up scenes where I'd hear a knock, get out of bed, put my slippers on, turn on a light, get my robe on, walk down the hall, open the door; there'd be Jack Warden, he'd grin, I'd grin, then we'd scream with laughter. I'd return down the hall, take off my robe, take off my slippers, get back into bed, hear a knock, walk down the hall; there'd be Jack Warden, he'd grin, I'd grin . . .

" 'Cotter's Girl,' Scene Twenty-one; Take Six!"

"Okay, I'm fine, just fine. Now let's *all* calm down." Jimmy stuck to his guns; nary a titter; we got on a roll.

Chester demonstrated to Clarey proper utensil use: "Well, you jes kinda stick the meat real good with your fork and then run the knife right down it. Then you change hands." He cut a delicate morsel, popped it into his mouth, chewed daintily, and dabbed his mouth with his checkered bib.

In frantic imitation, I attacked the steak, potatoes flew, while Chester did a chorus of "Well, I . . . Well, ah . . ." I finally succeeded in cutting off another chunk, forcing the whole thing in my mouth; I now looked like my brother, Tony, playing the tuba. Jimmy could hardly contain himself. He was sitting on a laugh so large, his face was puffing up. But he was determined to hold it down.

So was Chester. "Well, that ain't too bad for the first time."

"It ain't!" I sat straight up, filled with pride—mouth wide open, a wad of meat the size of a volleyball. I looked like Andy Gump.

Jimmy was visibly in pain. His voice went an octave lower, like a drunk overcorrecting. "Well, you should 'swallah' before you talk, Clarey."

I swallowed, then gagged: "It's still sittin' right there." Boy, was it ever.

"Well, you should chew before you 'swallah.' "

"You just said, 'Swallah.' "

"That's right, Mister Dillon, that's all you said is jes to 'swallah' it. You didn't say nothin' about chewin' it a'-tall."

"All right, Chester, fine. Let's just be quiet about the whole thing."

Jimmy didn't say that. He didn't say anything. Although he was making sounds. They were coming from behind the napkin he had stuffed in his mouth, tears pouring down his cheeks. He bit his lips, bit his tongue, bit anything to hold back the flood. Chester couldn't look at him; the camera couldn't look at him; no one on the soundstage could look at him, all just barely holding it themselves. Little leaky air noises, little *s-ss-sss's* were escaping from his mouth. But Jimmy was determined not to laugh. He would have made it, too, if Miss Kitty hadn't laughed off camera. Amanda Blake had this broad, hearty laugh. With that, everyone peed themselves.

Took another twenty minutes to sort out the set.

" 'Cotter's Girl,' Scene Twenty-one; Take Sixteen!"

I tried cutting another piece of steak; the steak flew across my plate, landing at the next table, while Chester muttered, "For gosh sakes alive." A lovely old character actor picked it up, walked over to our table, doffed his hat, and said so straight I wanted to die, "Pardon me, Ma'am, but I believe you dropped your steak." Gone. We were all gone.

Privately, Jimmy Arness is one of the funniest men alive. People pay to see his imitation of Robert Redford. But, he should never be a straight man. Straight men are supposed to be just that—straight men. Comedy is structured so that the straight man will always have the line after the laugh line, and you sure as hell can't get a shot when the straight man is under the table.

We'd just settle down and this small giggle would start low in his boots. All it took was a small snicker from Miss Kitty, and there'd be an explosion, like a sneeze, that set off a chain reaction. It didn't take much to set everybody off. All it took was silence contrasted with sound. When silence on the set was called for, the scuff of a sneaker would send them into mild hysteria, the scrape of a chair leg would bring down the house. Justine should have been there. They would have split their sides on one of her knock-knock jokes.

It got so bad that by the time Joe the cook delivered the next plate of steaks from the kitchen, they were already laughing. We had to break that night; we couldn't get the shot.

When Dad drove me to the set the next morning they were all business. Mumbled "good mornings," isolated donuts, silence in makeup. Time to play catch-up; time to get to work. Jimmy was half asleep; Dennis was reading the newspaper. Yesterday's hilarity long forgotten, we crossed sleepy-eyed to the set.

" 'Cotter's Girl,' Scene Twenty-one; Take Twenty-seven!"

Chester tucked his napkin under his chin; I did the same. Matt placed his napkin pointedly on his lap; Joe the cook set plates in front of us containing the T-bone steaks and roasted potatoes. I grabbed the steak; Chester giggled. Say "Bye-bye," Jimmy.

On.

The.

Floor.

It was all she wrote.

It took us about five hours to shoot that two-and-a-half-minute scene. Three hours in the evening, two hours the next morning.

If anyone's had the good fortune to see "Cotter's Girl" in a rerun, notice that the scene opens with a master of all three of us, but you rarely see all three of us together again. The rest of the scene, Matt's all alone; he's never in our shot. Two-shot of Chester and Clarey; one-shot of Matt. Two-shot of Chester and Clarey; one-shot of Matt. That's because they shot Jimmy's lines later, when we were all off the set. That's right. They had to send Matt Dillon to his dressing room and put the script girl in his place. It was the only way they could film the scene.

Dennis Weaver was just as bad, so they shot his lines, then sent him to a separate trailer.

That was one of the last times I saw Dad laugh.

FIFTEEN

All I could see from where I stood
Was three long mountains and a wood.

—EDNA ST. VINCENT MILLAY

I don't know if I will ever be able to understand why Dad did what he did. For many years, I took it personally. Then for a long time, I felt responsible. Not only responsible, but that I had caused it. I miss him sitting there, I miss him laughing, I miss seeing his pride when I performed. I guess there's even the fantasy that if he were alive we'd have a little house out back, and he could paint to his heart's content. He wouldn't have the pressure of having to succeed.

When someone drinks, you know he's running away from his feelings, but you never know what those feelings are. So you fill in the script. I guess he was made to feel he was a burden to the family—someone who could do nothing but cause pain and problems. He was the only one who tried to risk but never could go all the way. I think the rebel died in him because he had to abandon his art, his dream. He had to support the family.

And he never, ever, found the compromise.

It was a series of events that caused the death. A series of socks in the gut. One after the other.

A week after Mom had moved to L.A. and Dad's job fell through, he got another blow.

His brother, Howard, had been living in Pasadena for years. As soon as Mom arrived, they all made plans to spend the evening together; that evening brought a call from Aunt Ruth. Howard didn't feel well, something about his "tummy." Dad kidded her about his "tummy," told her "not to worry," and hung up. About an hour later, Ruth called back. I started joking with her, picking up on Father's tease:

"Oh, boy—you two—how's Howard's tummy?"

"Mariette, don't joke. Howard's dead."

Dad had adored Howard. Their mother had died when Dad was twelve and Howard seven, so he was paternal toward his younger brother, his only brother.

On top of that, Tom had stuck around.

That autumn of 1962, we had abandoned the beach house—and the mildew and the must—and moved to Brentwood Gardens on Sunset and Barrington, right by the Barrington Country Mart. It was a small two-story stucco containing about twelve apartments, with a garden area and a beautiful lawn. We were in Apartment B, first floor on the left—one main room, two bedrooms, two baths in the back.

Tom had moved with us, relocating to a bus bench in front of the Texaco station across the street. Court order after court order had done nothing to stop the hovering, the menacing that kept us all on edge. Mom and Dad had to drive me everywhere. That's when I was shooting *Gunsmoke* during the day and rehearsing *Antigone* at UCLA at night, getting two hours' sleep. I don't know when Tom slept. We'd drive into Metro;

he'd be on the lot. We'd drive to the theater; he'd be in the lobby.

At last he was subpoenaed for the divorce hearings. The day we went into court, I panicked. I feared the judge would think I was lying, overdramatizing. Called to the stand, I had barely scratched the testimonial surface, however, when the judge gaveled, "divorce granted." Suddenly, it was all over. Once Tom legally lost ownership, he also lost interest and drifted off.

Throughout the spring of 1963, Dad and Mom looked for a place to work and live. Dad had dreams of teaching senior citizens with his book *How to Paint,* so they went to several small towns, looking at houses. Finally, they found a charming little place in a valley near Laguna, smack up against a mountain. It had a huge barn, where Dad could paint and hold classes, and was extraordinarily inexpensive. The owners were getting a divorce and wanted to sell fast. Mom applied for a job in a dress shop in the area; Dad was ecstatic at the thought of teaching. Then the couple reconciled. No house; no senior citizens.

Running out of alternatives, they began to flirt with retirement in Mexico. A friend from Weston lived in the region of Guadalajara on Lake Chapala. Once more, Dad's sagging enthusiasm was bolstered. Hoping to find a good place to live, they set out in early April but had only been on the road a day or so—two or three hours south of Nogales—when Father doubled over with cramps. He was in a lot of pain, and frightened because there was blood in his stool. About midday, they stopped in a small town and were directed to a little shopping center where a Mexican doctor spoke English. He was kind but seemed frightened, too; he told Dad to go back home. "You're an ill man. Go back home."

They had no choice but to turn around. They sought out the same young doctor in Pacific Palisades who had "untreated" me for hepatitis. When he found nothing wrong, Dad was still determined to get to Mexico, but Mom had misgivings. The doctor dismissed them; he thought it was important for Dad to make the trip. So, off they went a second time, staying for about a week in Lake Chapala, putting feelers out, trying to make a go of it, until Dad had a relapse and had to go back to bed. Again, his stomach.

I suspect that may have been his last hope. He was depressed. He was sixty-seven and feeling his age. He honestly had something wrong somewhere, or there wouldn't have been blood in his stool. And, although we didn't know it at the time, he was in pain.

The month of May brought the final sock in the gut. Mom had to leave us and go to Chicago; her stepfather, Hal, Rary's second husband, was ill and in the hospital. Rary was also ailing and pretty helpless. She wore two sets of very strong glasses and was practically blind. Years later, I visited my mother in Scottsdale, Arizona. We spent a Saturday afternoon and evening together; we talked for eleven hours. It was there she was willing to recall:

"I had arthritis very badly in my shoulders—probably from tension—but I couldn't tell anybody. Seemed to me everybody was having more problems than I was. But it was difficult taking Mother to the hospital. I would go alone every morning to see Hal and take Mother in the afternoon."

Opening heavy hospital doors with those weakened shoulders was agony for Mom, but she kept her pain quiet. What outwardly looks like martyrdom in my mother seems to come from an innate sense that whatever is said won't matter.

"Finally Hal came home and somebody had to take care of both of them. So, it was little old me, which was . . . fine."

Mom stayed there three or four weeks. The pain began to get worse. As she watched her mother disintegrate, she also felt a disillusionment about Dad and his dreams.

"I'd look at Mother and think, 'God, I don't want to live that long. I don't want to be blind and helpless.' And it didn't look as if Paul and I were going anywhere. So I just took Mother's sleeping pills. And she found me. Just sitting in the chair. Gone. And they called an ambulance and pumped my stomach and brought me to life." Then she laughed. "Much to my disgust."

They called Dad. When she woke up in the hospital and looked into his face, she was furious.

"God, I didn't want to live. And they all treated me so strangely. They acted as though I'd committed the most horrible offense against them and the world. Same thing with Paul. There was such a coldness. No one hugged me. I kept praying for somebody to say, 'Hey, kid, it's all right, we love you. Thank God it didn't happen and we're sorry and let bygones be bygones.' No, nothing like that. I was just stunned.

"On the plane going home, Paul and I were very quiet. Finally I said, 'Paul, I'm awfully sorry you had to come to Chicago.' We were hard up and that cost money. And he said, 'It's all right. But just make sure, if you do it again, we do it together.' So we made a kind of 'suicide pact.'

And that was about it." Then she laughed again. "Now, what other little cheerful tidbit do you want to talk about?"

When I picked them up at the airport, I'll never forget her face. There was such a look of resentment, of fury at not being dead. But, until that Scottsdale talk, we never mentioned it again.

That was when the staring began, when Dad would just sit in the corner of the apartment staring straight ahead, almost catatonic.

He'd given up. All those years of grand ideas, and none of them had worked out. It hadn't helped when Howard had said, "Jesus, Paul, I know you're a painter, but at this point, why don't you paint houses?" Dad sat around in his bathrobe—with a Hemingway beard that Mom hated—rarely going out, rarely getting dressed, sleeping most of the day.

He just sat there . . . staring.

Mom's brother and his family visited in June, staying at a nearby motel. Dad liked Little John enormously; they had lively discussions. But even John felt something was wrong. Dad was very quiet, not himself. And, for the moment, on the wagon. Either rigidly on the wagon, or rigidly off. Not long after, he rolled back off.

He took to his bed. The pattern, when he was drinking, was to take to his bed—the green bed, the one he designed. Then remorse would set in, and he'd cry in Mom's arms, "I don't know why you put up with me. I'll never take another drink as long as I live." A lot of remorse.

One day he begged Mom for a drink, but she was firm. "Honey, I'm not going to do it. You're going to stop drinking, get out of that bed, and we're going to start over." He started to cry, but she still wouldn't do it. "Anyway, we haven't got any."

"Yes, we do. In the washing machine."

So she got it; she brought it to him. "Because he was about to get down on all fours," and she couldn't bear to watch.

She said she wasn't frightened about it, "I mostly think I got a little resentful. At least in Connecticut he once had ideas, enthusiasm, but in L.A., he wasn't doing anything. He was getting Social Security and very embarrassed about it. Standing in line with *those* people." Although Mom had just gotten a sales job in a store across the street, she still had no control over the checkbook, and her money was beginning to go for liquor. "I must admit that I was getting pretty . . . disillusioned."

Mom was of the old school: the husband sets the course, the wife follows. But when Dad lost his way, the family became rudderless. Once again, I became the cheerleader—determined to fill the void, be the parent, hold it all up—but I was leading hollow cheers in an empty arena. After the threat of Tom, after the debilitating "hepatitis," compounded by a bad case of immaturity, I needed a parent myself.

Doom seeped into that apartment. Once in, it never left. It got into the corners, the closets, the vents, the air. The darkness that had been threatening for the past few years silently moved in.

For survival, the three of us had reached out to each other. In that odd symbiosis known as family, we had grabbed on. Now, we hung on. We clung. A human rope entwined in misery, dangling over the abyss. Waiting for a parent, any parent, to stop the sway and pull us up.

But there *was* no parent. There was no one in charge.

Then, the last two weeks in June, Dad stopped drinking. And it got worse. Much worse.

He just sat in that chair, totally shut down.

Mom tried talking to him; I tried talking to him. But he just sat there, staring straight ahead. I don't know if he consciously couldn't hear us or if he was purposely blocking us out. We would plead to no effect, not even the blinking of an eye.

Day after day. No response.

He'd sit at the dinner table, barely eating, silent, staring into his cup. "You want some bread, Dad? Dad?"

I literally got down on my knees and asked him, begged him, to get some help—get to a doctor, get to an AA meeting, but he wouldn't or couldn't acknowledge that I was there. He was always very judgmental when he went on the wagon. But this was different. This was very different.

Frantically, Mom and I held whispered conferences in the kitchen. He needed professional help, but who, where? And how the hell would we get him there?

Day after interminable day. "You want some coffee, Dad? Dad?"

Horrible to say, but I began to long for him to drink. At least then he would talk. At least then he would laugh. At least, then, I could reach him on some kind of plane.

"You want the paper, Dad? Dad?"

He just sat there, staring . . .

We didn't know where to turn.

* * *

Then, by one of those seemingly innocuous quirks of fate, I was doing a week's shoot on *Dr. Kildare,* and the guest star was Mary Astor. We had a lot in common: careers at fourteen, nonworking fathers with "big ideas," Metro contracts, alcoholism. Mary Astor had been an alcoholic for years. Once, refusing an MGM renewal, she had entered a sanatorium for several months, following that with a suicide attempt. She wrote a book called *My Story* about her descent and recovery. I'd read every word, each page an odd kind of solace.

I was drinking a little too much myself at that time. To the untutored eye, it looked like youthful hijinks and hangovers. But fellow alcoholics can usually smell out a kid who looks lost, so she had approached me. I liked her; she liked me. Another one of those deep, "on the set," lifetime friendships that last a week.

She mentioned she was in AA. I'm sure it was a ploy to get me talking, but, instead, I talked about Dad. It all poured out. His not drinking, his not talking, his withdrawal, his depression. She urged me to get him into a home, a sanatorium. I told her I didn't know how.

"If we get him drunk he might agree to go. He sure won't go there sober."

"Then get him drunk."

So, the first day of July, Mom and I deliberately got my father drunk, successfully getting ourselves the same. It was like the back end of an O'Neillian drama. In my guilty memory, we were like the Furies, long fingernails beckoning: taunting him, tempting him, enticing him to drink with us. The plan had been hastily devised: we'd get him drunk, call the paramedics, he'd wake up in the sanatorium, he'd have help. So, we got him drunk, to save his life. That's the irony.

As always, it was more pleasant when we all drank. We were on common ground. We talked of the future, "dwelling in possibilities": jobs all around, sunshine, fresh air, billowing curtains in the kitchen sunlight.

Bobbing, weaving, surrounding him, leading him on.

Mom said, "Now, I have a job."

And I said, "And I have a job."

And Dad said, "By God, you're right. I'll go to the sanatorium. Then I'll get out and work across the street in the filling station. And we'll all live together."

We bobbed; we weaved. Taunting, tempting.

But he was back; a part of him was back. By the time we passed out, we were thrilled. And definitely relieved.

The next morning, everyone woke up late.

It was July 2, a holiday weekend; otherwise, it was just an ordinary day. Extraordinary things happen on ordinary days. Father was in the green bed, nursing a hangover. Mom and I were fixing brunch, pretty hung over ourselves. Everything perfectly ordinary.

It was around eleven o'clock when Dad called softly from the bedroom:

"Mariette."

So softly I wasn't sure I'd heard him:

"Mariette."

I went into his room. "Yes, Dad?"

He was out of bed, still in his pajamas and robe, standing near the closet door.

"Mariette, I can't find my glasses."

Something seemed strange. His behavior; the

fact that the closet door was open. The closet door was rarely open.

"Where did you leave them?"

"I don't know."

It was as if he wanted me to see something, but that's in retrospect. For at the moment, I spotted his glasses on the bed under a corner of the blanket. Nothing was mussed, nothing. They seemed to have been carefully placed.

I picked them up, puzzled: "Here they are. They're right here, honey."

"Oh."

Then I went out—because I didn't know he had that gun in the house. I suspect it was in the closet. Again, in retrospect.

I told Mom about his glasses. Idle conversation as we buttered the toast. She said she saw him get up earlier and walk to his desk in his bathrobe.

"He had this funny look on his face, like he was in a daze."

"Did he do anything?"

"Just wrote something down and put it in his pocket. Do you want cream cheese?"

"No, thanks. Did he say anything?"

"Yes."

"Good, he's still talking. What'd he say?"

"He said, 'Why don't you two go to some nice place for lunch?' "

"What'd you say?"

"I said we were fixing lunch."

"What'd he say?"

"He just said, 'Oh,' and went back to bed. Jelly?"

Not much later, we sat down to eat. Then we heard this "pop." It was like no other "pop" I'd ever heard. Not like the gunfire you hear in movies during "Cowboys and Indians" or "Cops and

"Big John" Watson, my grandfather, and the father of behaviorism. Children should be touched only as necessary.

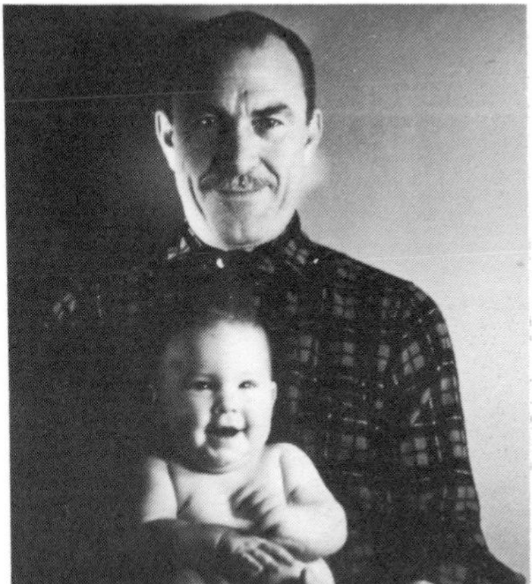

Father Paul Hartley and "the perfect baby," 1940.

With my brother Tony and mother Polly: touching, but not too much. The silences were growing.

Polly with yet another family pet.

Dad in his prime.

Dad quail-hunting. Once he lost his job, the drinking got worse. Mom's, too.

Halloween, 1945. I'm the tall one in the middle of the back row. Sandy Gjuresko is in the front, third from right, looking . . . perfect.

A Silver Nutmeg Theatre production in the early '50s. I'm the wicked fairy fourth from right. I always played the wicked fairy. Also all the kings, cavemen and trees.

At fifteen, with Tony. I was an honor student, a cheerleader, and I thought I was pregnant.

My movie debut in Sam Peckinpah's *Ride the High Country.* Joel McCrea's acting advice: "Stick in your stomach and go on."

At seventeen, a radiant picture. But the family was falling apart.

Christmas, 1961. A dreadful time. Dad was at his lowest ebb. I was married to a charming monster. But we looked good.

Drums of Africa, with one of the few live animals the budget could afford.

Dad, in his Hemingway beard, Polly and me in early 1963. My last picture of him. When we heard the "pop" from the next room, we knew instantly what it was.

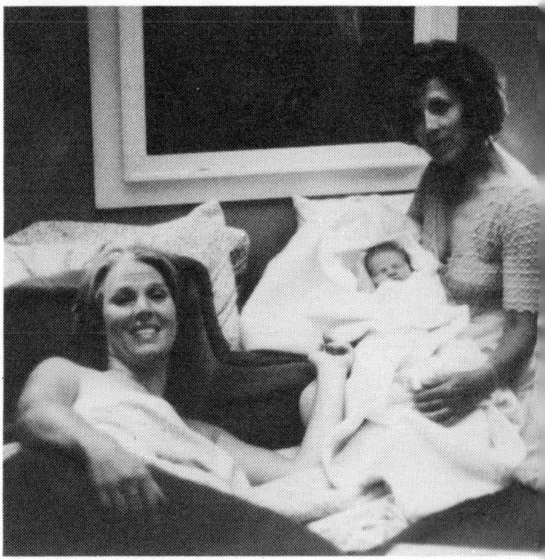

With Patrick's French mother, Jacqueline, and Justine, two hours old, in 1978. Confusion, polyglot hysteria and the Westside rapist—what more could you ask for?

Things hit bottom in 1966. But then the jobs came, the confidence came. Even better, Patrick came. Our first child, Sean, was born in 1975.

During the height of the Polaroid commercials, people really *did* think I was married to James Garner. (Copyright © 1979 Tony Korody/Sygma)

The great CBS *Morning Program* experiment, 1987. Here I am with Jane and Joan and Hizzoner Ed Koch. Why am I smiling? I was too tired to know any better.

With Candy Lightner, filming *M.A.D.D.: Mothers Against Drunk Driving*.

Closing the circle: With Eva LeGallienne in 1989. With Patrick, Sean and Justine.

Robbers." It was a very small "pop," like a cap pistol. Mom and I looked at each other and instantly knew. When we rushed into the bedroom, we saw Dad lying on the bed, the gun slack in his hand. He had shot himself behind his right temple. I remember screaming, "No! No! No! No!" while Mom grabbed the gun and hurled it against the wall.

Amazingly, he was still alive. Literally, half a head, but still alive, still breathing, making a kind of death rattle. His face wasn't distorted; I don't think he was in pain, but there was a lot of blood—on the sheets, on the walls.

Mom held him, encouraging him, hopeful, while I ran to the hall telephone. I don't remember who it was I called but I must have called the paramedics, the fire department, and the police, pleading with them to come quickly. Then I ran back to the room.

"He's got a good pulse, Mariette. He's got a good pulse."

She told him we loved him, told him not to worry, he was going to get better. But the paramedics seemed to take forever. I kept running out to the street, as if running out would make them come faster, because all I could see was this man with half a head, alive. It was a crazy jumble of out to the street, into the room, out to the street.

"Is there a note? Did he leave a note? He's got a good pulse, Mariette."

Whenever I drive by the corner of Barrington and Sunset, I still see myself running out; I still hear the screams; I still hear the sirens from far off; I still see myself flagging down the ambulance. The police arrived, followed shortly by the paramedics. I hurried them into the house, into the bedroom. Mom looked up at them, "He's got a good pulse."

As the paramedics set up the stretcher, one of the policemen found the gun across the floor—a squared-off revolver.

"Did you know he had a gun?"

"He was a gun person. But we didn't know he had a handgun."

"You never saw this before?"

I looked at Mom, she shook her head no. "He must have bought it in L.A."

"To do what he did?"

"I don't know. I guess. Maybe. I guess."

The paramedics placed Dad on the stretcher; the cop launched into more questions, seemingly routine.

"Was he depressed?"

"Very."

"About what?"

"He couldn't find a job."

"Anything else? You have an argument?"

"No. But he might have been upset about last night."

"What about last night?"

Suddenly, defensive. "Nothing. There wasn't an argument."

He picked up the gun, studied it, then studied us.

"Anybody see this happen?"

"We were in the other room."

"Sure you weren't in the same room?"

"I don't understand."

"Well, we can't tell what's happened here. Why isn't the gun on the bed? Why isn't it in his hand? Why is it on the floor, on the other side of the room?"

Mom was confused, "I think I threw it."

"You think?"

"I'm not sure."

"You touched it? Your fingerprints on it?"

"I guess."

"Anybody else here? Anybody see this happen?"

"I just told you. We were in the other room."

"Besides the two of you? No witnesses?"

"Isn't it obvious?"

"Never can tell."

I looked at the pain in Mom's eyes. We were both so full of shame. You feel the blame, you internally accuse, you don't need help. The other cop told him to back off.

The paramedics put a sheet around Dad and wheeled him out through the living room, through the study. He was still alive, he was still breathing, his eyes were still open. It's almost with fondness that I think back on his face, because it was the last time I ever saw him. There was—and this image keeps coming back to me—half a man there. I had been seeing half a man for years, but this time, literally, there was half a man. I had a terrible sense of guilt, an enormous sense of loss, maybe even relief, and terror. What would happen if he died? What would happen if he didn't?

Mom rode in the ambulance—sirens wailing—to the UCLA emergency ward, while I followed in the car. He was taken immediately to the operating room. Somebody, an intern, came down and said, "We can operate, but he'll have no mind at all. And practically no movement."

"No, no surgery."

It seemed like hours until somebody came down to us and said, "He's gone." Mom says it was a half an hour. Then an intern I'd never seen before, an intern dressed in blue, handed me a brown paper bag. Inside were Dad's bathrobe and his bloody pajamas.

The most brutal time was reentering the house. In the movies, suicide is romanticized: a leap from the bridge, a vial of pills, the sound of the ambulance. In reality, there is nothing so awful as cleaning up your father's brains that are all over the sheets, all over the wall, all over the white living-room carpet. Picking up something, not knowing what you're picking up, until you realize what you're picking up. Dropped as he was being wheeled out. And the smell. The smell of blood, the smell that never goes away.

As we cleaned, we tried to find a note. We searched his bureau, we searched his desk, we searched his books. No note. We did, however, find something else. Phenobarbital pills. Vials and vials of phenobarbital pills—behind cracker boxes, on top of the refrigerator, wrapped up in his socks. The doctor in Pacific Palisades must have been giving him prescriptions for pain. Along with a few other doctors. He had not only been drinking, he had been taking barbiturates. The staring, the catatonia, began to make sense.

Then Mom opened the brown paper bag and vacillated. Should she wash his bathrobe and his bloody pajamas or just throw them out? Instinctively, she prepared them for the wash; instinctively, she checked the bathrobe pockets. That's when she found the note—probably written on that early morning walk to his desk. It said the insurance premium was paid up until the fifth of July. He wanted to be sure Mom had some money. But that's about all it said.

We cleaned all day. Scrubbing, scouring—to make the sheets, the walls, the rug look as if nothing had happened. Even though it was a lie. We washed the sheets; we scrubbed the rug. And for years, we pretended that nothing had happened.

A few days after my father's death, Sandy came to be with me from Florida. We were sharing an evening with Dana Andrews's sons in Palos Verdes—both went to Staples—when suddenly, a blackness hit me. I turned to Sandy.

"I have to go home."

"Why?"

"Something's wrong. I have to go home."

Palos Verdes was almost an hour away from Brentwood Gardens. When I opened the apartment door, it was quiet. Everything was quiet, not a noise. And it was dark. Only a sliver of light under Mom's bedroom door. But as I entered the study, the room with the guns in it, there was enough light from the streetlight and the moon to see the note on the desk. A large, white piece of paper neatly folded over, her childlike, wiggly upside-down "M." And then the rest of it: "a-r-i-e-t-t-e." That's all I needed. The power of that note blew me against the wall. My body left me, everything left me. I saw it and I ran.

She was in the bedroom, same bedroom, same green bed. Pills again. I ran to the same telephone. They took us to the same hospital, the same emergency ward, the same goddamn emergency ward. And I stroked her head and I said, "Mom, you need help. You've got to get some help." But the next morning nothing was said. She didn't remember. And I couldn't remind her.

I took Mom to the beach, to Dick and Betty Wilson's, one of those great old houses on Santa Monica beach, an old fisherman's house. I walked her out onto the sand. As we stood there, everything went out from under me: the ocean disappeared over the horizon, the sand disappeared from under my feet; before I knew it I was looking up at Mom's face. "Darling, you passed out. Go into the water; maybe it'll do some good." I stood up, turned, and found it hard to walk away from her.

It was a beautiful day. The waves were gentle, but strong enough for me to bodysurf, something I had never done before. I stayed in the water for hours, determined to master it: waiting for a wave, joining it, riding with it. I could feel my body. Death takes everything with it; you forget you have a body. Being washed up on shore and back again, being washed up on shore and back again, scraped clean by the small pebbles that line the beach. I finally understood the concept of mother sea. There was something so huge, so loving, so steady, so nurturing and encompassing, I could go with the waves, back out and back in, back out and back in. Until life was breathed back. Like Millay's "Renascence," "I breathed my soul back into me."

After my TV son committed suicide in *Silence of the Heart,* I dreamed my father came to me in the kitchen—in clean pajamas, clean robe—and asked me what was the worst thing about his suicide. It was then, only then, I was able to say that the worst thing was that "we all became suicidal." What I was consciously talking about was my Mom. What I was unconsciously talking about was myself.

The real horror to me, however, is that on the ashes of my father, I was eventually brought back to life. I needed that kind of drama, that kind of explosion to bust me alive.

SIXTEEN

I tried for perfection but I failed at that. I tried to be a saint. I failed at that. And then . . . he wanted me to be a woman— I failed at that, too.

—CLAIRE MORTON

It has always struck me as ironic that a novel dealing with conflict between mother and daughter gave me the means to cut the cord with my own mother. When Allison Mackenzie left Peyton Place, I left the apartment at Brentwood Gardens.

After Dad died, Mom and I grabbed on; there was a desperation in our connection. We were locked together emotionally and financially, supporting each other's disease. It was as if Dad had sinned against nature, creating a fissure. We tottered on the crevice, not quite knowing whether to choose life or death ourselves.

We were walking near a street corner at La Brea and Fairfax when we turned and saw a car careening toward us, out of control. We both froze. Once again, all I could think was, "That's right, that's natural." Everything negative was natural. At the last minute, the car swerved away.

I got a small part in *Marnie,* one of Alfred Hitchcock's few failures. At first, Hitchcock was sweet to me; we had a repartee that was nice and light. Then we shot the first scene, and he didn't talk to me again for the rest of the film. With my fragile ego, I took it personally. Now I suspect he was so concerned about the movie, he just forgot I was there.

Whenever a car backfired or I turned my head quickly to the right, I would hear a gunshot. I got the part of the daughter in *Touch of the Poet* at the Pasadena Playhouse. Every night for four weeks, I listened for the sound of the gun when my stage father, Con Melody, went upstairs and pretended to shoot himself. I'd shake, then go home, and get drunk.

On opening night, in the middle of the first scene, I heard "jingle, jingle, jingle." I peered into the audience to see my mother, wrists smothered in bracelets, climbing belatedly over legs and coats to get to her seat. That night I got a standing ovation on my curtain call. Mom hurried backstage, thrilled, and asked, "Did you see the standing ovation?"

"Yes, I can't believe it!"

"Believe it. *I* started it."

For the last few years, I've told this story with laughter. There was no laughter then. It only added to the disintegration of our relationship.

Then in 1964, when *Peyton Place* was barely into its first season, I drove my hood car onto the lot at Fox. (At least my idea of a hood car—a Falcon with holes in the muffler. I liked the sound, cruising up Sunset with my V-8 engine. Besides, I couldn't afford anything else.) I was going to audition for the part of Claire Morton, a frigid doctor, wearing my three-piece charcoal-gray suit, pale-blue silk blouse, black alligator shoes—all very elegant, all very frigid, all serving to hide my escalating weight. Something worked. I was signed as a regular by Paul Monash for thirty-four episodes.

It was my first steady job, and I made good money—enough to afford my own apartment and a new 280SL. It was as hard for me to pull away as it was for Mom. She was never verbal about it, but the nonverbal message was, "If you go, I'll die." I'd talk about moving out and would get a disapproving silence.

Then one day I was lying down in my bedroom in the Brentwood apartment, and suddenly my right hand involuntarily reached up, as if it was reaching for another hand—the final grasp above the waterline—and I thought, "If I don't get out of this house, *I'll* die." I called a psychiatrist recommended by Betty Wilson and immediately started therapy. Dr. Monke helped me make the separation.

I found two apartments: one called Château Colline near Westwood, the other just off Malcolm. Mom couldn't afford Brentwood Gardens when I left, so she took the latter, gave me the furniture from Connecticut and bought hers from a friend who was moving to Palm Springs. Physically, we still weren't far apart. But Mom felt abandoned, and I resented it enormously.

When *Peyton Place* was first telecast by ABC on September 15, 1964, critics gave it one season. They should have bet on me. The show lasted five years; I was the one that lasted one season. The series was so popular, viewers were taping it. I'm not talking video, I'm talking audio. They just taped the sound.

It was the first nighttime soap opera, unless you're a stickler for accuracy and want to count *One Man's Family* with Mother Barbour, Father Barbour and all the little Barbours who lived in

Santa Barbour. At least that's what I thought for years; they really lived in San Francisco.

Peyton Place was a "bold, new concept"—a sanitized version of Grace Metalious's bestseller—that had everything: ripening sex, budding sex, brooding sex, repressed sex, wretched marriages, and a girl on the threshold of womanhood. Others, like loose-living Betty Anderson, had gone so far past the threshold they were in another suburb. Jack Paar called it, "Television's first situation orgy." The *New York Times* called it: "Life on the verge."

Similar in format to radio, it used an opening narrator, Matt Swain (Warner Anderson), editor of *The Clarion:*

> David and Doris Schuster have spent their first social evening in Peyton Place. They have been guests of Theodore Dowell, a man who has been presented with an opportunity and a challenge. Whatever Dowell decides to do, it will affect David and Doris Schuster—more than they know.

I was on *Peyton Place* long before Mia Farrow (Allison Mackenzie, later Harrington) chopped off her hair. I rarely worked with Mia Farrow. I just remember her arriving every morning in her quilted bathrobe, limousined in from Beverly Hills. I rarely worked with Ryan O'Neal (Rodney Harrington); rarely worked with Dorothy Malone (Constance Mackenzie Carson); saw Barbara Parkins (loose-living Betty Anderson Harrington Cord Harrington) once in a while, getting her hair teased. I was the "B" plot line. Or "D," depending on your mood.

There were three directors: Ted Post, John Newland, and Walter Doniger. The first day, I was sitting in makeup, pretty nervous, when Ted Post came up to me:

"How are you, honey?"

"Fine."

"Don't forget—she's frigid."

"Absolutely." I told the hairdresser to hit the Spray Net.

The second day, I was still nervous when Walter Doniger came up to me in makeup:

"How are you, honey?"

"Fine."

"Don't forget—she's frigid."

The directors were doing three shows a week—Tuesday, Wednesday, and Thursday—which was murder. At least I assumed it was murder, or why would they keep repeating themselves? Because the third day, John Newland came up to me in makeup:

"How are you, honey?"

"Aren't I playing frigid?"

"Yah, just don't forget, okay?"

And I never did. I neutered my hair, unblushed my cheeks, never smiled. No one smiled on *Peyton Place,* anyway, unless they were drunk. I crossed my arms, crossed my legs; every orifice was pursed. Compared to me, Marian the Librarian was a slut.

I was playing opposite Leslie Nielsen, not knowing he would soon show up with a twin brother and become Leslie Nielsen, Leslie Nielsen. He was my husband, the great Doctor Vincent Markham, the Al Schweitzer of the Andes. He and I had cured the Peruvian Indians of some dreaded disease and were receiving awards in captivity. I was flown to captivity for the awards banquet, then flown back out. I had to get to my new job at Peyton Place

Memorial, leaving my husband, the great Doctor Vincent Markham, to continue Schweitzering without me.

So, Claire Morton, newly arrived from Peru, unpacked her bags, drove to the hospital, parked her passion, and frigidly jumped into the story line. They like to introduce new characters on soap operas; it gives them a place to plant the exposition. The first ten episodes I was so bombarded by exposition, I'd go home and wipe it off my front. It got in my eyelashes, in my hair, in my mouth. I'd be walking down the hospital corridor, briskly, glacially, and notice handsome Dr. Michael Rossi, his chin on the linoleum floor. I'd ask innocently:

"Something wrong, Mike?"

"I shouldn't have brought Rodney here."

"Why not?"

"Rod was married to Betty Anderson."

"My nurse? I didn't know."

"How could you? You've been away." Then, there would be this long pause. Long enough to march Macy's Thanksgiving Day Parade through: "Betty lost a baby."

"How terrible for her. Here?"

"Yes, it was last Christmas. Just after Allison Mackenzie found out that Elliott Carson was her real father, a few weeks before he finally married her mother, Constance Mackenzie, only weeks after he'd been released from prison."

"I didn't know that."

"How could you? You've been away. Rodney married loose-living Betty Anderson because she told him she was pregnant, but she really wasn't. Actually she had been, but lost her baby in a car accident. That was right after Steven Cord came back to town, threatening the inheritance of his half brothers, Norman and Rodney Harrington. Have you met Norman?"

"No, but, as you say, I've been away."

"You may have seen him with Rita Jacks. Rita is an ex-girl friend of that ruffian, Joe Chernak, who . . ."

"Don't forget, she's frigid."

"I won't, Ted."

A soap opera is not a job I would recommend to anyone with an ounce of paranoia. I'd get these delusions of being killed off, even though, contractually, I'd been promised life for thirty-four episodes. Contracts in Hollywood are generally used for fish food—and the frigid issue didn't help. Whether or not Claire Morton will defrost does not put a viewer on the edge of his cliff.

We never knew the story line ahead. The script would arrive at my door the night before, I'd crawl into bed, reading avidly, reading warily: "Oh, Leslie Nielsen has a twin brother. Oh, for heck sake." I'd look for symptoms: a slight cough, a sizeable lump, a brakeless car, a deep ravine.

One of the first things they teach you in "soap opera training" is never to get behind the steering wheel of a car in a blizzard when the camera is locked on your face, the lights and horns from oncoming traffic are sounding ominous, and the windshield wipers are rhythmically swishing, "She's gonna die. She's gonna die." Amnesia's generally safe, but don't ever fall asleep in a hospital where a nurse with dark, brooding eyes is haunting the corridors, brandishing a large hypodermic. And never, ever, turn your back on an actress with wild red hair, long red fingernails, who has just arrived in Junction City, carrying Louis Vuitton luggage and a voodoo doll. I've just scratched the surface.

I don't know if this story's apocryphal—it's certainly ancient—but I heard that a bunch of writers got sick of the story line on "Helen Trent," put all the running characters on a bus, and sent them out to Oxnard on a picnic. The bus went over a cliff while a ukelele plucked out "Juanita." Twain used to do that. Whenever he got bored with a character, he sent him out back and had him fall in a well. Said he had to quit when the well filled up.

Non oblivisci, illa est frigidus, became my coat of arms. If Johnny Newland came up to me one more time and said, "Don't forget, she's frigid," I was going to whack him with my chastity belt. I couldn't have been more frigid if I'd had a stiff snort of engine coolant. Geez.

After a number of weeks, it became apparent to me that frigidity was not my only character trait; I was also becoming Vera Vague. In 1985, when Dick Clark did a retrospective on Hollywood, he included a speech of Claire Morton's as an example of one of the least understandable diatribes ever uttered. I had a flock of them. Like this verbal loop-the-loop from Episode seventy-nine:

I had just delivered my first baby, when I bumped into Dr. Mike Rossi, played by Ed Nelson. I started succinctly enough:

> "I would like to discuss the nature of panic. And of cowardice and failure."

Ed, knowing my "scriptual" tendencies and wanting to be home by ten, tried to warn me off:

> "Claire, you've had a long night."

No such luck, Ed.

"Tonight I went into Mrs. Sinclair's room. Her pains were intensifying. I put on my benign professional face and started my soothing 'there, there, everything is fine' speech. And suddenly that pathetic woman-child started to clutch at me; sobbing and begging me to help her. I wanted to run. All of a sudden I was back in Peru: the Indians staring at me, holding their quiet children, wanting to give them life. But I had life! I had all the life of the good food I ate as a child, and the warm home I came from! And all the life in my hands that came from my training as a doctor! And that was what they wanted: my life for themselves! It terrified me! I walked among them in constant terror, even while I put salve on their terrible sores . . ."

I suddenly stopped. With terrible control, I refilled my coffee and sat absentmindedly sucking at the rim of my cup. At least, that's what the stage directions said I was doing. After an appropriate amount of rim-sucking, Ed (Dr. Rossi) tried to console me:

"Don't judge yourself so harshly. How much of himself can anyone give?"

His pronoun alone lending little help to the rising syntactical confusion. Luckily, I wasn't listening. I retorted bitterly:

"And him. The great Doctor Vincent Markham, Peru's shining answer to the Doctor Schweitzer tradition. If they asked for tears mixed with their morphine, why, they received it. Sob with us, they cried. Bleed with us, pray with us, sleep with us on our soiled mats. Nothing was too self-abasing for the holy Dr. Markham to do."

Obviously, it was Dr. Rossi's turn as an expository foil.

"What about you, Claire? What did you do about the filth and the vermin?"

"I tried, Michael. I tried. I learned their dialect. I learned to eat their foods and I read their history. But that's not what they wanted. Growing up in Peyton Place didn't prepare me for what they wanted. In the tradition of Doctor Robert Morton, I tried for perfection but I failed at that. In the tradition of Doctor Vincent Markham, I tried to be a saint. I failed at that. And then . . . he wanted me to be a woman—I failed that, too."

With that, they cut to a commercial. To let things settle.

It wasn't too long after, that Dr. Mike Rossi—in an example of extreme altruism—took it upon himself to take Claire upon himself, to help her succeed as a woman. Ed Nelson had so many kids in real life, I didn't even want to sit on his chair, but despite his pollinating tendencies, I was thrilled; I could finally smile.

The writers created a scene in his beach house, a wonderful scene—soft, romantic, dark, sexy. On our walk to the bedroom, the camera discreetly lingered over the wine. I couldn't wait for the segment to be aired. I couldn't wait to prove to others, to myself, that I wasn't frigid. People would finally think of me as a sex object, or, at least, someone with sensuality, or, at the very least, someone capable of having a Pap smear. No such luck. As far as America was concerned, the rocket went off and Mike Rossi didn't.

The segment was to be aired on Thursday, June 3, 1965, the same night Edward White took a stroll one hundred miles out in space, untethered from his "Gemini" space capsule. Balloons, ha! Try a space launch, Claire Oleson! And, oh sure, wouldn't you know they'd preempt. So the only thing that went up that night was a rocket. It has been one of the best-kept secrets in television history that Claire Morton lost it with Dr. Michael Rossi at his beach house on a Thursday night, right after an Ipana commercial.

Thirty-four episodes after I began, I was to fly off to the Andes with Leslie Nielsen and never return to Peyton Place again. I didn't have a lot of choice; ABC had already purchased the ticket. It was excursion fare, and some restrictions applied. Leslie Nielsen and I were going to be written out at the same time, along with his twin brother. I always had a feeling if anybody was going to go, it was going to be Leslie. Then, when I found out he had a twin brother, I thought, "Oh, boy, we're all gonna go." I mean, three pins standing, what producer could resist picking up a spare.

So, on the fatal day, I left with Leslie Nielsen to watch him die in the Andes of some horrible nameless disease, having nary a cough myself. He didn't know what it was, but it was going to kill him. I knew what it was. It's called "soap opera" disease. It's so contagious, it can ravage a set in two weeks, spreading from one cast member to another. Its symptoms include a rash of new writers, an outbreak of new producers. Even the Peruvian Indians had come down with it.

I didn't work for Paul Monash again for a very long time.

I had a manager, at that point, who kept pricing me out of the business by making extraordinary demands. (He'd ask for a limo, while I was just hoping they'd let me park my Falcon on the lot.) One day I said to him:

"I'm curious. Why haven't I worked for Paul Monash? I did a respectable job as Claire Morton. Maybe not Emmy material, but heck. . . ."

"I'll do some homework. Let me find out."

About a week later, he called back. "I don't know how to tell you this."

"What?"

"I talked to the people over at Monash's office."

"What'd you find out?"

"Paul Monash won't hire you because he thinks you're frigid."

I swear it's true; I know it's true. Because Monash hired me a year later for *Judd for the Defense.* I played a frigid schoolteacher.

I don't understand any of it.

SEVENTEEN

All serious daring starts from within.

—EUDORA WELTY

Some drinkers end up in the gutter, some on skid row. I ended up at I. Magnin's in Budget Dresses.

Whenever I was released from a show—even though it was preordained—I took it as a personal rejection. I also lost another family. *Peyton Place* had given me a place to go, a boundary, a discipline. It was something to look forward to, and when my role ended, it was like slamming into a brick wall.

Not long after, I started shooting *The Hero* at NBC with Richard Mulligan and Victor French. It had a delightful premise: Mulligan portrayed a fearless TV Western star who in reality is a bumbling family man with a fear of horses. I played his wife.

We shot thirteen episodes, aired opposite Marlo Thomas's top-rated *That Girl* in the fall of '66, and got clobbered. I've always liked Dick Mulligan's work and so did the reviewers. They called it an intelligent comedy, but it was a major failure in the ratings. End of another family.

I was drinking through *Marnie,* drinking through *Peyton Place.* But it wasn't until *The Hero* that I started bringing little mustard jars of vodka to the set, mixing it with Snappy Tom tomato juice from the catering wagons. No one knew because no one knew me. There was a secrecy about me, a mystery. No one knew what was going on, including me.

And once I started drinking, it was hard to stop. I'd drunkenly squat in front of an open refrigerator, an open cupboard, drinking vodka, and eating everything, including Purina Cat Chow. I was a chub in *Marnie,* a chub on *Peyton Place.* I remember watching Lillian Roth on *This Is Your Life* while crying buckets for my ill-spent life.

For the past few years, I had been going to work with hangovers. I could get by but couldn't handle the tough stuff. A script arrived late the night before I shot a *Stoney Burke.* When I opened it, I found a two-page monologue about building a bridge and how it went up and how it went down. I came from Connecticut; what did I know about building bridges? I only knew I had to shoot the next morning at six. I got there fuzzybrained, hung over. When Jack Lord and I did the scene, I couldn't remember my lines. We went over it and over it. In exasperation, he said, "What do you do when you have to learn Shakespeare?" I wanted to say, I usually get the script a month ahead, but I didn't. I sat there, humiliated. There's a wonderful story about the actor who forgot his lines on Jack Benny's show, so Benny forgot his lines with him. The actor relaxed and his lines came back. Jack Lord was not Jack Benny.

I reached my bottom when I started drinking by myself and realized I wasn't drinking with anybody, at anybody. Having moved away from Mom, I was managing to be self-destructive totally on my own.

I had gone back to school, to UCLA (downtown), studying philosophy and psychology, trying to get a degree. But I had the same organizational problems I'd had at Carnegie Tech. I went two terms, got good grades—even an "A" in psych—but at an enormous cost. I'd have an attack of paralyzing nerves before each test and study compulsively all weekend, drinking almost a case of beer.

I was full of anxiety, still carrying Dad's death, drinking to forget, to anesthetize. After a while, it got to be something that my body craved; it became a daily thing. I'd love to be able to describe it so that it sounds different from other people's stories, but I can't.

I'd slowly walk up the stairs to parties, nervous, shy—I never felt as if I fit in—and say, "I'm not going to have anything tonight. I'm not going to have anything, and no one's going to care. I'm not going to have anything." The hostess would open up the door, and I'd say, "A very cold, very dry martini—thank you," as if none of that battle had been waged. Then I'd get drunk and be the perfect party girl. I didn't have any sense of guilt. Sober, I was a mass of moral adhesions, but drunk, the morality washed away. It was like a click in my brain; here we go, guys.

One day in therapy, while complaining of another hangover, I heard an impatience in Dr. Monke's voice which I'd never heard before. That did it. Hangovers might have no effect, but that kind of motherlike silence could. I stepped out of the race, joined an anonymous support group and a little theater over a Burbank bowling alley.

* * *

A few months later, I'd stopped drinking, I'd stopped overeating, but I'd also stopped therapy. I didn't stop, I ran. I had demons screaming, "Don't look inside; you'll hate what you find." I was absolutely terrified. And I didn't trust anybody.

I was living like a penurious old maid with my two cats, Pansy and Stanley Butterfly, and dying inside. Depression is seductive, whispering there will be no change. I was convinced I was going to live like this for the rest of my life.

I was standing on the corner of Bedford and Wilshire, and I was scared. My career was dead. No one was asking for me. I was down to my last thousand from *Peyton Place*, and felt I would end up rentless if I didn't get some work. I was too scared to call people like Mike Frankovich or Leonard Stern and say, "Hi, Leonard. Hi, Mike. I've lost weight. I've changed."

I was twenty-six and had been acting since I was ten. I wasn't sure if it was something I was doing compulsively or something I wanted to do. Stardom had been my father's dream. Was I in this business to fulfill my father's fantasy for me? My life was not working. No matter how much applause I got, nothing filled the hole.

I began separating my father's fantasy from my own. Could I do something else? Did I have a choice? I thought, "I can't do it anymore, Dad. I can't be a star for you. It's a fantasy." I walked across the street to the employment office at I. Magnin's and applied for a job. I started work the next day.

I was in Budget Dresses, which, in the summer of 1966, was right next to Better Dresses, two doors down from Better Shoes. Miss Betty ran

Better Dresses. Miss Betty was one of those ladies who had blue hair and wore black dresses with little white doily collars, who've been working for eighty-six years, scraping and scratching their way up from Budget to Better.

In one week, the buyer decided I'd make a swell assistant buyer, people began to ask for me, and my confidence soared. If Big John could sell coffee at Macy's, if my mother could sell dresses at the Separate Shop, then maybe this was what I was cut out to do.

When people from show business came in, or people recognized me from television, I wanted to hide, but they always bought something.

"I know you. You're that girl who was crippled on *Doctor Kildare.* Times are tough, eh? I'll buy this and this and this."

"I know you. You were that squaw on *Bonanza.* Can't you get work, honey? I'll buy this and this and this."

"Oh, my dear, weren't you the one that went blind on *Ben Casey?* I'll buy this and this and this."

I felt like a Hollywood Poster Child.

One day a woman felt particularly bad, "I loved you on *My Three Sons.* You would have made a terrific mother for those poor motherless boys," and bought a stack of clothes. We needed Rose, the alterationist, but she was nowhere to be seen, so I marched past Tina Turner in Better Shoes—not selling, buying—calling, "Rose!" I marched past pale-pink sofas with seated manikins, calling, "Rose! Rose!" I marched through the maze of fancy dressing rooms for Better Dresses—room after shuttered room—calling "Rose! Rose!" (You only get full doors in Better Dresses. In Budget you get curtains resembling zip strips that you have to center.)

I could hear a murmur of voices above the dressing-room stalls.

"Oh, I don't know. What do you think?"

"The plaid's nice."

"Rose!"

Somewhere in the maze, I heard Rose's timid voice, "Yes?"

"Rose, I need you. Where are you?"

As I went past another dressing room, I caught a glimpse of Greer Garson trying on a sequined red gown. Miss Betty was with her.

"Oh, that looks wonderful! Just your color."

"Sure it doesn't make me look fat?"

"Rose!"

That's when Miss Betty rushed through the curtains and hissed, "What are you doing here, kid!"

"I'm trying to find Rose. I need some alterations."

"What is that! A thirty-six buck dress! Don't you know this is where the minks and the diamonds are! You wanna wreck a sale?"

I said, "Gee, no, but is Rose in there?"

She said, "Get back to your position. I'll talk to you later."

I said, "Gosh, I don't think so."

That was the day I quit I. Magnin's—after only three weeks on the skids. By the end of the year, I was back to fringe and mules, shooting *Death Valley Days*. But I. Magnin contributed to the turnaround.

I was in that support program for over three years, at one point attending three meetings a day. I didn't just attend, I was hooked. I became the perfect groupie, falling into the same family mode that I did in my own family. I became a fanatic. I was going to be the best nondrinker in the West. When I developed a cough on location in Death Valley and the doctor gave me cough medicine, I drank the whole bottle before I realized it was full of alcohol. I blamed myself for months.

While the program had made me sober, I had still not dealt with the problems, only the symptoms. I continued to make myself the heavy so that I could avoid getting angry at Mom and Dad.

I was asked to speak a lot because I was an actress and young and funny and had a good story. Unlike Girl Scout Camp, I was getting applause and laughter for all those things I'd been hiding for years. But it got to be an act. I was still not in touch at all. Eventually I left the program with my rage and shame intact. I was not ready to face the truth for eleven more years—not until I joined ACA (Adult Children of Alcoholics), and was finally able to broach that recovery as a sober adult.

During that three-year period, Tony called from the hospital. Mom had tried again. Someone had found her in the garage. I felt helpless; I was helpless. I started to tremble and called an advisor:

"My mother has attempted again. What do I do?"

"Stop encouraging it. Don't do anything."

"But I have to go to the hospital."

"You don't do anything."

"But I can't just not show up."

"Yes, you can. You don't do anything. You break your connection with death."

So for the first time, I didn't show up. It was one of the hardest things I'd ever had to do, but the advisor was right. Although Mom took one more overdose, it was feeble, halfhearted. That was the final serious attempt.

But the estrangement with my mother lasted for a long, long time. Too long.

EIGHTEEN

The consumer is to the . . . advertising agencies, what the green frog is to the physiologist.

—JOHN B. WATSON

Having come from a long line of advertisers, I looked down on it. I remember sitting in front of a television set in the early sixties with a drink in my hand saying, "Those poor suckers—selling cars, selling soap." I was an Eastern snob, a the-a-trical actress. Hell, I did Shakespeare. Maybe my father had to lay down his paintbrushes, but I didn't. At least not until '65. At least not until I hit that the-a-trical bottom so hard that I bounced. It was a long fall from pride.

My first series of commercials was for Safeguard soap. You may have heard actors talking about subtext, the character's history, what's *not* being said. If you're playing a proper New England matron, the subtext might be that years earlier you smoked Indian hemp, turned nympho, and went through the local board of Aldermen. Although this does not show up in the dialogue, actors use the subtext to flesh out their interpretation. Lear, Hamlet, Blanche DuBois. I was a little surprised, however, when I was called on to use subtext for Marti, the drugstore lady. I mean, subtext when you're playing a Fruit of the Loom banana? Procter and Gamble sent me a fifteen-page history/biography of this woman standing behind the counter hustling soap.

Seems Marti had been happily married for years until she lost her husband. (I love that phrase, "lost her husband." I always envision the widow checking her pockets, rummaging through her purse, looking behind sofa cushions.) Anyway, one day while standing on a street corner, Marti's only child was hit by a car. Honest. In her grief, Marti decided to start her own drugstore. This was her subtext. I seriously doubted if any actress had been this challenged since a radio actress was directed in parenthesis to say her next line, *(tempestuously, brokenly, but with pride)*. Her next line was "How?" How, indeed. How was I to give the audience a sense of poor Marti in thirty seconds, while convincing a customer about the security of Safeguard with lines like, "Hi, honey, how you doin'?" How was I to give all that emotion behind "Hi, Mrs. Chester, what can I do for you today?" and not cry?

I had a real problem in "domestic cleaner" commercials. I don't know if it was a lack of subtext or a lack of elbow grease, but I never could get the stain off. With Favor, I couldn't get the stain off the tabletop. With Formula 409, I couldn't get the "x" off the refrigerator. I couldn't believe it, standing there feeling like a friggin' failure as a friggin' actress because I couldn't get the "x" off the refrigerator with the friggin' 409. (My mother's going to hate that sentence.)

I did the Toll-House cookie commercial. It was shown for four years. My godchild in Boston got so tired of seeing it, he almost threw up on the screen.

Then, one day, I'd had it. My first manager had said to me, in one of his more eloquent moods, "You can't do commercials, because you'll feel rejected and die." My first manager had enormous insight. I had slogged along from interview to interview carrying different outfits, different personas. One day they'd want my Ali MacGraw look, the next day my Candice Bergen look, my Grace Kelly look. My trunk was full of Jane Fonda clothes and Josephine the Plumber wigs. So I made the decision not to do any more commercials for scale. Scale, at that point, meant $220 plus residuals. After having done everything from Texaco to peanut butter, it was time to take a stand. Then I got a call from Arlene Dayton, my feisty new manager.

"There's a call for a Polaroid commercial."

"Scale?"

"Yes."

"I don't want to do it. Not for scale."

"Oh yes, you do, honey."

I got a call from Sandy Joseph, my commercial agent.

"Tomorrow, 2:15, Polaroid."

"It's scale."

"So?"

"Didn't Arlene tell you? I've taken a stand."

"No time for a stand, Custer. 2:15."

When I arrived, the casting office looked like the good witch had passed through and every woman but one had been turned into Homecoming Queen. I felt like Kentucky swill in a room full of bourbon. Worse yet, sitting directly across from me was this even more gorgeous woman. When I say gorgeous, I mean drop-dead gorgeous. How the hell could I compete with Morgan Brittany? With that great long blue-black hair, eyes the color of lapis lazuli, legs that didn't quit, alabaster skin.

I've always been conscious of my little slanted eyes. The minute I saw those ladies, my eyes got slantier. By the time I was called in to tape my audition, I was bowlegged, knockkneed, and had a hunchback. All this venom spilled onto the test tape, and I got the part.

So I was hired by Doyle, Dane, Bernbach as a day player to be one of James Garner's many wives. But on July 27, 1977, the first day on the set, magic happened. The dialogue set a tone that would continue for years. We were promoting the new Onestep camera. On the first commercial, Jimmy was doing the pitch:

"Just one step. Point it and push the button."

"That's two steps."

"We don't count the pointing."

"It's beautiful. But I still think pointing's a step."

"Well, it isn't."

"Well, it should be."

That was it, lovely, I thought. Well-written, I thought. And a one-shot chance to finally work with James Garner, I thought. Or so we all thought, until take four. Jimmy started out the same:

"Just one step. Point it and push the button."

"That's two steps."

"We don't count the pointing."

"It's beautiful. But I still think pointing's a step."

"Well, it isn't."

"Well, it should be."

Now, I don't know if it was the way I said it, or a latent elf in Jimmy, but he ad-libbed, opting for the final word. "We don't count it."

What was I going to do? Give it to him? Are you kidding, Lucinda? I hit him with as much finality as I could muster: "But you should." That's the one they aired.

By the time they asked me back for a second commercial, I was five-months pregnant with Justine; it didn't show. By the time they asked me back for a group of four in June, 1978, I was a week overdue and the size of a sofa. I was so large they shot me knitting a king-size afghan over my stomach, sitting behind a table wrapping gifts, standing behind a saddle polishing leather. In the last one, they placed me behind so many obstacles—Jimmy's golf cart, my golf bag—I was on a different network.

Arlene and I began sensing there was some kind of campaign here; they don't build sets around a nine-month pregnancy for day players. My contract came up for negotiations, and she went to town.

Over a six-year period, we shot close to 250 commercials: ten-, thirty-, sixty-second spots. Bob Gage and Jack Dillon, the creative writer-directors, lived near each other. When one of them came up with a commercial, he put it in the other's mailbox. The second-half read it, revised it, and returned it.

I think the woman I played—that gutsy, brassy dame—was based on Jack Dillon's wife, the kind of woman who, at a cocktail party, would turn to Jack and say:

"Jack."

"What is it, dear?"

"Is this the man I'm supposed to like?"

"Yes, dear."

"Well, I don't."

* * *

The commercials had a similar structure. Jimmy had the pitch; I had the put-down:

"Polaroid's Onestep is the simplest camera in the world. You just press one button."

"How many does it have?"

"One."

"Then that's all you *can* press."

"Polaroid's Onestep, the world's simplest camera."

"Can you prove that?"

"Don't you believe me?"

"I don't even know you."

We lived in 250 houses; owned stables, horses, pickup trucks, jeeps, and sailboats. When it got to the point that viewers thought we were married, I began to wear a T-shirt that said, "I am not Mrs. James Garner." Then I put a T-shirt on Justine saying, "I'm not James Garner's baby."

The structure of the commercials was simple. We sold cameras. The scripts were tight and wonderfully written. But once the legalese was out of the way, we could improvise. That rarely happens in the commercial world; they're generally rigid. And Jimmy was wonderful to work with. I swear, he never did the same take twice.

"Polaroid's Onestep. You just point it and press the button."

"Why not button it and press the point."

"I try. Heaven knows, I try."

I think one of the reasons for the phenomenal success of the Polaroid commercials was that they continued to shoot new ones. We filmed sixteen days a year, eight commercials a shoot. The first year were mostly thirty-second spots shot by

Ernest Caparos, one of the talented Cuban cinematographers who'd arrived before Nestor Almendros. Then we did some prestige spots for the bowl games, the Oscars, the Rose Bowl Parades.

"This Christmas give Polaroid film to someone you know has a Onestep."

"Lot of people I don't know have a Onestep."

"She's just here to complicate things."

"If you buy a Onestep for Christmas, you can get a roll of film and a flashbar free from Polaroid."

"And if you don't, you won't."

In 1981, there was a new wrinkle. I began to do the pitch in a kind of circular, silly way; then Jimmy would do *me*.

"Make sure you get enough Polaroid Time-Zero Supercolor for the fifth of July."

Jimmy: "You mean the fourth."

"The fourth is a holiday."

He still couldn't win. But I did. Selling those cameras changed my life.

NINETEEN

dah.
dah.
Lah
Wabah-dabah-dah.
Wabah-dabah-dah.

—WHISPERING CHORUS FROM
A MAN AND A WOMAN

Before I met Patrick, I was compulsively early for every appointment. Oh, yes, I was, Pat. I was between five and fifteen minutes early. Oh, yes, I was.

If I was compulsively early, Patrick was chronically late. I don't think this had anything to do with getting a slow start. I think Patrick has a pathological fear of waiting. Someone put him on hold at a very impressionable age. For self-preservation, I'd find something to do, like paint the vestibule. I'd get so absorbed, I'd miscalculate; then Pat would be waiting for me. He started out fifteen minutes late, I added five, he added five. We're now on Fuji time.

When Patrick cooks, we even eat late. Volunteering to fix braised tongue around four, he'll spend hours preparing a gourmet meal that will reach the table around ten. Pat says, "It's southern European." My mother says, "We're southern Californian." My mother has a point, Pat.

It's not that he tarries. It's not that he's flaming

the beef. It's just that he's not cooking; he's cleaning the kitchen. Patrick refuses to cook unless the kitchen is immaculate, and it remains immaculate throughout the cooking process. You see, Patrick is very neat. I don't mean neat; I mean NEAT. When Patrick cooks, surgeons could perform a triple bypass on the kitchen counter. He's the only man I know who can grate carrots without getting carrot curls all over the floor. When he chops, the celery hugs the cutting board.

Now I don't mind eating that late, but the houseguests get whiny, and the children seem a little haggard. They've also spoiled their dinner.

"Sean, what are you eating?"

"Macaroni and cheese."

"But it's frozen."

"I don't know how you American children could ever get through the Algerian War. I mean, what would you do? You couldn't have hot dogs; you couldn't watch MTV. Eef they dropped an atomic bomb tomorrow . . ."

So when I cook, the kids are relieved. They get to eat the same day. But Patrick's not relieved, because when it comes to cooking, the house rules are clear: I clean up after him; he cleans up after me. After Patrick cooks, the kitchen looks like a double-page spread in *Gracious Home.* After I cook, the kitchen looks like Galveston, after the storm. Patrick can never understand why there's salad dressing all over the oven (actually, I can't either). But even though I cook in a flurry, I cook on time. The kids will ask, "Who's cooking tonight?" If the answer is "Mom," they nod and go back to their homework. If the answer is "Dad," they call out for pizza.

Another puzzler to Pat ("eef everyone ees so hungry") is why we all arrive late to the table after he announces, "Dinner." Simple. Each of us has made the mistake of coming when called, only to sit there drooling into the bread basket while politely waiting for everyone else.

There was only one period when we ate on time. That's when we hired a couple to help around the house. The wife cooked; he served. To say the husband was morose is to say John Poindexter's lighthearted. By midweek we had nicknamed him Lurch. When he'd call us to dinner, we were all so terrified we'd run like hell, sit straight up, and eat as it was served. We ate everything on our plates because he'd hover over us: "What's the matter with the salad? Something wrong with the beans?"

Patrick's lateness infested us all. We were late for everything: church, soccer, even a twelve-hour flight to Bombay. We raced out of the house, fourteen pieces of luggage, two kids, raced onto the San Diego Freeway, hit a traffic jam, took the offramp to Sepulveda, hit a traffic jam, merged back onto the San Diego, same old traffic jam, off, on, merge, off. Patrick, for once, seemed concerned:

"When we get to the airport, we need a plan of attack."

"Plan of attack!" I roared. "We've *never* had a plan of attack! Okay, here's our plan of attack. When we get to the airport, I'll open my door; you open yours."

It was impossible to teach the kids the concept of time. The "big hand, little hand" theory was open to interpretation.

"When are we goin'?"

"In a minute."

"When's the movie?"

"In a minute."

I only know the cast of a movie if the credits are shown at the end, so a minute to my kids was anywhere from one to five hours. There was a conceptual leap, however, the day Sean came into the kitchen and asked:

"When are we goin' to the Galleria?"

"In a minute."

He wasn't having it. "How long is a minute?"

"A minute? About as long as it takes to walk from here to the bedroom."

"Fast or slow?"

"Medium."

He raced out of the room, jubilant: "Hey, guys, we're goin' in a minute! And I know what a minute is!"

But we learned to live with it; we found the compromise. If the soccer game was at ten, the ritual would start around nine.

I'd be in my robe, relaxing over the remains of breakfast—morning hair, morning face—stroking one of the kittens on my lap. Coco, the Amazonian parrot, would be muttering and spitting kernels from the chandelier, flirting with a blue jay in the window. Coco was my confidant. He rewarded me with the most profound silences.

Patrick would be in the bathroom, buck-naked, squeegeeing the glass in the shower. (I told you he was neat.)

"Mariette, it's almost time to go!"

"I'm packing up!" That's when I'd decide to give myself a henna rinse.

Sean would saunter in, attempting to play Scrabble with his friend Brendan. Since he had yet to start school and couldn't read, it was difficult.

"Hey, Mom. What does t-o-r-k-t-i-s spell?"

"Torktis."

He'd race out, thrilled. "Hey, Brendan, I spelled 'torktis'!"

Patrick would start shaving, "Mariette, we're going to be late!"

"Almost ready." By this time, I'd have my hair in a towel, cleaning out the compactor.

Patrick would climb into the shower. "Darling, I'm getting in the van!"

"I'm right behind you, sweetheart!"

And that's how it went. Until the two of us would tear for the car, screaming, "We're late, guys!" Then it would be every man for himself. Random houseguests knew enough to be packed and standing at the door because if anyone wasn't ready when Pat and I finally decided to make a break for it, the guy not at the door got blamed and had to put up with snide remarks—albeit witty—for the rest of the day.

I don't know how the kids are going to live through their childhood. They're going to be so shaken about always being late, they'll have to live in India and be a day ahead. I figured it out.

The day I officially met Patrick I looked awful.

It was the spring of 1974. I was still living alone at the Château Colline—after moving out of Brentwood Gardens ten years earlier—and was taking the Thursday red-eye from L.A. to New York for an Orange Plus commercial. I was to be Margaret, the town-greeting lady, welcoming newcomers to town. I guess she was supposed to stand at the gates of the city and wait for an unfamiliar face. "Hello, I'm Margaret, the town-greeting lady. Do you want orange juice? Fresh-squeezed." Hell, I don't know. This was the morning after I had killed my sister with a wrench, then run her off a cliff on *Barnaby Jones.* They loved me to play heavies because no one suspected this cherubic face until the last minute.

The "red-eye" isn't called the "red-eye" for nothing. With only one week's notice, I arrived at JFK on the 5:52 tired and red of eye. Benton & Bowles sent a limo to pick me up, but the St. Regis had problems with my reservation. By the time I got to my room, there was no time to change out of my jeans, no time for a nap; I just had time to wash my hair and jam on some curlers before the driver took me to the studio. I arrived about 8:00, hurried into the lobby, the elevator door opened and . . .

There's a memorable scene in *Indiscreet* when Ingrid Bergman opens the door and Cary Grant is standing on the other side with those dancing black eyes. Bergman proceeds to talk while nonchalantly removing the cold cream that's all over her face. Well, on the other side of the elevator door was the producer of the commercial, Patrick Boyriven. He was French, he was gorgeous, and as we were introduced, I nonchalantly fumbled with my hair curlers. When I finished taking them out, I did not look like Ingrid Bergman sans cold cream. I looked like Shirley Temple sans comb-out. In short, I looked like hell.

We spent most of that Thursday together going up and down the elevator, on and off the set. Patrick was very businesslike, aloof, and talked about French philosophy. Even worse, he seemed devoid of humor. By lunch, I realized there was no way I could marry him and have his kids. Although he did have a terrific-looking left thigh.

I had met his thigh unofficially six months earlier when he had been casting for a Brim commercial that had called for a woman cattleherder. I hadn't gotten the part, he was now telling me at lunch, because I was too attractive, too sophisticated, too well-bred to ride a horse. I blushed tweed, and gave him my Kate Hepburn whinny with my Bryn Mawr teeth.

He told me he was impressed with my professionalism. He said he had taken the red-eye several times and didn't know if he would have the patience to be polite.

"Listen, Meess Hartley, you have been such a good sport. Eef there ees anything we can do for you while you are in New York, please do not heseetate to ask."

"Well, I would like to go to the theater."

"What would you like to see?"

"*Candide.*"

"But, of course. I'll see what I can do."

That night after shooting, I returned exhausted to my hotel and as I opened my door, I saw the most exquisite autumnal spray of flowers "to the epi-tome of sunshine" from Patrick Boyriven. That's how he singled me out from a field of 250 candidates to be a spokesperson for Orange Plus. To convince others, he and a copywriter put together a presentation. The copywriter had waxed eloquent over my attributes, calling me the "epitome of sunshine." Patrick had never run into that word before, so when he was doing the presentation, he railed on about my talent, my loveliness, and hammered home with, "More than this, she is the epy-*toam* of sunshine." Pat thought the polite smile on everybody's face was because of his eloquence.

He had also given me two tickets to *Candide.* He thought two tickets, because a gentleman would never give a single ticket to a woman. It assumes she has no friends. Patrick, a gentleman to the core, would never presume to assume. In his presumptive unassuming, however, he assumed I had a friend in a high rise on Park Avenue who would be delighted to spend the evening with me. But by Friday morning, I had nobody to go to the theater with, and curiously thought of Patrick. The director was not sure it was a good idea. "Don't touch him! He's not quite divorced, he's got a mistress, and he's sleeping with everyone in town."

The more he told me, the more interesting Patrick got. So when he sauntered onto the set, carrying an aluminum attaché case, I invited him to *Candide.*

He stood there for a beat, his face unchanged, "I may have a complication, excuse me," and left the room.

I found out later that his complication was a long-legged dancer in the Poconos. Immediately after the shoot, he was to jump into his car and drive there. Thus, the aluminum attaché case. On top of that, he had made it a rule never to get involved with an actress on the job. Then again, the invitation came from me. Then again, there was "legs" in the Poconos. Then again, I was right there—a bird in the hand, so to speak—and "lovely and beyond" what he'd hoped for. Then again, if he went to the theater with me, he'd probably end up spending the weekend by himself. Then again, he could take me to theater and dinner then hurry to the Poconos, covering all bases . . .

He stood there for a beat, his face unchanged, "I may have a complication, excuse me," and left the room.

As we shot another take, he returned, stood behind the camera, and smiled, "Yes."

We finished the shoot late in the day, and Patrick was stuck with two cans of 35mm film and his aluminum attaché case. Not wanting to check them at the theater, he dropped them off in my hotel room, and we were off to see *Candide*. That's when I smelled his after-shave. But I can't marry him, I mantra'd through Act Two: "no humor, no humor, no humor."

We went to Sardi's after. The waiter seated us at a banquette, brought the rolls, we ordered dinner, and I said:

"So. Tell me about your mistress."

He choked on his hard roll, and said, "What would you like to know?"

"I understand you're married and have a mistress. Maybe more than one."

He was candid, French candid. That's candid. He said his marriage was over; he was in the middle of divorce. He said on several occasions he'd almost gone back because he was distressed about his son, but he knew it would just continue to promote a lie. He said suddenly a ghost from the past—a dancer with whom he had been lecherously in love—had showed up in his office, a gorgeous blonde with legs that wouldn't quit and a body that sent men howling into the night. He said they'd had a long but complicated relationship before he was married, but now she was back and even more gorgeous because she was more mature and he preferred older women. He said there were no promises made from either side, except to have a good time. He was also having a good time with several other ladies. He said, "What about you?"

I mumbled something about my cats and an old boyfriend named Phil. I said we played pinochle a lot.

Then he said, "What are you doing this weekend?"

"I'm either going up to see my brother in Syracuse or I'm going home."

"I'll drive you to see your brother in Syracuse."

"Then I'm going to see my brother in Syracuse."

When we got to my hotel room, Patrick picked up his two cans of film, his aluminum case, walked to the door, and turned to say good-bye. He looked down at me, still formal, still reserved.

He said, "Excuse me, please," and tossed his aluminum attaché case on the bed.

He said, "Excuse me, please," and saucered a can of 35mm film; it landed on top of the aluminum case.

He said, "Excuse me, please," and saucered the other can of film; it landed on top of the first.

I thought, "Oh my God, he really has done this before." Then he kissed me resoundingly.

But we didn't do anything. We couldn't if we wanted to, there was so much junk on the bed. So our relationship was not consummated that night. I won't say when it was consummated, but trust me, we have two kids. If we'd had the two kids first—who always want to sleep in our bed—the marriage would never have been consummated. God is wise.

The next morning he picked me up at nine o'clock, loaded the suitcases, put the top down on his little brown Ferrari, and we were off on a six-hour drive to Syracuse. I felt like Anouk Aimée in *A Man and a Woman.* As we drove, a chorus of Frenchmen whispered breathlessly in my head: Lah-dah-dah. Wabah-dabah-dah. Wabah-dabah-dah. Not that I could be seduced by a little brown Ferrari, but I did hasten to tell myself that he had no sense of humor. Wabah-dabah-dah. Wabah-dabah-dah. It was a beautiful day for a drive. The countryside of upstate New York turned into the Loire valley, cumulus clouds were nimbusing in the distance, the cows were lowing, the ducks were honking in a soft French patois. Wabah-dabah-dah. Wabah-dabah-dah.

After a lunch of bread and Brie and a quiet Bordeaux, Patrick was still cool, reserved, formal, straitlaced, charmingly pompous; in other words, he had a broom where a broom should not be. I, in turn, was getting warmer and warmer, which was strange for October. When we stopped to share the view, I needed to break the heat, let off steam, reduce the tension, SCREAM, so I leaned over and made pig sounds in his ear. Relieved, I sat back. There was a long silence. Then he leaned into my ear and squealed the most horrendous boar sounds, like a male pig en route. That moment—this will show the kind of Gibraltar our relationship is built on—that moment I knew I was in love.

Monday morning we headed back to New York. I was leaving that evening for Los Angeles; Patrick was leaving two hours later for France. We shared a cab to the airport, holding hands all the way. I boarded the plane, but it was detained for an hour. I sat there watching Patrick, who couldn't see me. With his face pressed against the window of the departure lounge, he was nose-to-nose with the 747 two feet away. For one solid hour, he never moved—until the plane pulled away.

As far as I was concerned, when I had left Phil in Los Angeles, the relationship was over. But that Saturday morning, when Phil called me at the St. Regis and the girl at the desk said, "Oh, they've gone," I think it stirred his interest. He met me at the airport, drove me back home, sat me down and said, "I want to marry you." Then Patrick sent me a telegram from Paris and said, "I want to marry you."

I didn't know what to do. I was in love with Pat. Then again, I had three years invested in Phil. Then again, I had never felt my soul fly like that. But I didn't know Pat; I might be just one of his women. Then again I might be in love with Phil and not know it—a bird in the hand, so to speak. Then again I was walking around in Anouk Aimée flats, hearing zithers. Then again . . .

I finally wrote Pat. I acknowledged that I had had a "swell" time with him, that I cared for him very much. Then I proceeded to tell him at length about Phil, that maybe I ought to give that relationship a chance. I ended with: "Perhaps it was just an infatuation."

Pat rushed to the nearest Western Union. I still have his reply:

LOS ANGELE
S, CALIFORNIA
THE HELL WITH INFATUATION STOP YOU HAVE BECOME THE CENTER OF LIFE TO ME STOP I LOVE YOU STOP BLESS THE UNEXPECTED STOP
PATRICK

He then put on the pressure. He sent flowers, wrote every day. A week later, he was assigned three more commercials and managed to schedule them in California. In two months I was pregnant, and we were in Big Bear trying to decide what to do. It was a huge decision. We didn't know one another. We only knew that we'd been thrown together. It was the most powerful experience either one of us had ever had, but we sure didn't know one another. But we decided, in spite of the problems with the divorce, to have the child. We came out of that weekend with a strong bond.

In a matter of two weeks, he was hired by EUE-Screen Gems on the coast. He had to stay in New York one more month, waiting impatiently. Our phone bills were astronomical. During that month I suddenly miscarried, but we decided to try again.

Patrick felt his divorce was imminent, just a matter of procedure, but his lawyer kept saying, "You have to prove this; you have to prove that." Patrick didn't want to prove anything except that there were two people who couldn't live together. He thought the divorce would take less than a year. In fact, it took three.

But all was well. We were deeply in love. He came out to California, moved in with me, and I stopped talking.

TWENTY

"Would you like to go to the bitch?"
"What bitch?"
"The bitch. Zuma bitch."
"Oh, beach!"

—PATRICK TO MARIETTE AND WHY WE SOMETIMES MISUNDERSTAND EACH OTHER

Patrick always said that if I were trapped somewhere in the Antarctic on a three-day shoot with an attractive man and I had one of those *accident de parcours,* the French equivalent of a one-night stand—(why does it always sound so romantic in French and so tawdry in English?)—I should tuck it away for a pleasant reverie and move on. Patrick was very specific:

"The rules of marriage, my darling, are very simple; the absolute does not exist." (This from the same man who will not bend a single Hoyle while playing Canasta with his children.)

"If you're alone and vulnerable and you shoot a love scene and the guy's right there and I'm not and the son of a bitch has absolutely no morals and things get out of control and you wake up in the middle of the night in torpor and think, 'Oh my God, what have I done?,' it's an *accident de parcours*—you tripped on the combat course. What are you going to do? Jump out a window? Feel guilty for the rest of your life? In my way of thinking, you have two choices: you can just chuck it out of your mind or you can come home and tell me. Then I have to deal with it and two things happen. First, it upsets me. Second, I start to think about why you told me. Then, two more things happen." (Patrick's speeches tend to subdivide.) "If you tell me, it's because you know it will hurt me. And if you want to hurt me, there's something wrong with our marriage to begin with. So why not just make light of it and move on."

I, in turn, told him that if *he* ever had an affair, he'd be tossed out ass-over-end in a Buffalo snowstorm before you could say, "Aga Khan, John Profumo, and Porfirio Rubirosa." So the rules of our marriage were very clear.

Pat had his first affair at the age of fourteen. *His* with an older woman named "Martine." Mine with a kid named "Sandy." (Why does it always sound so regal in French and so sleazy in English?) Pat's sexuality was much more sophisticated, more nonchalant, more natural. I don't know if it's the double standard or the different cultures, but mine was more desperate, more guilty. He once went through the entire building at Ogilvy & Mather before he started on Doyle, Dane, Bernbach. He did it a floor at a time. But then, he's always been methodical. If one were to look at that closely—if one dared—one would have to assume he was trying to prove something to someone in his past, but that's just a rough guess.

Suffice it to say, when it comes to sex, Patrick is very secure.

I was doing a television movie called *No Place to Hide,* which shall go nameless, playing a "baddie." It was my interpretation of Joan Crawford. Maybe Jack Palance playing Joan Crawford. Maybe Sheldon Leonard playing Jack Palance playing Joan

Crawford. Anyway, Keir Dullea was playing the other bad guy. The day of our first meeting, I stood by Keir's Winnebago and shook his hand.

He said, "Hi, how are you?"

I said, "Oh God, I'm a fan. I loved you in *2001, 2010.* I loved you in *David and Lisa, Hoodlum Priest, Bunny Lake Is Missing, Madame X, The Thin Red Line, Il Diavolo nel Cervello.*"

He said, "I'm a fan of yours, too. I loved you in *The Long Ships.*"

I said, "That wasn't me, that was Rosemary Forsyth."

One hour later, we had the first of two very long, very passionate scenes together. We entered the location cottage, shook hands, and began to neck. We necked all day long while I wondered if Keir was fantasizing Rosemary Forsyth.

Thus, I was very—what's the word?—"primed" as I left the set that first evening. I barreled down the entrance ramp onto the Santa Monica Freeway like a bull coming out of the chute and raced home. Patrick saw me tear up the driveway, opened the door to greet me, and—like a Tom and Jerry cartoon—he was flattened. Doooooii-innnnnngggggg. I scooped him up like a rampaging Valkyrie and hauled him into the bedroom. It was quite a lovely evening, actually—warm, intimate, fast. Patrick lay there purring.

One week later, the same thing happened—minus Keir's foreplay: "I loved you in *The Long Ships.*" We met on the set, shook hands, walked into the cottage, and necked for three more hours. I had my usual midafternoon stirrings and by evening was burning rubber down the Santa Monica. Patrick greeted me at the door—this time with some expectation. I scooped him up, hauled him into the bedroom, and in a matter of minutes, Patrick lay there purring.

About a week later, Pat and I were sitting in the breakfast room having coffee when he turned to me and said,

"Is this your last day?"

"Yes."

"Gee, I'm gonna miss Keir."

Years later, I ran into Rosemary Forsyth and told her about Keir's compliment and my reply, "That was Rosemary Forsyth. I was never in *The Long Ships.*"

Rosemary laughed, "I wasn't either."

"Pardon me?"

"I wasn't in *The Long Ships,* either."

"Then who was in *The Long Ships?*"

"Rosanna Schiaffino."

"Oh. Gee. I knew it began with an 'R.' "

So, there it was. During all that necking, Keir wasn't fantasizing Rosemary Forsyth; he was fantasizing Rosanna Schiaffino. It had to be Rosanna Schiaffino; I looked it up. The only other actors in the movie were Richard Widmark, Sidney Poitier, and Russ Tamblyn. Unless he was fantasizing Oscar Homolka.

Patrick gave up everything in New York to move to California and live with me. Divorces are costly. He arrived in California—sans lock, sans stock, sans Ferrari, just barrel—and he was wearing it. He had one suitcase containing everything he owned.

The day he moved in with me at the Château Colline, we were on a high. He loved my apartment, proclaiming it ideal for romantics. He fantasized our neighbors: Romeo and Juliet in A1;

Tristan and Isolde in A2; Dante and Beatrice in B1; and Mariette and Patrick in B2.

By the second day, Isolde went into a funk. Since he wasn't used to my funks in those days, he took it personally. A funk to him meant the dissolution of the relationship. It meant, "I hate you; go away." It meant, "I never want to see you again as long as I live—in this life or any other life, not on Wilshire Boulevard or anywhere in the cosmos." He used to pace the streets of Westwood thinking, "What in God's name did I do?"

If he didn't know, I wasn't telling. How do you tell someone that the reason you're having a Class A snit is because he was born. It wasn't his fault, poor bastard; I knew that. It was his mother's. I was having a hell of a time adjusting to someone moving in on my territory. I had lived alone for ten years, treating myself like a guest in my own house. Then came this intrusion with unusually high expectations. For one thing, he expected to talk in the morning. I hadn't talked in the morning for ten years. I was used to having my coffee, reading my paper, having my two ounces of cheese in cathedral silence.

In his own book—if he wrote one—Pat would defensively describe those early breakfasts as a cross between the rack and taking a sponge bath in jalapeño peppers:

"Mariette was a little old maid—weighing her cheese, making her coffee *just* the way she liked it, preparing her morning forage *just* the way she liked it. It was like watching a rite, a ceremony. I learned very quickly to dispense with conversation, to do what I had to do with efficiency: get my breakfast, get the newspaper, put it on the table with the headlines facing her, sit down, pick up my fork, and quietly disappear.

"I learned to soak my toast to make less noise when I ate it. I learned to swallow an egg whole to obliterate the sound of chewing. If I did make the crude mistake of uttering a civility, she would glance over the paper without expression, then return to her reading. Mistakenly thinking she hadn't heard me, I would therefore repeat. Once again, she would glance over her newspaper, but this time with marked annoyance—amazed at my vulgarity, at my audacity, as if one of her dominion had not had the sense to keep his place, interrupting *le grand silence.* Invested heavily in schmuckdom, I would think that perhaps she had misunderstood, so I would repeat it a third time, slowly, in concise English, but in the middle of my sentence it would finally dawn on me that the Volga was indeed frozen. So I would just stay quiet and try to figure out something else to do.

"I didn't want to leave the table because I didn't want her to think I was pissed off. I didn't want to remain at the table because I had finished my breakfast and was sincerely bored. So I would wait for her to finish a section of the newspaper like a starving dog waiting for crumbs. When she would imperiously shed Section B, I would throw myself on it and recline in feigned comfort, knowing I was now safely within the bounds of acceptable morning behavior. That's when I took up the crossword."

Patrick soon learned to avoid taking the temperature of our relationship before noon.

I also had to make room for him. You know, "sh-sh-share." I graciously cleaned out half my dresser drawers—giving him the smallest—and resented every inch of it. Sharing half my drawers was enough to send me into deep depression.

There was one other problem. Patrick had inherited more than royal blood; there was a genetic trait passed down from Boyriven to Boyriven over the centuries: unguent bipeds. His smelly socks in my small, unventilated closet were enough to spell the end of Tristan and Isolde; they even kept me awake at night, reminding me of his presence, his existence, as the clock ticked out the hours of three A.M., four A.M., five A.M. I'd crawl out of bed exhausted, my pillow smothered in resentment.

By the third night, he was sleeping in a hotel on Pico. And rightly so.

That morning we were going on a picnic with friends and were told to bring chicken salad. I didn't know we were told to bring chicken salad because Patrick was the one who was told to bring chicken salad and forgot to tell me. The sparks were flying, but it wasn't about chicken salad.

He was in a robe, making coffee—quietly, unobtrusively. I was in a robe, getting out a salad bowl—silently, martyredly. He handed me juice; he handed me "morning."

My automatic and muffled "morning" dropped to the floor.

The only sound was a bang whenever one of my objects met an immovable surface—i.e. sink, stove, or white tile. With each bang, there was a perceptible flinch from French shoulders.

I put three eggs in a pan, filled the pan with a torrent of angry water, and placed the pan smackly on a burner. I calmly went to the produce bin, calmly took out an onion, and calmly slammed the produce bin shut. As I sliced the onion thinly, the silence grew thick.

"There is no chicken, Patrick."

"I know, Mariette."

I opened a cupboard door and whipped the

lazy Susan at ninety rpms until I found the olives, slammed them on the counter, and rifled through the drawer.

"There is no mayonnaise."

"I know."

"I thought you were going to buy some."

"I thought you were."

I got out the olive oil, bang; the vinegar, thud; and the kitchen door thwacked as I exited. Another thwack on reentrance, as I carried in dill from the garden.

"We're going to Jan Costeau's this morning, right?"

"Right."

"And you inform me we have to bring the salad." Bang. "You've known for four days. And now we're going to be late."

"I've got an idea," said Patrick. "You go ahead and I'll follow with the chicken salad."

"No. You go ahead and I'll follow with the chicken salad."

Patrick stuck out a three-year-old chin and said mockingly, "I said it first."

I didn't know whether to howl or deck him, but I secretly admired his audacity. Especially since we had only one car. That's when I said, "Patrick. I really think. I'm really afraid . . . I might be too much for you."

"WHAT!!" I think he had sat on his feelings a little too long. "THE GALL! THE GALL that you would even SAY THAT! THE GALL that you would even SUGGEST that you might be TOO MUCH FOR ME! THE GALL that you would even ASSUUUME that you might be TOO MUCH FOR ME! Which is not to say that you might not be. BUT HOW CAN YOU EVEN THINK OF YOURSELF WITH such GALL, such

AUDACITY, such BRASS! Did it ever OCCUUUR to YOUR OVERSIZED EGOOO that I MIGHT BE TOO MUCH FOR YOU! Obviously not! Did it ever OCCUUUR to YOUR SMUG SELF-CENTERED SOUL that I MIGHT ALSO HAVE 'trepidence' about going into a SECOND RELATIONSHIP so quickly?"

I said, "Trepidation."

He said, "What?"

I said, "Trepidation." And started to leave.

He said, "WHERE ARE YOU GOING?"

I said, "OUT!"

He said, "WHAT! You make this SELFISH, SELF-CENTERED, EGOTISTICAL remark. And you're the one that gets ANGRY! You're the one that's going to SLAM THE DOOR and walk out of here in a PUFF."

I said, "Huff."

He said, "WHAT?"

I said, "Huff." (Patrick has trouble with colloquialisms, especially in a colloquy.)

"Puff! Huff! You're a selfish, spoiled, obnoxious, old maid!"

So I threw the telephone book at him.

That's when he spent the night in a hotel on Pico.

The fourth night we made up. It was glorious. The fifth night, he was taking a shower in my little shower stall where his head rose above the sliding glass doors, when I came in—he still maintains—with a smile all over my face and said:

"I've got terrible news for you."

He thought, "What now?" but said, "Oh?"

"Actually, I have terrible news and good news. The good news is I got a job: a two-hour movie of the week with Dennis Weaver. The terrible news is I have to go to Mexico City for a month, maybe a month and a half."

Patrick maintains I continued to smile during the entire terrible pronouncement. His turn in the funkhole.

We share a legacy of abandonment. So we both have trouble with good-byes. Pat gets really snarky a day before; I say a mental good-bye to people I love two seconds after I learn their departure date. They of course don't know this, and wonder why I take to in-depth conversations with the ticket clerks, flight attendants, anyone in the next lounge chair, ignoring "the loved one" completely. I think that's why I arrive late at airports, no long good-byes. I'm lucky if I can get out a hasty "see ya" as I do a Bruce Jenner across a receding expansion gate, barely landing in the plane.

So Pat drove me to the airport in my little brown 280SL, and after a truncated good-bye, found himself in the middle of L.A., not knowing anybody, wondering if I was ever coming back, if I ever wanted to. Somehow he was lucky enough to get a commercial to direct at E.U.E. and, on the first weekend, flew to Mexico City. We had a wonderful weekend, probably because it wasn't my turf, and returned with a glorious souvenir. There's a sign on Sean's bottom: Hecho en Mexico.

A few months later one of the questions on *Hollywood Squares* was, "What is the most traumatic thing that can happen in life?" The answer contained one of three things: having a baby, moving, or getting married. I was doing all three and reentering analysis with Dr. Monke.

Pat and I had found a handyman's bargain, a dark, little peasant's cottage in Rancho Park with tiny windows. But the move from my marvelous old castle on Wilshire terrified me. Every move in my childhood was downward—from Larchmont and my beloved Montessori, from the big house to the nightmare of the little house to the final abyss of Brentwood Gardens.

Along with that, the words "commitment" and "intimacy" made me want to put on my Nikes. I had never been that intimate with anybody and still was having trouble with the good feelings. That morning, when I had said "I may be too much for you," I meant, "I think I'm unfillable; my needs are too big." When Pat could hear what I meant, he answered: "Not for me, they aren't."

I had finally met a man who wouldn't run (even though I had given him a bouquet of reasons) and I didn't know what to do. I didn't have the road map; I didn't have a model for this kind of affection. The feeling of big was coming down to the feeling of not so big, of things finally in proportion. So when the "always unfillable" was filled for the first time, it all came in on me like a blackness—extreme claustrophobia and terror.

I stood in the middle of my bedroom and started to shake. There was something extraordinary going on both physically and psychically. I went to Pat in the breakfast alcove, "I need your help. I don't know what's going on, but I really need your help." He got me onto the bed, I contracted fetally, and he held me while I cried and talked. I just kept rambling, while Pat hung on. When I finally stopped shaking and the terror left, I asked him what had happened. "What was I talking about?"

"You kept talking about two-months old. You didn't want to grow past two-months old. You didn't want to get married, you didn't want to move, you didn't want to have kids, you didn't want to grow up."

I called my mother. "Did something happen to me when I was two-months old?"

"What an odd question."

"I just need to know."

She hedged, then somewhat guiltily, "You were in a nursing home by yourself for a month."

"When I was two-months old?"

"I didn't want to leave, but your father wanted it to be a kind of a honeymoon, and you got whooping cough."

If I hadn't believed in the power of the subconscious before, I believed it then. How the past bleeds into the present, infecting it. Big John often maintained that the absence of mothers had no adverse effect at all on small children, only positive ones. And once more, Mom believed him.

Patrick held me that day; that was the greatest gift he could have given me. That and the children.

About three or four months after Sean was born, we bought that house in Rancho Park, tore down walls, gutted the living room, put in a cathedral ceiling, put in French doors, and made it magical. We filled it with some of the happiest days of our lives.

Patrick finally got his divorce, and we got married. At the wedding, Sean toddled around saying "Is this a party? Why are you here? Whose birthday is this, anyway? Where are *my* friends? How come they're not *my* presents?"

Through the years Patrick and I have had enormous problems in our relationship. It hasn't helped that we both chose careers that, by their very nature, foster unemployment for weeks, sometimes months. So every time Patrick was out of work, I'd look at him in his robe, cooking, and see my father. The first sign of depression on his part, and I'd go under, convinced the future was irreversible, that there would be longer periods of unemployment, longer periods of depression, ultimately leading to suicide and another loss. I'd close up, hoarding my emotions like a squirrel, preparing. The more depressed I got, the more depressed he got. The more depressed he got, the more depressed I got. The fact that Patrick wasn't used to expressing what he felt, wasn't used to talking things out, only added to our misunderstandings. We'd both climb in the hole.

It took me a lot of years to let Patrick be Patrick. I still fall into that hole, but not as often. He's learned to talk; I've learned to disassociate—at least with my father.

It took me longer with my mother.

It's not the big things that separate; it's the minutia. One day she came into my bedroom when I was nursing Sean and said:

"Well, I hope you're not going to nurse as long as Barbara did."

The way she described it, I was sure my sister-in-law had nursed my niece and nephew through college, possibly graduate school.

"How long did Barbara nurse?"

"Och, it must have been six months."

I was very silent.

During those years of pull away, nothing my mother said was right. I was overcorrecting. All those years of buying it all, I now bought nothing. I didn't give her an inch.

Sean was fourteen months and mid-wean, when I shot an episode of *The Oregon Trail* with Rod Taylor and Andrew Stevens in Arizona near Sedona, Sonoma—I know it begins with an "S"—somewhere near the Grand Canyon. Now I had never been away from Patrick or Sean for more than a week, and I was lonely. An attractive young actor and I would have a beer or two together. One night I called Pat in California from the coffee shop, and he asked me how I was.

"I'm really terrific. I've met this awfully nice guy. He seems to need my help running lines; we're having a drink right now in this funny little cowboy bar."

"What's his name?"

"John Lawlor. He's funny; you'd like him. We've had a good time together."

I hung up, finished my beer with John, and we went up to our mutual motel rooms—his was right next door. I was very attracted, as was he. We stood outside my door, looked at one another, and tacitly agreed that it was probably a good idea that we didn't have a good idea. We were both married; there was a lot at stake. But John, thank God, was mature. At least that's what I was banking on, because I sure as hell wasn't; I was about ten meters away from tripping over tires on the combat course.

We said good night, I went into my room, took a cold shower, and tried to sleep. Six o'clock in the morning, there was a tentative knock on my door. So much for maturity. I yelled, "Just a second!" put on my robe, hit the Binaca, took a deep breath and opened the door. There was Patrick. He had found a baby-sitter in fifteen minutes and had driven his Volkswagen from L.A. to Arizona. I had visions of this little green bug racing across the desert trailing a cloud of dust. Charge!!!!

I felt so claimed.

TWENTY-ONE

Balls.

—MADAME EVELYN WALSH

When I announced to Mom that I was involved with a Frenchman, there was a long pause. "Oh my God, darling, do you know what you're getting into?" She should have said, "Have you met his relatives?"

She was an aristocrat. Indeed, she was an aristocrat. She had the smell of an aristocrat, the bearing of an aristocrat, even the nose of an aristocrat. She was Patrick's grandmother, she was Madame Evelyn Walsh, and we called her Mamouche.

She was a tall, thin, erect woman in white gloves and pillbox hat who never got her nails done, never went to a beauty parlor, bought very good suits and hats—Chanel suits, pillbox hats—then stored them away for years on end, so they all smelled of mothballs. And she always carried a purse with nothing in it, except for a comb with about seven teeth, a clean handkerchief, and maybe, at the outset, a $1.50. She kept fondling it to be sure the latch was facing her stomach so a pickpocket would have to disembowel her to get her $1.50 and the comb with the seven teeth.

An earlier stroke had paralyzed the left side of her face, oddly adding to her imperious demeanor. Once, after turning eighty, she was holding court on her Jamaican verandah in a lovely African dress when the manager of Round Hill came up to her and said, "Madame Walsh, you look so beautiful tonight." She beckoned him nearer. As he leaned down and put his face next to her, she muttered, "Balls."

We took her to New York one day, from her Rittenhouse Square home in Philadelphia, on a trip to the Museum of Natural History. All of us were bouncing along for two hours in the Volkswagen van: Patrick and Mamouche (pronounced Mamoosh) were in the front; I was in the back playing Scheherazade, trying to keep three screaming kids away from her. She wasn't the most wonderful person with children. I mean, that morning she sat at breakfast, holding her purse, checking the latch: "Justine, my God, what are you doing? What is that child doing? She's got her hands in the butter. Oh my God, it is *dis*gusting."

"But she's only three and a half."

"I *don't* care."

Patrick couldn't find a parking place, so he dropped us off in front of the museum, the one with all those tiny little steps, and I had to get a wheelchair. There I was with three kids chomping at the bit, pushing Mamouche in a wheelchair up all those tiny little steps while she said, "Oh my God, I d-d-d-d-don't know if we should do this b-b-b-b-b-because I'm not very comfortab-b-b-b-le."

"It's okay, Mamouche: I won't let go."

"Where's my p-p-p-purse?"

I angled the wheelchair and three children awkwardly through the turnstile and entered a very loud, very public museum. Naturally we chose to go to the museum on Memorial Day. Every child in New York was at that museum that day, running, punching, hitting, slugging. Patrick was still driving around the block; I lost Justine; a cop brought her back, gave me a dirty look.

"Oh my God, what is she doing? What is that child doing? She's got ice cream all over her face. Oh, my God, it is *dis*gusting."

"Mamouche, she's only . . ."

"I *don't* care."

Now I neglected to mention one important thing. Mamouche couldn't see very well. It was like bringing Mr. Magoo to the museum.

"Where are we now?"

"In the coatroom, Mamouche."

"Oh, all right. It's a nice coatroom, don't you think?" She clutched her lap.

Since Patrick had volunteered to make breakfast but had been diverted by crumbs in the ridges of the waffle iron, the kids were starving. So we decided to head for the cafeteria downstairs, which meant that I, Mamouche, and the wheelchair would have to descend two more flights of tiny little steps, b-b-b-b-b-b-b-because the elevators looked like the Japanese subway with hands and arms hanging out. I lost Justine again. The same cop brought her back. Another dirty look.

Somebody whispered to me that the freight elevator was working, "but don't tell anybody," so we ended up in the freight elevator with half a dozen kids, screaming, biting, kicking. Someone, not me, had told everybody. Mamouche was oblivious. She sat quietly, holding her purse, checking her latch: "Where are we now?"

"In an elevator—the freight elevator. We're going down to the restaurant."

"Oh, all right. It's a nice elevator, don't you think?"

The elevator opened wide, and we found ourselves in the basement, the innards of this museum, and on the sides of the walls there were hoses all wrapped up and put into rolls, fire hoses. As I pushed by them, she said, holding her purse, checking her latch:

"This is very interesting."

"Mamouche, we're . . ."

"What is this exhibit? It is fascinating. That is a very interesting thing on the wall there. Who is the artist?"

I read the label on one of the fire hoses that said INSPECTED BY and gave her the name of the fire inspector: "John Renaude."

"Ah, he is French. I knew it. He is very good, don't you think?"

"Yes, very good."

"And he's done all of these."

I looked at other tags on other fire hoses, and she was right. "Yes, every one."

"Oh, my God, what's she doing? What is that child doing? She's got her sticky hands in that ashtray. Oh my God, it is *dis*gusting."

"Mamouche, she's only . . ."

"I *don't* care."

We arrived at the restaurant and total bedlam: paper plates saucered through the air, straw wrappers were in lift-off, and hot dogs were being used as Cruise missiles. Oh, I neglected to mention one important thing. Mamouche was slightly deaf; and she was also much lower than I was, because she was sitting in the wheelchair. So she was oblivious to the noise, oblivious to the UFOs, oblivious to everything. As far as she was concerned, we were having a quiet little luncheon on the Rue de la Paix.

We fought our way, battled our way, just to get to the line. It was like trying to reach the hot-dog stand at Omaha Beach. "Okay, kids, what would you like?" I wanted to be ready to yell my order fast—knowing if I didn't get the chocolate milk, there'd be one wailing kid and lines like, "I like Stephanie's mother better."

After twenty minutes, I finally caught a concessionaire's eye and yelled: "Four hot dogs, four fries, one coke, two orange, and one chocolate milk!" Then, I leaned down to Mamouche's ear: "Mamouche! What would you like to eat?" Mamouche just sat there, ruminating, for a long time. I tried again, "Mamouche! What would you like to eat?" Mamouche ruminated some more. Then, clutching her purse, she looked slowly up at me and said:

"I would like . . . I would like a quiche."

I stuttered, "I do . . . I don, I don't think they have quiche here. Anything else?"

"What?"

"I don't think they can do that, Mamouche. There are a lot of people here."

"What?"

"There are a lot of people here! People!"

"Oh, what a shame. *Quel dommage.* What else do they have?"

"I don't know—there's hamburgers, hot dogs!"

"Oh my God, no."

"They have, I don't know, they have sandwiches—tuna fish . . ."

"Oh God, no."

"Ham, ham and chee . . ."

"Oh, yes, ham and cheese. That's all right. I'll have a ham and cheese."

"Great!" I started to give the boy the order: "Okay. Four hot dogs, four fries, one . . ."

"And I'd like it heated."

By this time eight hundred people had cut in front of us; the concessionaire had lost interest hours ago. So we fought our way through the line again, got our food, got a table, cleaned off the ketchup and loose french fries, sold our collective bodies for four chairs, and as we finally began to eat, Mamouche turned white as she looked at Justine and said:

"Oh my God, what is she eating? What is that child eating? It is *dis*gusting."

"It's a hot dog, Mamouche."

"Oh my God, I thought it was a suppository."

We finished lunch while Patrick was still driving around the block, and Mamouche had to go to the bathroom. I told the kids to hug a column and not move on pain of "no Twinkie." I parked the wheelchair outside the bathroom, and slowly the two of us shuffled shuffled shuffled . . . in. We ended up in this tiny, tiny stall and she said, "I don't, I don't know how to do this anymore."

"You mean, you want me to undress you?"

"Yes, it's so difficult."

"It's okay. I mean, I'm just not sure where to start." Here we were—in this tiny, tiny stall—me pulling up her skirt, then pulling down her girdle, then pulling down her panty hose, then her underpants. While she grabbed on to the walls saying, "It's no, no, too much. No, oh no," because it's hard to undress someone gently in a tiny, tiny stall.

Now you have to savor this picture. There we were, the two of us, in this tiny, tiny stall. I, on my knees in front of her—my legs protruding out from below the stall—when I heard the door open and the sound of two talking mothers and a bevy of children. Needless to say, the talking stopped.

Now, I neglected to mention one important thing. Mamouche had a delicious sense of humor. So when I said, on my knees, "Oh my God, Mamouche, either your reputation is going to be made, or mine is going to be ruined," her shoulders heaved with mirth.

"Oh, ho, ho, ho, ho, ho. Oh, ho, ho, ho, ho, ho. Oh, ho, ho, ho, ho, ho . . . Where's my purse!"

When I did *Skyjacked* at MGM in 1972, I played a pregnant passenger who went into labor while a plane was being hijacked to Russia by Jimmy Brolin. Chuck Heston was in the cockpit. Yvette Mimieux, Jeanne Crain, Susan Dey, Roosevelt Grier, Walter Pidgeon, Leslie Uggams, and I were screaming in the rear cabin.

They fitted me with a gigantic pregnancy pillow at Western Costume, weighted it down, strapped in the crotch, and I walked outside to see how I felt. I felt large. I also felt like a wounded bird in a nest of Boy Scouts; men from everywhere rushed to help. ("Quick, sit down." "Want some coffee?" "Want a Coke?") But when I went back into the costume shop, they said, "We made a mistake; we gave you the triplets pillow from *My Three Sons*." So they put me in a solo-size pregnancy pillow, I went back out, and people were only a third as nice.

I attended Lamaze classes for research and Rosie Grier taught me to needlepoint a butterfly to use as a focal point. The day they filmed the birth scene, I focused on my butterfly and pushed and pressed and pressed and pushed—take after take after take—as Jeanne Crain was urging, "Push, Mrs. Stephens, push!" and Yvette Mimieux, the stewardess, staggered up and down the aisles in total revulsion, going "Yuck." After a few hours of this, my face was the color of Jeanne Crain's lipstick and I started to hyperventilate. When I finally stood up, I almost passed out. I also broke down in tears.

After all that labor, I had nothing to show for it. God, I wanted a baby.

So the first time I met my Parisian mother-in-law-to-be, I was *very* pregnant with Sean and should have been *very* happy. I wasn't. It was my first trip to France; I had been sick for seven months with constant nausea; I was worried about my inadequate French; and I felt ugly, fat, and bloated. "HEY THERE, HEIFAH!" As I stood there with a mountain of motherhood in front of me, Jacqueline opened the door of her little apartment in a suburb of Paris, went from my belly button to my eyes and back to my belly button with glee, then shrieked, *"Comme tu es grosse!"*

It did not bode well.

Small, with a beautiful face, Jacqueline entered our relationship shyly, with a great desire to be accepted and loved. So did I. The basic problem was the language; we could only understand one another superficially. Patrick was left with the task of interpreter, which he fulfilled with spotty accuracy, depending on the nature of the topic and his interest level. So Jacqueline and I just stood around smiling, agreeing to god-knows-what.

There was a grief about her. Her life—and by association, Patrick's—read like a French melodrama. She was born, as they say, out of wedlock. Her mother, who was tossed out of her "respectable" home, legally denied Jacqueline's birth, and the child was sent away to live with a nanny.

Arriving for her first visit ten years later, the mother impulsively scooped Jacqueline up and took the child to live with her in Paris. Quite a leap. By that time Jacqueline's mother was directress of a successful fashion house.

So when fifteen-year-old Jacqueline met fifteen-year-old Sammy Boyriven, there was an immediate bond. A child of divorce, Sammy had also been neglected. His mother, Mamouche, a direct descendant of Sir Francis Drake, grew up in a family that owned a string of European hotels. His father, a sterling member of Paris's social elite, was a fighter pilot in World War I. One of the last of the romantics, he straddled two centuries.

When Jacqueline became pregnant, Mamouche was adamantly opposed to the marriage. She wanted Sammy to marry the daughter of her dear friend, Elsa Schiaparelli. If Mamouche had had her way, Patrick's father would have been the father of Marisa Berenson; Patrick would have been her brother; she would have been Sean's aunt; Tony Perkins would have been my brother-in-law, and I wouldn't have been able to take showers ever again.

But Patrick was born and ironically became Mamouche's *raison d'être.* She gave his parents an apartment near the Elysées Garden, and life was sweet. Until Hitler entered the picture and things fell apart.

It was June 1940, and Panzer divisions were steamrolling through Europe, knocking off country after country: Poland, Belgium, the Netherlands. Paris was seized only ten days after the battle of France began. Refusing to sign an armistice with Hitler, the French government resigned; Marshal Pétain was hastily voted the new premier, hastily formed a cabinet, and agreed to

Hitler's terms. Handing over three-fifths of France, he left only an unoccupied zone in the south whose capital was at Vichy. Vichy France was supposedly free to govern itself, but the Germans kept adding pressure to collaborate.

Sammy was in the military. Rather than do forced labor in German factories, he decided to leave for Africa. So the day I was born, when German tanks were parading down the Place de la Concorde, Patrick and his family were fleeing, along with two million other Parisians. Since Patrick was only two, he doesn't remember the trip across France. He knows they passed the Vichy demarcation line clandestinely, ending up in Marseilles. Boarding a ship, they then went by way of Casablanca to Abidjan in French West Africa, then took a train north to the Upper Volta, to a place called Bobo-Dioulasso. By that time, Sammy was sent back to the army for more training.

Patrick's memories begin in Africa. He and Jacqueline stayed in a thatched-roof house in that little village of few whites with a backyard that stretched into the African bush. Fences kept out the African livestock: lions, tigers, an occasional hyena. By four, Patrick was smoking cigarette butts and running wild with the natives. They then moved to a small house in Dakar on a little street called Rue du General de Gaulle. It is here, dear reader, that we finally get to one of the two Battles of Algiers, known far and wide at our dinner table.

Early in the war, most of North Africa, including Algeria, had fallen into German hands. In November of 1942, combined allied forces landed along the top of Africa—Casablanca, Oran, Algiers; Rommel was trapped at El Alamein, and

Algiers became the headquarters of Charles de Gaulle.

A lone voice in the early French resistance, de Gaulle came to Dakar in the spring of 1944 and all its sons threw a parade to welcome him. He was there to gather the 2nd Armored Division to march with Eisenhower and Montgomery through the boot of Italy right up to the Champs-Elysées. Organizers had given each black African a five-franc note—in those days, the equivalent of a penny—so that they'd shout, "Vive de Gaulle!" Unfortunately, black Africans had no idea who the man was that was saluting them from the top of a jeep, so they shouted, "Vive Pétain!" while waving their five-franc note.

There were very few whites in the crowd that day. When the retinue passed Patrick and Jacqueline, de Gaulle turned and looked at them and continued to turn with his eyes on them until the jeep disappeared. Patrick remembers it vividly; he's always felt there was a loneliness about de Gaulle. So Patrick teethed on the first Battle of Algiers. As did I, as did Justine, as did Sean, as did any of our emaciated houseguests.

In hasty summary: Once back in France after the armistice, Sammy fell in love with another woman and left on Christmas day. In tears, Patrick begged him to stay. When his father came back the following Christmas, Patrick refused to see him. Disappointed, Sammy sent word that he'd return for Patrick's tenth birthday, March 29th. He never made it. On March 29th, Sammy left his home in the south of France and died when his car hit a tree. Years later, Jacqueline married a man named George. In 1972 they bought an old sheep farm, with plans to restore it. George never did. On March 29th, he was driving with a friend of Pat's and died when his car hit a tree.

Emotionally shaken, Patrick went to France for his stepfather's funeral, returned to New York, realized his marriage was over, and moved out. I met him two years later. That's when he moved in. That's when we went to France.

Patrick has always loved my enthusiasm, so he couldn't wait to show me his France. But the pregnancy had put a slight dent in it. He'd point at paintings in the Louvre, and I'd yawn because I had something inside of me that was a real creation. He'd say, "Look, there's the Eiffel Tower" and I'd snore because I was carrying the ninth wonder of the world. Everything paled: Versailles, Notre Dame, the Tuileries. Somebody's kicking here, Pat, come on.

I also threw up every day; I knew all the fields in France. I could give you a Michelin Guide to every clement tree, but I couldn't begin to tell you where the Place de la Concorde or Arc de Triomphe were. I didn't care.

We borrowed his mother's car, we borrowed his mother, and went down to the Loire Valley, touring château after château, until I was châteaued out. And every day Jacqueline would say. *"Oh, tu es grosse—incroyable—très grosse."*

One day I'd had it. The three of us were outside the Château de St. Germain-en-Laye at one of those little bistros sipping cassis, sitting on little ice-cream chairs that you can hardly sit on because you're gross, and I had to go, but didn't want to. It had a lot to do with where I was going—to the French version of a countryside toilet, what they call a little too graphically for my taste, a Turkish hole. Turkish toilets—a ceramic platform where you place your feet in two indentations and squat with your bottom coincidentally hovering over a hole—have been a custom in France for a long time, and I don't know why. All I could think of was squatting and losing my kid.

It was a parting shot as I was leaving that did it, a despicable lowball as I walked the stone path to the bathroom. *"Oui, très grosse,"* Jacqueline yelled, *"Très grosse, comme tu es belle!"* All I could hear was *"très grosse"* in reverb. Her voice followed me, getting louder and louder—*"Très grrrooooosssse"*—while I trudged the road of unhappy destiny toward this Turkish hole where this fat, ugly person, this gross *côte de boeuf,* was going to lose her kid. To add to the indignity there was a line, an actual line of people waiting to get into this hell hole. I started to sob. Reading my heaving shoulders, Patrick hurried over to me, "Honey, are you all right?"

The whale wailed. "I'm going to lose my baby. It's going to go down the Turkish hole and end up in China."

He laughed. "Oh, is that all that's bothering you."

"No, that's not all that's bothering me."

"Then what else is bothering you?"

"If that woman doesn't stop calling me gross, I'm going to belt her."

Patrick stopped laughing—wisely sensing the depth of my hostility, wisely sensing that he was standing naked, midbattlefield in an opening volley between his future wife and his present mother.

He said, "Darling, you don't understand." Not the smartest way to begin. Not only did I feel hurt, now I felt misunderstood.

He said, "It's very simple. Mother is not saying you're *gross*. She's saying, you're *grosse*."

"Swell."

"No, there's a difference. She means you're round with child, in a beautiful state of motherhood. It's a compliment."

He knew he had found an opening because my eyes started to unsquint. That's all it takes for Patrick to get pedantic, flowery, and Frenchly chauvinistic.

"The French don't hide their pregnancies, my darling, they flaunt them. Why be pregnant and hope no one will notice? This is a vain Hollywoodish vanity that a woman should not be distorted. You're not in America now where every blemish is a sin. Here every blemish is part of the character. If you're pregnant, that's a beautiful state of being. If you're grossly pregnant, it's even more beautiful. Imagine the amount of life in there."

Well, I bought it. And my child was not born in Taiwan.

So Jacqueline and I made a kind of truce. One night we were sitting in her kitchen having *café au lait* and croissants—her two little dachshunds, Nora and Sara, yipping around our legs—while she told of her plans for her sheep farm in the west of France, and I told her the story of how Pat and I met. I asked Patrick to translate.

"When I met your son, I thought he was wonderful."

Pat translated; she smiled.

"I fell in love with his left thigh."

Pat translated; she smiled.

I said, "But sometimes I feel . . . well, sometimes I feel . . . he really has a broom up his ass."

Patrick didn't miss a translated beat; she roared.

'Ah, oui! Mais depuis qu'il te connaît, ce n'est qu'une

brosse à dents." In essence, she said, "Ah yes, but since he's met you, now it's only a toothbrush."

When humor became our language, we fell in love.

TWENTY-TWO

Well, if my wife wants flowers on the day of her daughter's birth, she's entitled to flowers.

—PATRICK BOYRIVEN
TO HIS MOTHER

How do you bring up children when one parent believes in a very strict, very rigid, European kind of discipline, and the other one—the more rational one—approaches it differently?

I was on location in Atlanta, Patrick had flown in with the kids, and we were having a wonderful time. We went to a wonderful doll museum; strolled through a wonderful shopping mall—everything perfectly wonderful—until I made the mistake of giving Sean responsibility for the shopping cart.

She was right, it wasn't fair. She was right, I should have shared it. Because if I was going to give Sean responsibility, Justine wanted some, too. Anyway, after two choruses of "S'mine!" the front of the cart dropped and papaya juice went all over the floor. Patrick got furious, "I don't want to hear anozer word out of either of you for the rest of the day." And there was a part of me that went, "Oh my God, it's only three o'clock."

The rest of the day was a long way away.

(This is from the same man who when Sean lost

one shoe, turned to his son and said, "Zis ees eet. I will not buy you anozer pair of shoes for as long as you live.")

So there we were, returning to the hotel, when Justine in her inimitable style turned to him and said:

"Great, so now we can't talk for the rest of the day, right?"

And I went, "Oh, my God."

Patrick said, "No, this is not what I said."

And I went, "Oh, my God." Because I knew I had an irrational need to keep the record straight; I knew I'd open my mouth. I did.

"Wait a minute, Patrick, that *is* what you said. However, I think what you meant was that you didn't want them to give you any more trouble."

I guess that's not what he meant, because he said, "Fine. Then I will never discipline them again."

Which I, of course, took to mean: for the rest of their lives.

"Oh c'mon, Pat, you always do that."

(Did you know the phrase, "you always do that," is the major cause of domestic violence in the United States today?)

Patrick's pronouncements ring of finality.

I once flirted with having the kids wear bilingual earphones with U.N. translator's mikes, so when Patrick said, "I don't want to hear from you for the rest of the day," the kids could say, "Come in, Mom, come in. Is this literal, is this literal?"

Then I could say, "I don't think your dad meant for the rest of the day. I think he meant for the next five minutes, or at least 'til we get out of the car. On a deeper level, he probably means he'd rather not hear from you until you've married or at least left home."

Or, when Patrick said, "If you lose anozer shoe, I will not buy you anozer pair as long as you live," I could interpret.

"What your father means is: scour the house, try to find that shoe. If you can't find it, go to your mother and she'll buy you a new pair."

How do you punish a kid without punishing yourself? It can't be done. See, what kids know and we don't seem to grasp is, if we tell them they can't go out, they stay in . . . with us. The problem is: good threats are finite. I tried them all.

I tried "Mumbling" threats: "If you don't turn that TV off, I'll askpuffegngdidngsan."

"You'll what?"

"Never mind, just do it."

I tried "Guaranteed-To-Backfire" threats. "If you do that again, you can't go to church."

I tried "Hasbro-Coleco" threats: No Barbies, no Kens, no G.I. Joes.

Come October, I generally drudged out the old "There'll-Be-No-Christmas" threat. They knew I couldn't stop Christmas. Christmas was going to come whether I liked it or not. I lost credibility fast.

Some of my threats were so limp, they hung in the air like a bad smell. "Okay, that's it! No back-to-school clothes!" Now, what was I going to do? Send them to school in last year's gravy stains? First of all, they'd have loved it.

One night, when I was trying to get them unglued from the television set, I heard myself saying, "If you don't turn that thing off, you can't watch television." I called that the "Redundant" threat.

Punish a kid in a crowded store and guess who's punished? "No, you can't have a balloon. Not when you ask that way." A wail goes up from Aisle 9, a siren that sounds like a prison break, and it continues from Bullock's to the May Company. All the kid wanted was a balloon. Now, you'll promise him anything to stop the attention you're getting. "You want ice cream, you want Coke?" All the kid wanted was a balloon. "You want a bike, a stereo-tape deck?" All the kid wanted was a balloon.

Then I discovered a system of warnings—first warning, second warning, third warning—announcing the punishment after the third. Since the kids usually moved on a two-count, I rarely had to waste a threat. For years, it was gold. Until the night I told them to get to bed over and over. Second warning: Turn off the TV; get to bed. Third warning: Turn off the TV; get to bed. Over the years, the system had slightly eroded. By now, I was up to, "Okay, this is the third warning of your third warning." That night, Sean called my bluff, "What's after the third warning?" By the time I came up with it, they were watching David Letterman.

I must have been rattled, because the next day on the way to New York I moved into the risky territory of "Unenforceable" threats. I was furious with Sean:

"You do that again, you can't get on the plane."

Now what was I going to do? Stuff him in a locker until we got back? Luckily, he heard the tone and obeyed on "second warning." Until we were up in the plane and he wasn't doing his homework.

I said, "First warning . . ."

He yawned.

I said, "Second warning . . ."

He smirked.

I said, "Third warning . . ."

"What's after the third warning? I don't land? If *I* don't land, *you* don't land."

The party was over. He'd caught on. And immediately turned to his little sister and passed the word.

Justine Emelia Boyriven was born June 22, 1978. Barely. The same day her father was arrested as the Westside Rapist. Almost.

But I'm getting ahead of myself.

For this story starts back even further—back to August of 1975, back to the birth of Sean and the preparations surrounding that birth. Patrick and I were euphoric. We did Lamaze, we listened for the heartbeat, we gauged the kicks, we lay in bed reading *The First Nine Months of Life:* "This is the month the toes are forming; this is the month the ears are forming." I had waited thirty-five years for this and didn't want to miss a thing.

It was a glorious time. Glorious right up to August 30, to the day of Sean's birth.

The morning started serenely enough; the contractions came slowly. We noted the times, got the suitcase together, called the doctor. I felt like I was floating, riding the contractions like a skiff. Here it comes, be ready, ride to the crest, up and over. There was pain, but a kind of natural pain—rolling with the rhythm of the sea. Calmly, methodically, we went to the hospital, prepared to continue Lamaze.

I have always suspected that the problem was caused by a fundamental lack of trust between the doctor and Mother Nature. She dictated one pace; he another. (Patrick's theory is much more complex and involves a golf game.) But after two or three hours, the doctor seemed impatient. "You're not dilating enough; your contractions aren't strong enough." He gave me an intravenous—of what, I'll never know—but whatever it was, everything changed. The baby was coming and coming fast. It was like banging, banging, banging against a brick wall. The head was pushing, forcing dilation, so it could go into the canal. I wasn't prepared for this kind of pain. I remember thinking, "My God, I'm lost." Pat didn't know what to do, either. He was as lost as I was.

We later learned the IV might have been Pitocin. The label warns of the danger in inducing premature labor. If "Pit" was used, I wish someone had let me in on it.

I felt like a failure; I felt robbed. After all the lessons we had followed, nothing we expected happened. I didn't need a drug; I could have had a natural birth. But implications in that hospital room were subtly dropped: maybe it was because I was too old; maybe it was because it was my first child.

Patrick and I resolved this would never happen again, should we find ourselves in the same position. Not long after, there we were . . . in the same position.

Doctor Number Two pronounced infallibly, "It's due June 4th." So you count backwards and say, "Oh, yes, I remember. That was a lovely evening. Okay, June 4th."

I was thirty-eight and knew Justine would be my last child. Once again, I wanted to have the baby naturally, but I needed help. We found a little place called the Nachis Birthing Clinic that specialized in the Bradley Method.

Now, it is important to note that the Nachis

Birthing Clinic was on Washington Boulevard near Venice, not the loveliest of neighborhoods. Nestled between a hardware store and a coffee shop, the building looked more like an abandoned grocery store. It didn't help that the windows were glazed with tinfoil for sun protection, so pregnant ladies could avoid being sauteed in the waiting room. Aesthetically, Tijuana would have been an up.

But the inside belied the outside. I knew I needed protectors, people on the sidelines coaching. I knew if I heard enough friendly voices, like directors in a play, I could be guided through it. But even more important, the voices would be there when the time came. Not at the hospital, but at Nachis. Not just in classes, but at the birth.

We were given two midwives. One we called "Pregnant Barbara," the other "Wanda Woman." We were also given a therapist. After the experience with Sean, I was terrified of the pain. Wisely, she confirmed my fears: "You're right, there is pain. But we'll be here to help you through it." The choice was either no pain and no experience, or experience with pain. After all those years spent avoiding pain, pretending it wasn't there, anesthetizing my feelings, after all those years of numbing out, I was determined to experience everything.

We exercised dutifully—every movement to the letter. No one was going to rob us of the miracle. Not this time.

My mother-in-law, Jacqueline, arrived from Paris in the middle of my eighth month. Since money was scarce, she had traveled with the aid of a discount fare and the usual inflexible departure date. But Jacqueline was no fool; she had scheduled her Paris return for June 23rd, three weeks past the "June 4th" due date. She was determined to be there when the baby was born.

She was also determined to predict like a seer exactly when this would be. She took to following me around like a shadow, timing my contractions with a stopwatch.

"Demain, it will be tomorrow. I know this."

I'd had cramps for months, electric shocks that went down my leg, making it hard for me to move. Since they always startled me, I'd let out a yelp: "Oh God, hold on just a minute! I can't move." This would send Jacqueline into a deep panic:

"Mariette! *Maintenant! Maintenant!"*

"No, no, it's not now!"

"Oh, oui, oui, oui, oui, oui! Je suis sûr!Je suis sûr! Je vais téléphoner à Pa-treeck!"

I'd lie down and have trouble getting up:

"Maintenant! Maintenant!"

"No, no, it's not now!"

I'd freeze on the steps or wince on the sidewalk:

"Maintenant! Maintenant!"

"No, no, it's not now!"

A Frenchman once wrote: "If you take a country and put half the people in one hand, and half the people in the other hand, then put them together—you would make an addition. In France, you make a division." I'm not sure how this applies; but, trust me, it applies.

The major division was language. Jacqueline—aka Manny to her grandson—did not speak a word of English. I, however, spoke a little French; or thought I did. Before I married Patrick. Before I met his mother. I'd say something like, *"Comment vas-tu, Maman?"*

And she'd say, *"Comment? Comment? Patrick, qu'est-ce qu'elle a dit? 'Comment?' "*

And he would say, I swear to God—exactly the same way—I swear to God: *"Comment vas-tu, Maman?"*

And she'd say, *"Ooooohhhh! Comment vas-tu!? Très bien! Très bien!"*

The whole family prepared for weeks.

Sean attended classes with us, saw movies of births (yuck), listened for the heartbeat, joined us in bed: "This is the month the toes are forming; this is the month the ears are forming." He was eager to have a sibling. (This eagerness lasted only as long as his sibling was tucked safely away in the womb where she couldn't get at him. A few days after her birth, he casually inquired, "When can we dead her, Mom?")

Patrick cut out a Styrofoam mattress for the back of the Honda hatchback, taped the Birthing Center phone number to the wall, packed a suitcase, filling it with a whole list of things: robe, slippers, toothbrush, tennis balls; things for me to chew on, things for me to focus on, things for me to massage on (that's why the tennis balls). There were things for him too: the latest Ludlum, the latest Follett, the latest Clavell, and a camera.

Jacqueline bought a layette, stocking it with the numerous wares of Mssrs. Johnson & Johnson. She knitted booties, hemmed diapers, alphabetized the pins and powder. And when she wasn't busy . . . she watched me.

When I sorted the mail, she watched me. When I tended the basil, she watched me. For the duration of the pregnancy, she watched me. I felt like a watched pot. A watched pot that dared not wince.

"Mariette! *Maintenant! Maintenant!*"

"Jacqueline, honest, it's not now."

"Ooooh, oui, oui, oui, oui, oui . . ."

Every morning, as we sat around the breakfast table—Patrick reading the *L.A. Times,* Sean eating banana pancakes, I picking at my food, hoping to hold it down—Manny would stare, hanging on to my every breath. Around the second cup of coffee, we'd get the daily prognostication: *"Demain,* it will be tomorrow. I know this. I have *mouton* and I know." And she did. She raised goats and sheep on a *mouton* farm in the west of France. She would discuss the lambing process at its earthiest, while I questioned with horrid fascination and Patrick translated:

"But what if there are complications, Maman?"

"Je mets mes gants en caoutchouc."

"You put on rubber gloves and reach in! You just reach in?"

"Naturellement, je sorts l'agneau en tirant par la tête ou par les pieds . . ."

"Where! The canal! You reach into the canal? Pat, did she say, 'You pull it out?' "

Patrick would elaborate. Needlessly. "She pulls the lamb out by the head or the back legs, whichever comes first . . ."

Sean would stop pouring maple syrup long enough to ask: "Is there blood?"

While I changed the subject: "What's in the headlines, Pat?"

"The Westside Rapist struck again."

"Swell."

There had been a series of gruesome rapes in southern California. Older women. Women my age. Since the Westside Rapist had his practice in the same area as the birthing center, I didn't want to hear about it.

We practiced by the hour—relaxation techniques, birthing positions: the down on all fours, the squat, the stirrup. I was taught to surround myself with something familiar (I chose my flowered pillows); I was taught to "tune in" to my body; to "think open, think open." Any way to facilitate the birth of a baby.

Our favorite exercise was what the clinic called "love talk." Patrick was very good at this. He had . . . you might say . . . savoir faire. During a mock contraction, I'd take a deep breath, rest my head on my flowered pillows, and he'd talk to me: recreating powerful moments in our life together. I'd breathe deeply, he'd wax eloquent:

"Lie back, my darling, and relax, just relax. Remember our first trip alone together, Death Valley?" (Yes, in sin.) "Remember the heat, the beating sun, the extraordinary silence, pierced only by the flapping of crow's wings. Relax, darling, take a deep breath and relax—feel the exquisite beauty of life. Remember the cold nights, Zabriskie Point, making passionate love in the dunes."

You know. Love talk.

It always sounds so idyllic in those classes. Giving birth, blithely, in little white dresses.

June 4th arrived. The morning of. And Patrick was a nervous wreck. He reinstalled the Styrofoam mattress, repacked the suitcase. Jacqueline reorganized the layette, recounted the pins. Everybody rushed around, determined to finish their preparations early so they could watch me. The cat watched me, the bird watched me. I felt like the centerpiece in an Ingmar Bergman movie—everyone sitting around the breakfast table . . . with silent faces . . . watching, watching . . . while the clock ticked loudly. Patrick pretended to read the newspaper; Sean poured more syrup:

"Does the lamb just pop right out and start to walk?"

"What else happened today, Patrick?"

"The Westside Rapist got another one."

"Swell."

The 4th of June came; the 4th of June went. Nothing.

The 5th of June, the 6th of June. Nothing.

The 9th of June, contraction, wince. *"Maintenant! Maintenant!"* Nothing.

The 15th: *"Demain,* it will be tomorrow. I know this."

The 19th: *"Demain,* it will be tomorrow. I know this."

By June 20th, everybody had lost interest.

Patrick was bored with the exercises; his enthusiasm for "love talk" was lost in the face of my yawns. Sean returned to C-3PO and Obi-Wan Kenobi. And even though Manny was still counting the days, it was for a far different reason: her discount fare would expire in seventy-six hours. Not only was she feeling personally insulted because Justine had not had the *délicatesse* to show up, but there was the very real possibility that Maman would be celebrating the birth hoisting champagne solo on a *mouton* farm in the west of France. The spotlight was finally off . . . and I kind of missed it. It's not easy being replaced by Wookies. Then my birthday came up.

It was June 21st. Pat had surprised me with two-on-the-aisle for *Side by Side by Sondheim*— a real treat. Until the overture. Then I began to feel a little funny.

"Pat."

"What?"

"Never mind."

Music, pain, deep Bradley breath.

"Pat."

"What?"

"Never mind."

Music, pain, deep Bradley breath. As I scanned the row, I noticed everybody kind of hunched over—fascinated by this whale of a woman hyperventilating with gusto. It was like a *New Yorker* cartoon; every time I'd breathe in, Row G would breathe in with me. Contraction finished, I'd breathe out; Row G would breathe out with me.

"Pat!" The row breathed in.

"What?" The row held.

"It's fine, it's okay. Never mind." The row breathed out.

11:30. We hurried home. Nothing.

11:45. We readied for bed. Nothing.

11:46. We took a poll; this had gone on long enough.

At 11:47, we began our own natural birth inducement which we had learned at the clinic (i.e., Patrick waxed eloquent, we reprised the dunes). Forty minutes later, I was on the floor of the bedroom, the waters had broken, and I was in transition—the head was in the canal.

Patrick, losing a modicum of savoir faire, tore down the hallway to summon Jacqueline. "I think this is it! I think this is it!" Jacqueline was thrilled, but hardly surprised. Of course, this was it. Hadn't she told us "this was it" only yesterday morning?

She threw on her robe, raced into our bedroom—*"Maintenant! Maintenant!"*—hurled herself down on all fours, prodded, poked, and declared in high French that the baby was, indeed, on its way. After all, she delivered sheep and she knew.

But that was the problem.

All I could think—as I lay on that floor—was that this sweet urban peasant woman from a *mouton* farm in the west of France was going to come at me with an enormous rubber glove and pull my baby out. This shepherd from Normandy was going to rip my baby out. I didn't want her anywhere near me.

I kept whispering, "Patrick, don't leave me with her. Patrick?"

But Patrick was busy. He couldn't find my robe; he couldn't find his wallet. He, did, however, find the suitcase. Everything in it was either stale, used, or gone. He also found the phone number for Pregnant Barbara:

"She's broken her waters! She can't move—she's shaking all over!"

"Just get her in the car. We'll meet you there in fifteen minutes." Then Barbara calmly began to give directions . . . among other things.

"Yes, I remember, I remember." After all, hadn't he done the trip a thousand times?

It was like Gary Larson's "Far Side" dog. You say to him, "Roll over, Duffy. Roll over and I'll give you a big, fat, juicy bone," and all the dog hears is, "Blah, blah, blah, blah, Duffy, blah, blah, blah, blah, blah." All Patrick heard was, "We'll meet you there in fifteen minutes." The rest was, "Blah, blah, blah, blah, Patrick . . ." Oh, how I wish he'd heard the "three little words" that were included . . . "among the other things."

But I'm getting ahead of myself.

For I was still lying on the floor, shaking, colder than I've ever been. Cold and alone, alone with Jacqueline. She was pretending to be helping, pretending to be nervous, pretending to be hunting for my robe. But I knew better, so I watched her.

As she tore around the bedroom, I watched her. As she looked in the closet, I watched her. She was waiting for her moment, waiting for her minute, just waiting to grab the rubber gloves under the bathroom sink and spring on me.

My whispers gained urgency, "Patrick? Patrick!"

But Patrick was busy. He couldn't find his socks, he couldn't find his car keys. He did, however, find the film to the camera.

He also found he'd have to carry me. I couldn't walk.

Has anybody ever tried to carry a five-foot-nine woman when she's pregnant? When she's pregnant and shaking and it isn't the movies? I was gigantic. As he huffed and puffed an angular route to the front door, I thought he was going to collapse. Although he couldn't let me know he was about to collapse because he's supposed to be the one I can rely on; but I knew he was about to collapse. And we looked out the door and wondered how in God's name he was going to get me to the car. While I shook.

The shortest distance between two points is a straight line. I had never seen a night so short on straight lines. Point "A" was the front door of the house. Point "B" was the Honda sitting at the mouth of the driveway. Since there was an enclosed patio between Point "A" and Point "B," Patrick had to perform an "L"—carrying me from the front door to the front gate, hang a right, carry me the length of the sidewalk, past the bottlebrush tree, and deposit me in the hatchback.

In retrospect, it was about thirty feet. In Patrick's retrospect, it was about four years.

He started down the steps tentatively, while I began ticking off lists. In an emergency, a rush of adrenaline clears my head, allowing me to direct the proceedings calmly and with authority. In other words, I get bossy. I remember everything that must be done, right down to the last detail. And when I run out of the last detail, I make up more last details—comforting myself in a swirl of minutia. As Jacqueline ran ahead of us to open the gate, I started my swirl:

"Did you bring the suitcase? Did you call the clinic? What did they say?" He maneuvered us carefully down the sidewalk. "Should we wake up Sean? Should we take him along? I thought you wanted to include him. You always said you did. I think we should discuss this, Pat." He made it to the bottlebrush tree.

"Do you think Sean should take clarinet lessons when he's older? Oh sure, I know that silence. It's the money, isn't it? You don't want to drive him, right?"

Jacqueline opened the hatchback. With a sigh of relief, he began to ease me onto the hard, flat floor of the hard, flat bed of the car. The Styrofoam mattress wasn't there.

"Oh, my God, don't move! I'll think of something, don't move."

I couldn't move; I couldn't do anything. He stood there stalling for time, considering his options. What was he going to do? Prop me against the car? Carry me back in? He had to stash me somewhere until he found the mattress, but where? Then Patrick did what anyone would do. He dropped me on the sidewalk and ran into the house.

There I was. Lying on the pavement of Balsam Avenue, dressed in a flimsy nightie, still in transition—glad that we weren't living in New York City and that it was not winter. "Oh, my God, Pat, my pillows. We forgot my flowered pillows."

Luckily, Jacqueline was lurking nearby. "*Jacqueline, Jacqueline, les oreillers . . . les oreillers avec les fleurs!*" She "*oui, oui, oui, oui, oiued*" all the way up the sidewalk, then raced into the house screaming: "*Mariette . . . des oeillets, des oeillets!*"

I lay there, desperately trying to breathe, desperate to be on our way, thinking nasty thoughts in rhythm: "Where. Breath. Are. Breath. The pillows? Where. Breath. Are. Breath. The friggin' pillows!" Shortly, my rhythm quickened: "Where are the friggin' pillows, where are the friggin' pillows, where are the friggin' pillows!"

Years later, Patrick barreled out the door with the Styrofoam mattress, followed by Jacqueline carrying a large vase of flowers.

Full of water.

I didn't know how to tell her that that's not what I wanted, so I thanked her profusely, "*Merci, merci,*" and took the vase. I was already soaking wet—my nightgown, my hair. All I could see on our trip to the birthing center was water pouring out of the vase, pouring out of me, swishing back and forth as it filled the car. I was going to give birth in a traveling Maytag.

Patrick detected confusion: "Mom said you wanted flowers."

"What flowers? I said *oreillers.*"

" 'O-yay' means carnations. 'Or-yay' means pillows."

"Oh."

Years later, Patrick barreled out the door with pillows, leaped into the car, revved up the engine, and we tore out of the driveway. There I lay, with every pillow in the house and a large vase of flowers, like a pampered, pregnant Homecoming Queen.

As the Honda bounced, I circled like a dog

seeking a comfortable position in which to nest, and every position was agony. We were halfway to the birthing clinic when I moaned, "Patrick, I've got to push!"

"Don't do that to meeeee!"

"What do you mean, don't do that to youuuuu? I have to push!"

I'd heard stories about pushing too early, so I gave myself an internal examination to find out where her head was. I found out where her head was; her head was right there. I could feel the tip.

"Patrick, I have to push!"

"Don't push! Think of Death Valley!"

"Stuff Death Valley! I have to push!"

Going west on Washington Boulevard, he made a hair-raising U-turn, screeched to a halt at the curb of the birthing center, leaped out of the car, banged on the front door of the clinic, threw open the hatchback, pounded on the front door of the clinic, glanced at me in panic, kicked the front door of the clinic. But there was nobody home.

"Patrick, this baby's coming. I have to push!" With an audible wimper, he leaned in to help.

Well, there we were: one-thirty in the morning, parked in front of a deserted building, the hatchback up, Patrick leaning in on top of me—his left shoulder under my right leg; his right shoulder under my left leg—while I lay there in stirrup position, my nightie wrapped around my neck, screaming.

It was then that he saw, out of the corner of his eye, a Los Angeles police car cruising west on Washington Boulevard.

I swear to God, this is a true story.

It was then that he remembered, in a corner of his brain, the Westside Rapist.

I swear to God.

His life passed in front of his eyes before the spotlight hit us. Another lifetime sailed by before the siren wailed. Then, red lights flashing, the squad car made a smoking U-turn on Washington Boulevard, screeched to a halt behind our Honda. Doors flew open, guns were drawn, two cops jumped out like a miniature SWAT team and yelled, "Freeze!" Patrick shot both arms straight up. "Don't shoot! Don't shoot! She's giving birth! She's giving birth!" My legs, of course, were already up.

The tall cop moved warily toward our car. "Oh sure, oh sure." Then he saw me. "Ooooo-oooohhhhhh shit, she's giving birth."

The paramedics arrived in three minutes—two ambulances, six paramedics. One of the cops had recognized me; the word was out. "Say, isn't that Mariette Hartley?"

Suddenly, the heavens parted. A sweet whispery voice was heard throughout the land: "Mariette, it's me. Think open. Think open." Now, I figured, if I thought any more open than I already was—with ninety-two people looking in and asking for autographs, my nightie up to Zanzibar, and my insides about to come outside—I was going to be on the front page of every tabloid in the grocery store check-out line; but it was Pregnant Barbara and Wanda.

And what the hell took them so long? And where the hell had they been? The same place we should have been. Around the back, of course. Remember the blah, blah, blahs? Remember those three little words? The part Patrick heard: "We'll meet you there in fifteen minutes." The part he missed: "Around the back."

They had both been waiting for us . . . *around the back.*

Then the two policemen, the two midwives, the six paramedics, the one husband, the one guerney with me on top, all ran toward the tiny little door of the birthing center. Then the two policemen, the two midwives, the six paramedics, the one husband, the one guerney with me on top, all tried to get through the tiny little door all at once. Like the Keystone Cops, everybody politely backed off. Realizing that everybody had politely backed off, everybody grabbed hold and tried again. The guerney wouldn't fit. I knew that; I kept telling them it wouldn't fit.

Especially when it got stuck. Half of my body was now in the birthing center; the other half was on Washington Boulevard, lowing like Elsie, Borden's prize heifer. Wanda kept saying: "Put that sound into a push, Mariette. Put that sound into a push." Until some young wiseguy of a paramedic, who had been through Lamaze and knew what he was talking about, said: "No, don't push! Blow!"

I said, "I've gotta push!"

He said, "No, little lady, blow!"

"I've gotta push!"

"Blow!"

"Push!"

"Blow!"

Needless to say, I was confused—and sincerely trying to be helpful—when I told him kindly and with some force, "Oh, go blow yourself." And with that, the whole guerney popped into the birthing clinic.

Justine was born four minutes later.

They wrapped a robe around me; Wanda handed me a glass of cold cranberry juice that tasted like nectar. I had such a sense of quiet victory: to sit in the rocking chair and rock her; then, to bring her home and sit with Jacqueline and Patrick and Sean in the big bed . . . and watch the sun rise.

TWENTY-THREE

You scum-sucking shits! You should be rolled in bat guano and served on a bed of excrement. You scum-sucking shits.

—A CENTRAL PARK RESIDENT

Want to know how to clip a rabbit's tooth? It's not easy. Because the front paws dig into your stomach at a ferocious rate of speed, making a too-too-too-too-too sound, while the back paws really knock the wind out of you. What you have to do—if you can catch it—is to wrap the rabbit in a terry-cloth towel. It has to be one that the rabbit likes, else he gets very threatened. You wrap the rabbit, pull it toward you, open its tiny little mouth, insert these big things like fingernail clippers and . . . you have to be careful 'cause the rabbit is still kicking you—too-too-too-too-too—in the stomach while you're trying to insert these things. I don't know what rabbits who live in the wild do; they don't have clippers. Anyway, you're supposed to clip the part that's kind of greyish. Now I'm a little myopic these days, and if you clip any part that's not greyish, blood spurts all over you, so you think you're killing the sweet helpless rabbit. Once you get the top teeth—too-too-too-too too—and you haven't made it bleed, then the real trick is to stick your finger underneath the top teeth, which are now pretty sharp because they've already been clipped, and try to get the bottom teeth. I still haven't gotten the bottom teeth.

Our rabbit has very long bottom teeth.

A lot of decisions are revocable. You take a job; you quit a job. You take a husband; you quit a husband. Deciding to have children is irrevocable. Once that tiny person pops out, you can't change your mind. There aren't any lemon laws to protect you. Say good-bye to entering a bathroom unaccompanied by a minor. Say good-bye to reading anything longer than milk of magnesia bottles. Say good-bye to sounding sane on friends' answering machines: "Hi, luvey, it's moi, Mariette. I just wanted to call and say how much I missed you and . . . Stop it!"

And these problems will multiply. You don't just take on one or two children; you take on one or two turtles, three or four cats, and five or six bugs in a jar. Say good-bye to wearing black velvet. Say good-bye to suede, linen, or wool. Remember the light scent of outdoor lilac that used to pervade the house? Say hello to the heavy scent of indoor ammonia.

Now I happen to love animals, but Patrick doesn't. He says he does, but he doesn't. He loves Donald Duck. He loves Mickey Mouse. He thinks animals are witty, warm, a part of life. He just doesn't think they belong in the house. Except for the fish. He doesn't mind them because they're low-maintenance, and they don't go on the rugs. Although we did have a little run-in when he turned the air pump off because the sound was not "harmonious."

The beginnings of our ménage went sensibly;

we adopted two brothers, Bilbo and Max. (Bilbo was once "Mister September" on a Purina Cat calendar, but they had to spiff him up; he generally walks around in jeans and a torn T-shirt.) Then Sean saw a stray sleeping under the house, "This poor cat, how could we?" Pat could. Pat absolutely could. But Sean couldn't. So Pat spent weeks encouraging Tigger out with bread crumbs. Then Bruce Lee was found near a dumpster. We went from none to four without shifting.

Then there was the Polaroid commercial I did with a golden retriever puppy. Poor Pat; poor Daisy. She had a barren womanhood and took to nursing the cats. They'd lie on the floor kneading her belly, purring so loud they sounded like snowmobiles. In the autumn of her years when she was gray about the muzzle, Daisy had six puppies—one of which, Mickey, was overly friendly, totally untrainable, and the size of the Berlin Wall. We couldn't go into our backyard without sprinting until we found him a home.

Then came Mean Joe Greene, aka Coco, who sat on Patrick's wooden valet. Part Amazonian parrot and part snapping turtle, I have no idea how many fingers he'd stored away. Coco was so mean he dismantled his perch, but he was brilliant at mimicking our voices. At a very early age, Justine went through her screamer period, a sporadic, "Aaaaaeeeaaa!" Then she'd tear into our room with her version of Sean's latest transgression, usually a crime against humanity so odious it would have repulsed Amnesty International. We prayed she'd grow out of it. She did. But Coco didn't. Coco had that scream down cold and brought it out daily for the next five years: "Aaaaaeeeaaa, aaaaaeeeaaa, aaaaaeeeaaa." Worse yet, when the phone rang, Coco said "hello" so convincingly, varying our voices, we all thought it had been answered.

At some point we added Cujo, a pebble-size Shih Tzu with a helluva name to live up to. There are now so many strays at our house that no one sits down without first checking the chair. I once emptied a dustpan into a wastebasket. A paw reached up and out, then another paw, and Max the kitten raised his head—dangling dust balls from each whisker. He climbed out of the basket and walked away—giving one back leg a final dusty kick.

When we uprooted to New York in December of 1986 to do the *Morning Program*, Patrick begged me not to bring the animals. I won. And continued to lose for the next two and a half years.

They traveled by Jet Pets. Why does that sound like gold-filled cages with brocade cushions? It's not. It's the same old gray cage with prison bars, and it still cost CBS $1600. Sixteen hundred dollars to send Daisy, the four cats, and the bird. Patrick will never get over it. The outrage of having to fly a bird. Poor Coco, with those redundant wings, flying Pan Am ignominiously cross-country.

The ménage arrived in Manhattan looking a little harried and had to adapt quickly to brownstone living: no grass, no birds, no trees, just stairs. Floor after floor of stairs. For the first week, they huddled in terror on the first floor. Initially, Patrick made a brave attempt to keep them all in one room, but that was impossible because children are biologically incapable of closing doors. I think it harks back to the philosophical question: If a father yells in the forest, "Close the door!" and only children hear it, will there be a sound?

In a matter of weeks, Patrick and I were a furball away from divorce.

Then there was *the dog problem.*

Fellow dog walkers are behind trees filling you in: "Pssst, lot of rangers around, keep your dog on the leash." "Psst, dog romp, 3:15 at the Basin, pass it on." "Pssst, if they give you a ticket, never carry ID, never give them your real name."

I don't mind curbing our dogs; our dogs are highly curbable. But I do mind the $50 fine or two years at Riker's for letting the dog off the leash. This includes eight o'clock in the morning when very few people are in the park, and dog owners—all armed with Baggies, all ready to pursue their squatting dogs—convene on a large lawn area to let the dogs play together. Try letting twenty-eight dogs play together on twenty-eight leashes; you have dogspaghetti in twenty-eight seconds.

There's another problem. Daisy is a Valley Girl, proud, fastidious. She won't lift her skirts in front of just anyone. The only way I can get Daisy to go is by taking her off the leash.

The first time I was caught and the ranger asked, "Name?" I just stood there. Dumb. First of all, I was doing *The Morning Program* with this mug plastered all over the screen. Second, if I gave him a phoney name and he knew my real name, would it be perjury?

"Name?"

The sweat was pouring down. I had rehearsed a *nom de chien* for hours. I chose Mariette Hardline—figuring if the ranger didn't know, he'd take it down; if he did know, he'd think I mumbled.

"Name?"

"Mariette Hardline."

The ranger laughed, "Oh, sure."

So I got a lot of tickets.

Patrick didn't. Patrick went to greater lengths.

One day he was in the park with Daisy momentarily off the leash, doing what she had come to do, when a ranger leaped out of the bushes with full regalia—the jacket, the pants, the decorations for bravery—and demanded his name.

Pat said, "What's the matter?"

"Your dog is off the leash. I've got to give you a ticket."

"Look, I always clean up after my dog. I'm not soiling the city. I have the poop right here in my hand."

Just the day before, Sean had been mugged at knifepoint for his bike. A week before, our cook had been mugged while carrying $1700 in savings; she left New York in a frenzy. A month before, Justine had been knocked off her bike by a crowd of sixteen-year-old boys who then ran off with it, even though she tried to bite them. She looked everywhere for them, cruising Manhattan in a police car like Charles Bronson. Patrick had had enough. His fondness for New York was in obverse proportion to mine. He lashed out.

"Where were you guys when my son was being mugged? Where were you guys when my daughter was pushed off her bike by five 'hurligans'? You're going to give me a ticket! You're going to bug me because my dog's not on a leash. Your priorities are completely cockeyed. You're totally absolute, and obsoletely ridiculous."

Patrick was upset. The park ranger was confused, but he stuck to his guns. "One doesn't excuse the other."

"To me it does."

"Fine. Give me your name."

"I'm not giving you my name."

"Then I'm going to have to call my superior."

"You do that. Call your superior. Call your mother. I'm not giving you my name."

The park ranger was furious; he signaled a ranger buddy and said, "Call Central."

Pat thought, "Fine. Call Central." He collared Daisy, turned in a "puff," and walked out of the park.

Nice bluff, but the ranger walked out right behind him. Pat crossed Central Park West, the ranger crossed Central Park West. Pat walked down Eighty-seventh, the ranger walked down Eighty-seventh. Pat couldn't believe it; was this guy going to follow him home and get his address? Yep.

Now you have to know, this is Daisy; this is no "Devil Dog, Hound from Hell." So Patrick walked right past the house without a glance, threatening Daisy out of the corner of his mouth, "You walk up those steps, Daisy, you're dog food. You hear me? You're horse meat." I'm proud to announce that Daisy walked right by that house with nary a glance of recognition. Pat kept on walking, past our house, past Columbus, all the way to our parking garage on Seventy-ninth. The ranger was right behind. So Pat drove around for a while, in rush hour, with Daisy. Just to save on a ticket.

Only in New York . . .

I've always been a magnet to strays and not necessarily feline. My man on the street is never the one on television interviews. My man on the street has just been released.

Whereas most people don't engage these people, it's my meat; it's what I live for; it's why I love New York. The town's alive, it swarms. Stand still on a street corner in Los Angeles for one year and no one will talk to you. Stand still on a street corner in Manhattan for one minute, and nine people will call the paramedics.

I was standing in the middle of the subway station, waiting for the Broadway local, when a woman came up to me. She had on one of those red jersey hats that kind of wrap around, a red slicker, a small red purse, big hands like mine, red nail polish, and not a lot of teeth. She said in a lovely Tallulahesque voice:

"Excuse me, I don't want to bother you, but I know who you are. I won't disturb you."

I smiled and looked fervently down the track.

"Every time you go up for an Emmy, lady, I just cheer. I think you are terrific. I am in your corner. Would you sign an autograph for me?"

"Sure. What's your name?"

"Veronica."

I wrote the usual, "Dear Veronica, we must stop meeting like this," gave it to her, didn't think any more about it, and got on the train. It was pretty crowded, but I managed to hip my way into a seat, scrunched up my legs, secured my purse, and stared vacantly at the red slicker in front of me. It was Veronica. She introduced me to Mack, her boyfriend, who was a fan, too. There was no place to go.

"I gotta tell ya," said Mack, "you are absolutely, spiritually wonderful. I've seen you in everything you've done, and you have a thing that's very special, and it comes out on the screen. My God, you are just such an artist. We are such fans."

Now, you've got to realize, I was torn. Veronica and Mack were really quite pleasant, their dialogue was certainly pleasant, but a part of me—the part whose cook was mugged, the part whose second-born was growing up to be Charles Bronson—was sitting there thinking, "Is this dangerous? Is it time for the net?"

They told me about themselves. Mack used to have drug problems but was now clean, and I was nodding, "That's terrific." Veronica was working with drug addicts, and I was nodding, "That's terrific." I looked across the car and saw this sweet Japanese baby lying peacefully on its mother's lap.

"Oh God, look at that."

Mack looked over and said, "Yah, we're tryin' to do that."

"Have a baby? You know how, right?" (Okay, so it was a feeble retort.)

Mack sloughed it off. "Yah."

There was an uncomfortable silence, then Veronica leaned in, "We really are. We're tryin' to do that."

I couldn't leave well enough alone. I had to say, "Oh, is there a problem?"

Mack nodded toward Veronica, "He's a guy."

"Pardon me?"

"Veronica's a guy."

Well, call me from Minnesota.

It was midday. I was late and waiting for a bus on the corner of Ninety-second and Broadway, looking nondescript but decent: wearing a nondescript dress, nondescript bag, nondescript shoes. This woman was standing next to me, all three-hundred pounds, but you couldn't tell because she was dressed in black. She had on a hat that looked like a black lamp shade, a dress that looked like a black tent, and a black bag that looked like a black bag. (People in my stories tend to be color-coordinated.) And this woman, this combination of Marie Dressler and Victor Mature, had the nerve to look *me* up and down, had the nerve to give *me* the once-over, before she said,

"So. You a prostitute, too?"

Now I have to admit I was a little taken aback, but it would never occur to me not to answer a direct question. So I checked my hemline, checked for leather, and said, "Well, actually, I'm not, actually. Are you?"

"Hell no! At least I don't get paid for it."

I thought about that for a minute. "Neither do I."

But I learned to get around, I learned the ropes.

I was standing in a subway line at Eighty-sixth and Broadway, trying to buy a token—one of those lines that went up the stairs and out on the street—and I was late, later than usual, that's really late—when a thin-haired man came over:

"I have a token."

"Oh, wonderful." I handed him my dollar.

"For a profit. Two bucks."

"You're crazy!"

He shrugged and went to a few others who gave him the traditional New York greetings: "Get lost"; "Up yours." I could hear the train coming, but the line was barely moving.

"How much is it again?"

"Two bucks."

"A buck fifty."

"Nah, two bucks."

I rummaged through my purse for change, but all I had was a five in my wallet and the dollar in my hand and was damn well not going to give him a five. As the train pulled to a stop, he stood there indifferently, tantalizing me with the token between his finger and thumb. I watched the passengers pour out.

"C'mon, a buck."

"Two bucks."

"One buck!"

I threw the dollar at his feet, snatched his token, bolted through the turnstile, leaped into the subway, pushed through the crowd to the opposite side of the car, and splayed myself against the inner doors, just as the outer doors closed. Safe! There was a spectacular feeling of elation, of adrenaline. I felt like Rocky. At least that was my first feeling. My second feeling was, "Oh my God, it's come to this."

Then we moved from the Upper West Side to the Upper East Side. I hate the ritzy East Side; it doesn't have as many street people. But dog-walking should be better, right? Wrong. It was early evening, the third of July, 1988. I know it was the third because not only does Daisy have leash problems, she can't "perform" when she hears fireworks. She gets very scared. So with my friend and general factotum, Vicki, along to help, I had to drive her in the van with Cujo, who can perform just about anywhere. Our plan was to park the car near the park, rush out, then pray that Daisy would go between bangs.

Fifth Avenue is gorgeous until Ninety-seventh Street. That's where you find dog alley—Alpo wrappers, Kal Kan tins. Unemployed dogs lying around in a sea of old beef bones. Afghans washing car windows. Puppies gone bad. Daisy hates that section, but there was nowhere else to park, so she crawled out of the van shaking. Cujo didn't care. As we passed a fourth-or-fifth-world family that had started Independence Day festivities a day early, the mother smacked one of her five kids, then grabbed another, screamed at him, and knocked him against a wall. Now I have a very low tolerance for child abuse that I had better get over, because one day I'm going to get killed, but I did my imitation of Mother Teresa. I went up and gently said, "COOL IT!" This lady with this stringy hair said, "You mind your own business." And as Vicki and I and Daisy and Cujo slunk away, her five kids—each child to a man—came up to me, hands on hips, and said, "You mind your own business."

The park was deserted as we backed into it, except for one fellow lying on a bench. As I let Daisy off the leash, I could barely make out a lump of black fur next to him and a faint, low rumble.

"Okay, Daisy, hurry up." Another firework went off. Daisy trembled. "It's okay, Daisy. Hurry up, you can do it."

Suddenly, through the gleam of a lamppost, I saw snarling teeth in the lump of black fur—teeth owned by the man's killer dog. The rumble grew louder. Then a German barrage:

"You scum-sucking shits!"

By now, I was missing Veronica and Mack and the friendliness of the Upper West Side. I whispered, "Vicki. Is he talking to us?"

Vicki didn't move. "I think so."

"Get your dogs out of here, you scum-sucking shits." He sounded like Klaus Kinski—okay, Arte Johnson doing Klaus Kinski. Okay, Kenny Mars doing Arte Johnson doing . . .

Daisy shook. We stood frozen, but not Cujo. To Cujo, "You scum-sucking shits," sounded like, "You handsome, sweet Shih Tzu. Come over and I'll give you biscuits, you handsome, sweet Shih Tzu." So Cujo trotted over for a sniff.

I said, "Cujo! Get over here!"

His killer dog emitted a steady, "Grrrrrrrrrrrrr," while Cujo licked and wagged his tail saying, "Hi, hi, hi, hi, hi."

"Cujo! Get over here!"

It was at that precise moment that Daisy chose to go, looking up at me sheepishly in that terrible squat position that God has deemed. Would this happen to Mother Teresa? I said, "Oh my God, Vicki, what'll we do? Vicki?"

But Vicki was in advanced apoplexy.

"You scum-sucking shits. Clean up after your dogs, you scum-sucking shits! You should be sent to Israel with the Israelites. You should be dipped in pigmy larvae."

Now Vicki and I were no longer Manhattan tourists. We certainly knew how to clean up after our dogs. You stick your hand in a Baggie, pick up whatever, loop the Baggie inside out and voilà—like Houdini—there you are, neatly sealed. We were experts. But it was dark, and I made the mistake of taking my eyes off Daisy for half a second to check the whereabouts of Cujo, and lost the place where Daisy had squatted.

His dog growled low. "You scum-sucking shits. You should be pickled in teeth plaque. You should be simmered in whale puke."

I was frantic; I looked everywhere. God, it was dark. "Vicki where is it?" I whispered urgently, "Do you see it? Vicki. Vicki!"

Then I heard this lilting voice. Now Vicki and I do not have a lilting-voice relationship, but that night she said musically, "Did you find it, Mariette? Did you find it?"

"No, do you see it!"

"It's right there, Mariette. Don't you see it? It's right there by your foot." She sounded like Cousin Melanie at Tara.

"Yes, oh lordy me, here it is," I lied angelically. "I found it Vicki, I found it."

"Are you cleaning it up, Mariette? Are you cleaning it up?"

"Why, yes, Vicki. I'm cleaning it up."

That's when Cujo went into stoop position. I scooped him up, we tore to the van, and drove back home shaking with Daisy. That man's voice haunted me all night long.

"You scum-sucking shits. You should be put on a morning show as entertainment and have your armpits pecked out by the news media, you scum-sucking shits." At least, that's what it sounded like.

And that's just what happened.

TWENTY-FOUR

Dear Mariette:

Just to say that you handled a tough situation with grace and class and that I hope our paths will cross again soon in much more favorable circumstances.

—DAN RATHER

Being the host of a morning news program is like being on the seventh floor of a burning building, and as you look down you realize that the people yelling, "Jump! It's safe!" are behind you wearing asbestos jackets with network logos, and there's no one in front of you with a net.

I've tried it twice. Each time reminded me of the day Justine caught me putting color on my hair.

"Ooh, Mommy, can I do that?"

"No, honey, it's too messy."

"I know, but I love my hands in it. Can I help?"

"Oh, honey, please. It's gonna get all over the rug, all over *your* clothes, all over *my* clothes. Why don't you just give me some moral support?"

She was absolutely thrilled. "Okay. Where is it?"

That's what I wanted to know when I did the *Today* show in 1979. I'd wake up at four in the morning, take a shower with Patrick (it was the only time we saw each other), go over my notes, then arrive via limousine at NBC about five-thirty. But the longest part of the trip wasn't from my hotel room to the studio. The longest part of the trip was the elevator ride.

To put it mildly, I was not terribly accepted. For one thing, I was filling in for Jane Pauley while she was on her honeymoon, and there were rumors that I was to replace her. No one knew the true story, including me, but the secretaries were very protective of Jane, as well they should have been. For another thing, I came from California, which meant I consulted channelers, consorted with beach balls, and had bikini brains. I was not only from California, but I was a woman from California. I was not only a woman from California, but I was an actress from California. The triple crown of imbecility.

I would get on the elevator—feeling particularly inadequate, not having been a journalist—and the secretaries would greet me with, "Did you read the column in the *Post* today? You should. How 'bout the *Times?* The *Daily News?*" The way they were saying it, I knew the articles were bad. By the time I got to the seventh floor, I felt like Angie Dickinson coming off the elevator in *Dressed to Kill,* covered with blood. Then I'd crawl forth, slap on a smile, and say, "Good morning, Phoenix!"

The apprenticeship was rugged. I was not reading very well—tripping over Somoza's and Walesa's and Khomeini's and Muzorewa's—but the toughest part was finding the right camera. With a little practice, I could peter-piper-peck with the best of them, telling America that the Pope was welcomed by one million to Warsaw; but as I was doing so, I was looking left to Omaha when I should have been looking straight ahead at Kokomo. Patrick suggested they use flight-deck flags instead of those little red lights to point me to the appropriate camera, because if I'd stayed on that show much longer, they'd have dubbed me "the great profile."

Interviews are also tough. When you're inexperienced, they're tougher. I learned to listen; I learned to wait. I also learned not to be too specific. In a lovely precamera chat with Margaret Truman, she told me that her *husband* had encouraged her to write the book she was promoting; that she'd been awfully busy, just had time enough to *play the cello;* and that having a famous father had its drawbacks. She *hated the sycophants.* She was aware of the sycophants from the time she was *seven.* Terrific, great quote, and we could trade cello stories. Then we went on camera.

"They say your husband encouraged you to write."

"No. My father, maybe. Not my husband."

"Uh-huh," I crossed out a line in my copy. "I hear your main source of relaxation is the cello."

"I've never played the cello in my life."

"Uh-huh," I crossed out another line in my copy and began to sweat.

"Is there anything you hated about having a famous father?"

"Yes. The sycophants. All those sycophants."

I was on a roll. "Since you were seven?"

"No. Since I was four."

By the time we got to "Good morning, Sandusky!" I was an ad for Safeguard.

At one commercial break, Tom Brokaw lowered his newspaper long enough to say, "Why are you so nervous?" I said, "Tom, if you were given a large part in *A Winter's Tale,* then had to perform it in front of a live audience with only three days' preparation, how would you feel?" I don't think he understood.

But Jane Pauley was generous and Willard Scott

was wonderful. He'd plaster down his toupee, stick a flower in his lapel, and tell dirty jokes at 6:59 in the morning to get my heart started. In spite of everything, by the end of the third week, I really began to enjoy it. That's probably why—when CBS beckoned—I had the bikini brains to try it again.

In September of 1986, I wrote in my diary:

> Bob Shanks called, secretly, regarding the revamping of the CBS morning show. The show would be based on me, on comedy—an *Arthur Godfrey*-type show in the morning. No one knows; no one can know; and if anyone finds out we're . . .

Bob called a few weeks later, "firming things up," and scheduled a secret meeting at the Beverly Wilshire. Arlene and I went, sneaking off the elevator masked like Muslim women. Then Bob went back; talked to Gene Jankowski, Tom Leahy, Laurence Tisch. "Can you come to New York?" Secretly?

We were met at the plane by a limo and instructed to be discreet in front of the driver. I've never been great with the gag rule, but Arlene and I were very careful. When we arrived at the Ritz-Carlton, we were speedily ushered to our rooms, then surreptitiously whisked to a secret meeting with Jankowski and Tom Leahy in his private CBS dining room. Concerned with the wagging tongues of New York society, we were to meet Tisch in a secret, designated place, the whereabouts to be issued at a secret, designated time. At last the call came, the rendezvous given for the summit, the pinnacle of hush-hush. Our meeting was held in the middle of the main dining room of the Jockey Club, New York's trendiest watering hole.

The next day the negotiations began.

We talked about taking the humanistic rather than journalistic approach, planning a balanced show with information and spontaneous, lighthearted humor. It was to be like the old "Don McNeill's Breakfast Club"—put your feet up, have coffee, let's become old chums and sneak into the day, that sort of thing. Meant to woo viewers who preferred casual fare with their crullers, I was to cohost with Rolland Smith; comedian Bob Saget would be our "sidekick"; and former disc jockey Mark McEwen would do the weather. Dubbed by Tisch an entertainment-information show, dubbed by Bob Shanks *The Morning Program* (later to be dubbed in our house the *Mourning Program),* we were off.

By all accounts, CBS had been trying to win that time slot since Walter Cronkite and a puppet-lion named Charlemane went up against NBC's *Today* show with Dave Garroway and J. Fred Muggs in 1954. The network had a conga-line of replacements: Jack Paar, Dick Van Dyke, Will Rogers, Jr., Mike Wallace; twenty-five different anchors in a rainbow of formats were now yesterday's toast.

By the time I came along, CBS had given up. Treated as a stepchild at CBS News, that morning period had gone through five executive producers in the past three years. But the success of *Good Morning, America* had given CBS the feeling that the *Today* show could be beaten. So Van Gordon Sauter announced midsummer that the responsibility for *CBS Morning News* would be moved from the network's News Division to its Entertainment Division in order to unshackle a producer from the restrictions of the news. It was to be a show, not a news broadcast.

No one told me that handing over news to entertainment was akin to ceding Mississippi to Iran. No one told me that in four months CBS would announce the biggest cutback in the history of CBS News. No one told me that 215 would be fired; bureaus would be closed in Seattle, Warsaw, and Bangkok; others would be crippled. No one told me that the time slot had been called the "Bermuda Triangle of Television." No one told me that starting at 7:30—one-half hour after the competition—was like limping out of the starting gate on a nag called "Gladys." And certainly no one told me that the News Division and Entertainment Division had about the same relationship as the 29th Infantry and the 18th Panzer.

What did I know? I was planting King George roses in my backyard in Encino.

So in December—while Patrick and four vans of furniture started off for New York—Sean, Vicki, Justine, Arlene, and I boarded Pan Am with the animals, and I finally had time to think. And think and think. Had I lost my mind? Even though we'd had a family powwow, even though we'd all agreed, I felt like the epi-tome of selfishness. There I was, uprooting my family, putting the kids in new schools, tearing them away from friends. Pat was leaving his business connections, leaving television city, and there was little work to be had in New York. Would the kids be okay; would Pat be okay; would the family come through this intact? To smother the internal chatter, I picked up Linda Ellerbee's *And So It Goes* and read her description of a certain type of woman reporter:

> We call them Twinkies. You've seen them on television acting the news, modeling and fracturing the news while you wonder whether they've read the news—or if they've blow-dried their brains, too?

I said to myself, thank God I won't be a Twinkie. I'm not a reporter; I don't pretend to be a reporter, and the show won't pretend, either. I can do what I didn't do on *Today.* I can be *me,* not a pseudo-journalist. Oh, ho, ho, ho and Bob's your uncle. At that moment, twenty-eight male executives were probably sitting around Black Rock saying:

"I still think we should have gotten Lesley Stahl."

"I told you, she's too short."

"Then let's turn Mariette Hartley into Lesley Stahl."

"Even better—a little snip here, a little tuck there, and in no time at all, she'll be Pauline Frederick."

My naiveté had me in high-Twinkie status in the blink of the CBS eye. Once again I was handed a dead fish and walked around for a year, showing it to everybody.

I was terrified. Every day throughout the first week of January we rehearsed. Every night I had dreams about trusting people and death.

For years, whenever success loomed, I felt uncomfortable, strangely doomed, and didn't know why. Then one day, when I had a pile of offers, I heard myself use the phrase, "I feel like the top of my head is about to blow off." That's the day I figured it out. My success on *Ride the High Country* was linked with Dad's suicide.

It didn't help that there was a slew of pre-publicity.

Bob Shanks said, "We are not parading as a hard-news program."

I said, "When I did *Today,* I got a lot of mail from people who told me they enjoyed seeing a human being up there, reacting, making mistakes, being open about it."

Bob Shanks said, "We are not parading as a hard-news program."

I said, "On this show, I'll be able to react as much as I like." Oh, ho, ho, ho, and Sal's your aunt.

But the really telling phrase in that avalanche of pre-publicity was from a producer at CBS who said, "Look, there is nowhere to go but up. The show doesn't have to be much to succeed."

The press wasn't interested in our disclaimers. The press was interested in a bigger issue. What would happen, they kept asking, if there were a major newsbreak—an assassination or hostage crisis? What would CBS do with "the actress"? I don't know what the fear was. At the first sign of a flashing newsbreak, Rolland could have yanked the mike from my blouse, the camera could have whiplashed away while they wrestled me to the floor, and Forrest Sawyer delivered the "hard news." I always wondered if they were afraid I'd go screaming across the set, "There's been an assassination! Oh my God, there's been an assassination. We're all gonna die!"

Bob had designed the show in segments. The first half hour included the weather, interaction between "the hosts and the studio audience," a comedy club, a viewer poll. There were also regular weekly segments: Monday, money; Wednesday, music; Friday, sports. National news would be wedged in at 7:45 and 8:15, followed by the local.

The 8:00 A.M. half hour featured the weather, a daily "celebrity" interview, "Who's News?" with columnist Bob Osborne, and a "Personal Health and Medicine" segment with Dr. Bob Arnot. The final half hour featured the weather, a "comedy segment that changed daily," financial tips with Betsy Ashton, a round table on assorted topics, and a feature titled, "Across America" with Roy Blount, Jr.

The pace was incredible. On the ship's log, the first hour of the first show looked like this: HOSTS TEASE :15 seconds; MAIN TITLE MUSIC ANNOUNCER :10 seconds; HOSTS CHAT 1:00; WEATHER NATIONAL :45 seconds; WEATHER LOCAL :15 seconds; BILLBOARD :05 seconds; HOSTS CHAT :41; HOSTS INTRO :10; MONEY WATCH 2:30; HOSTS SHOW TEASE :10; COMMERCIAL #1 2:02; INTRO-COMEDY CLUB :45; COMEDY CLUB 3:00; HOSTS REACT :40; HOSTS SHOW TEASE :15; BILLBOARD :05; COMMERCIAL #2 2:02; HOSTS INTRO NEWS :10; NEWS-NETWORK 2:15; BUMPER-TIME CHECK :05; NEWS-LOCAL 2:25; LEAD IN :35; BUMPER-TIME CHECK :05; HOST INTRO :15; INTERVIEW #1 (Sharon Gless, Tyne Daly) 4:16; BUMPER-TIME CHECK :05; COMMERCIAL #3 1:02; INTRO-PERSONALS :20; PERSONALS 2:00; HOSTS TEASE :10; STACK PROMO :20; SYSTEM CUE :03; STATION BREAK 1:04; HOSTS TEASE :15; MAIN TITLE MUSIC ANNC :10; HOSTS CHAT :40; WEATHER NATIONAL :45; WEATHER LOCAL :15; BILLBOARD :05; HOSTS INTRO :15; INTERVIEW #2 (Madden, Simms) 5:50; HOSTS SHOW TEASE :15; COM-

MERCIAL #4 1:02; HOSTS INTRO :15; WHO'S NEWS WITH OSBORNE 2:45; HOSTS SHOW TEASE :15; COMMERCIAL #5 1:02; BUMPER-TIME CHECK :05; HOSTS INTRO NEWS :10; NEWS NATIONAL 2:30; BUMPER-TIME CHECK :05; NEWS LOCAL 2:25; LEAD IN :35; BUMPER-TIME CHECK :05; BILLBOARD :05; HOST INTRO :10; PERSONAL HEALTH AND MEDICINE WITH ARNOT 4:10; COMMERCIAL #6 2:02; BUMPER-TIME CHECK :15; HOSTS AD LIB (Daisy enters) :32; HOSTS SHOW TEASE :20; BILLBOARD :05; BUMPER-TICKET INFO :10; STACK PROMO :20; SYSTEM CUE :03; STATION BREAK 1:04.

By 7:40, America was exhausted.

When we went on the air January 12, 1987—orange-juice logos, legs dangling off barstools—I went into Mach 1. I babbled profusely, describing the set to the audience like Julia Meade on angel dust: "And this is an actual working fireplace, this is an actual working refrigerator, this is an actual working mailbox. We want to be your friendly morning wake-up call, so stay for the day." I couldn't help remembering my own morning mood on Wilshire when Pat so much as coughed. All those lousy risers across America being accosted by Cheerful Edna at 7:30 A.M. Aaargh.

Convinced that the American public had the attention span of a pea and could only handle information between gulps of coffee and razor strokes, Bob had so tightly plotted the show that there was no time to relax or let a good interview continue. Even Daisy came in on cue, found the red light, wagged her tail and left. I looked forward daily to the round table at 8:15 where I could put my feet up and converse with people for more than 120 seconds.

* * *

In the beginning, CBS was firm. *The Morning Program* was meant to be light, informative, easy, and entertaining. When it went on the air and reviewers called it light and insubstantial, everyone at the network panicked and started to fix it. Have it funny, but not too funny. Be spontaneous, but don't veer from the script. Have it entertain, but keep it serious.

We got panned for being what we were supposed to be. We were unqualified if we talked about Iran, and fluff if we talked about pom-pom queens. But I learned many things.

I learned that if a pea falls to the floor during the cooking segment, don't pick it up and put it back in the pot.

I learned that when the camera's on, you should be too.

I learned you're only as good as the person you're talking to, and if he isn't talking, it's a long show.

I learned that my tongue could go on trips of its own. "And now, here's our own financial adviser, Betsy Ashton, with more taps tix."

"And now, psychiatrist Tom Cottle will tell you how to talk to teenagers about vital issues like sucks and drugs."

"And now, Dr. Bob Arnot will shaw, show . . ."

I massacred Nicaraguan webels, cystic fibroshus, meteor—logical. One day I said, "Most people are used to thinking of Jimmy Stewart as one of our quintessential film actors—a lanky pioneer of American acting style. This Sunday he will be hosting the Jimmy Stewart rely, relah, reloo . . ." I was so busy getting "quintessential" out, I tripped all over "relay."

* * *

I learned that you have to be on top of things:

"Next, we'll ask the former governor of Nebraska . . ."

"We did that."

"We did that."

"Karl Malden is . . . We're going to weather first?"

"In our next . . . Oh, that's you, go ahead."

I learned you have to know where you are, along with the rest of your cast.

"Today, Mark's in Louisiana."

"Mark isn't in Louisiana."

"Mark isn't in Louisiana. Mark's in Kentucky."

I learned I was terrible with names. I strangled Hauge, Fermalicht, Tamalo Otsuki, DeBartolo, Knipe, Oterkirk.

"Paula Begun?"

"Begone."

"Begone."

The day I was to interview Ruth Canow Weinstein, I went to everyone. "Is it Winest*een* or Winest*ine*?" They all said, Winest*ine*.

"Today we have Ruth Canow Winest*ine*."

"Cay-no."

"Cay-no."

I learned to trust my researcher. Or not. I was my own verbal self-correcting white-out tape.

To Karen Valentine:

"Now, you were raised by nuns."

"I wasn't raised by nuns."

"You weren't raised by nuns."

To Jane Curtin:

"Allie is supposed to have a boyfriend this year?"

"Allie has a boyfriend."

"Allie has a boyfriend. But you started out in Second City?"

"No, I didn't start out in Second City."

"You didn't start out in Second City. But you started out in Chicago, right? And then you went to *Saturday Night Live.*"

"Then I went to New York."

To Hunt Block:

"You went to Princeton."

"I've been to Princeton, but I went to Harvard."

To Geoffrey Holder:

"Now, you came from Tahiti."

"Trinidad."

"Today we have Eddie Albert."

"Eddie Rabbitt."

"Now, you studied Kung Fu."

"Tai Chi."

"Now, you have one stepdaughter."

"Stepson."

"Grace, your husband is also paralyzed."

"He's not paralyzed."

"He's not paralyzed."

Once I said to an entire audience, "I hear you're all from Japan."

The entire audience said, "No."

By the end of three months, Margaret Truman was looking good.

But the show began to settle in. There were memorable interviews. Liv Ullmann, emotional, full of passion; Lillian Gish ("Dorothy was the talented one"); Betty White (who rose to my knock-knock jokes by reducing herself to my level: "You know how to catch a unique rabbit? Unique up on it. You know how to catch a tame rabbit? Tame way, unique up on it"); George Burns, Dabney Coleman, Ken Kercheval, Rita Rudner, Roseanne Barr, Don Rickles, and Billy Crystal made me laugh so hard I fell out of the frame. I spent a delightful week cohosting with George Segal, who had as much trouble as I did, imperfection pouring across the screen ("We're on, George").

In that quieter last half hour, there were some terrific roundtable discussions. A moving segment had the Bergenfield students talking about the four children who committed suicide from their school. But the best, the absolute best, was the round table with Colleen Dewhurst, Maureen Stapleton, and Zoe Caldwell—three friends who showed their affection for each other through tease and banter.

The show got better. I got better.

I also fell asleep a lot.

To get up at four in the morning, it would be wise to go to bed at eight, or at the latest, nine. But I wanted to be with my family during those evening hours, so I rarely got to sleep before ten or eleven. That's probably why all informal snapshots from 1987 have me nodding off.

In future years, Sean will go through his scrapbook of New York memories: "Here's where my mom fell asleep at my birthday party. Here's where my mom fell asleep at the Museum of Modern Art. Here's where my mom fell asleep under the coats at Princess Yasmin's party." I'd take Justine over to Central Park to play, sit on a bench, and promptly drift off. I'd go to mandatory parties at night, and Patrick would walk me down the stairs holding me up by the arm, a scene out of *Notorious*, muttering "Stay awake, here comes President Reagan. Stay awake!" The combination of an overheated room and a couch was lethal. I wanted so badly to see friends, but it was hard zeroing in on any sentence lasting longer than compound-complex. Simple sentences I could handle. Even better: "go store," "buy boots."

I had so looked forward to moving to New York, having little *soirées* at the house, going to the theater. One month into the show, I didn't want to go to the theater; I envied Justine her slumber parties. I sat drooling through my birthday party; I sat drooling through Christmas. The children preferred me instead of their father because I said "sure" whenever I heard a question mark at the end of a sentence.

"Can I go to Janie's?"

"Sure."

"Can we have some ice cream?"

"Sure."

"Where to, lady?"

"Sure."

And sleep deprivation did not help anyone's behavior at CBS. Trying to deal with those Machiavellian corridors when you're nodding out like a Korean POW makes reactions extreme. We became a dysfunctional family—childlike, paranoid, petty, with trench mentality. It was like playing hopscotch in the DMZ.

All around was a swirl of distrust, hallway gossip, court intrigue. CBS pronounced you queen, sat you on the throne, but behind the dais the Duke of Gloucester was whispering to the Earl of Kent, while the Duke of Affiliates slipped blood money to henchmen.

It got to the point where I didn't know what

was real and what was a dream. Bob would make promises he couldn't keep: he'd talk to Tom Leahy; he'd change the format. I would be pulled in, trusting, then feel betrayed when things stayed the same. He also became the critical parent, and the tension between us grew. I brought Vicki in as my secretary. Arlene came in from California, every other month, to run defense. She had several conversations with the brass, telling them I didn't want to do it anymore, not the way it was being done.

I was juggling feelings of guilt about the show with feelings of guilt about not being home. The whole family was in trouble. In the classroom Justine couldn't infiltrate the already-formed cliques. Sean was with his friend Ethan so much it was hard to get him to talk. Patrick couldn't find work. I'd look at him staying home, helping, cooking, but I'd only see my father—pulling away, sinking into depression—so I'd pull away. Our marriage was at its lowest ebb.

By May I was hiding in the bedroom, not knowing how to ask for help, writing in my diary:

> Why is it when we most need hugs we most reject them? Justine does it, too. She's called every girl in her class for a sleepover tonite—now it is 6:15 and there are no takers. As she walked past me I asked her if she wanted a hug. She said, "No!"
>
> The last two weeks have been enormously difficult, full of backtracking, regressing, reliving old patterns, old feelings. The critiques of me whip me back to a time where I did everything to please my family. The truth is that I am in very much the same family at CBS as I was in my own home: high expectations, low

reality. Every morning after the show, I wait for the criticisms. Corporate daddies, corporate mommies. "Don't be spontaneous. Don't touch Rolland, but it's okay if he touches you. (I feel in good company. The only other person at CBS that's gotten that note that I'm aware of was Judy Garland.) No slapstick. We like you safe." Too many don'ts and not enough dos. Every message I had at home. Sometimes I think the best things in me make people afraid. I want to run away, to scream.

Justine opened the door, saw me, and shut it. The Saturday before, she had attempted to spend the night with a friend. We got the call in the evening, late—that she was homesick, crying. I asked her what was wrong, what were the feelings.

She said, "Number one, Tracy 'forced' me to watch *Mommy Dearest.* It was about this woman who beat her children and they had to call her 'Mommy Dearest.' "

"I imagine the fact that the mommy was an actress didn't help."

"No. Then I wanted to keep on my Halloween makeup, but Tracy told me to take it off. She was bossy."

The next morning, Justine had yelled from the shower: "And Tracy doesn't believe in God! She doesn't believe that there's a spirit within us!"

As if the movie and the makeup weren't enough.

Hardly seems possible that Sean will be twelve in three months. He looks older, sophisticated, sure of himself. He seems to be holding his own. I wonder.

The Morning Program was canceled on September 28, 1987, after nine months. The announcement was a pleasant one. No blame. CBS and I are pals, etc., etc. The toughest part, and there were a few, was that the last couple of weeks were the best. It was closer to what I thought the show could be. But doing entertainment isn't what did it in. It was a failure of nerve. It tried to be all things to all men; it started out a simple egg salad sandwich, then someone added roast beef, then someone added tuna, until it became totally indigestible.

A week later, I wrote in my diary:

> October 20, 4:30 AM. Sean broke down last night finally. He's been holding these fears down with his cool exterior. When he says something wrong in class he's afraid to turn around because someone might be laughing at him. "Soccer is all I'm good at." He feels tremendous humiliation and fear that he'll cry. God, I love him. At least now we know what's going on inside.
>
> Last night we went to the Joffrey Ballet's *Le Sacre du Printemps.* Justine sat in Patrick's lap and Sean came to sit next to me. I wrapped my left arm around him. When he rested his head on my shoulder, tears started down my face. The musts—the primitive Rite of Passage—filled me with a sadness. My son is passing into young adulthood—he is preparing to leave and as I held him in my arms, I grieved.
>
> So this weekend, we're all together, separating sooner than I thought.

On November 12, 1987—when CBS was kind enough to let me out of my contract ahead of time—I bid a hasty good-bye to Rolland, Mark,

Bob Osborne, Amy, Leonard, Joanne, Shiela—all very supportive, helpful, gentle—and went down to Georgia to shoot Ernest Thompson's *1969.* Months later, my dreams were still filled with *The Morning Program.* One night there was no producer, no one on the floor, no teleprompters, and a quarter of an audience. We had one guest, a woman selling oversized Barbie-doll furniture. I dreamt I opened the show in a platinum Barbie-doll wig.

TWENTY-FIVE

When I've worked long enough and my services are no longer needed, I intend to fulfill the greatest of my dreams: To live in the country, surrounded by trees, flowers, and "millions and millions" of animals, and "millions and millions" of books.

—EVA LE GALLIENNE

On May 3, 1989, Patrick and I went to visit Miss Le Gallienne at Toscairn. We'd called ahead the week before, but her caretaker said we needn't call ahead. "She won't remember. Just come." Two mild strokes had left her with short-term memory only; she could remember the past, not the present—as if that insatiable brain could contain no more.

I wanted to put it off, wait until next week, next year, the year after. What would she look like? Would she be feeble, distant? Would she remember me? I overslept, woke up tired, and asked hopefully if it was too late to go. "Not at all," said Pat.

I fretted all the way up the Merritt Parkway. Would she feel invaded, shoo us away? Would she remember me? As we turned off the Georgetown Road onto a newly-named crossroad, I prayed we wouldn't find it; markers had changed. But there, at the top of the rise, stood the same old stockade fence, the same small blue sign, now faded, that announced quietly, "Le Gallienne."

"Let's turn around, Pat; we can't just barge in. Pat?"

Ignoring me, he drove into the compound, crossing shadow bars laid down by the trees across the path. He drove past the outbuildings, parked near the rock fence in the lane, got out of the van, and took Cujo for a walk, leaving me to face my fears. Clusters of violets were blooming everywhere as I reluctantly walked up the stone walk, up the stone steps. The door was ajar. I dinged the tiny wrought-iron bell, and there she was—there, through the glass door, with her sweet small face.

"Yes?" she said.

"Miss Le Gallienne?"

"Yes?"

"I don't know if you remember me. I'm Mariette Hartley."

And her smile began. "Oh yes, my God." She was frail, bent over, but sharp, funny and alert. My fear melted as we went into each other's arms.

"You look wonderful," I said.

"I don't know about that. I feel pretty good for my age. I was born in 'ninety-nine, I guess. So that tells you how old I am." A tiny dog ambled over. "Here's my duckie. Here's my duck." She scooped it up. "She's a good girl. Aren't you, Dimpy?"

Pat peeked in the door.

"Do you remember my husband, Patrick?"

"Come in, dear boy."

We went into the blue room, the library, that cozy repository of years past, escorted by Dimpy. When I entered that study, when I entered that room, it all came back. I felt safe.

"I like Yorkshire terriers," she said. "They have the temperament of big dogs, yet they're so little.

She's never really known anybody else, so we're very close. Aren't we, Dimpy?"

She sat in her corner, behind her book stand, with Dimpy on her lap—constantly cossetting, cooing, comforting at the same time as she was being comforted. She was grounded by the dog, by the petting, by the stillness she created in it.

"I hope we didn't interfere by coming unannounced," said Pat.

"Of course not. I'm delighted to see you."

So we stayed, and she showed us her mother's large wooden box with her maiden name, "Julie Norregaard," written in ink on the inside. She showed us two magical bookmarks: one with a silver arrow, one with another set of initials.

"Did your father live a long life?"

"I can't remember. I didn't know him, you know. He and mother separated when I was four."

She showed me her *Mask* magazines, 1908–1909, all bound. She showed me her copy of Sarah Bernhardt's book, copied in her neat hand. She seemed particularly proud of the riding crop from *L'Aiglon*. She adored *L'Aiglon*.

"I've never read it. Who wrote it?"

"Rostand," she said, luxuriating in the pronunciation.

"Did you know John Houseman died?" I asked.

"No."

"Just about three months ago."

"I didn't know him, did I?"

"Yes. A little, I think. God, it's good to see you. Do you know how much influence you had on my life?"

My sentimentality sent her straight to Dimpy. "I didn't think I had *any*. She likes her tummy rubbed. That's enough, Dimpy—you're a naughty, greedy girl."

"Do you think in English or Dutch or French?" Pat asked in French.

"Je peux changer, j 'ai été élevée à Paris," replied LeG.

"Au collège de filles?"

"Non, seulement une école."

"Je suis allé chez les Jesuites."

"Ah, oui."

She showed me her father's books.

"And they were divorced by the time you were four?"

"I can't remember now. Is that what I said? Dimpy, don't scratch, lovey. No, don't scratch, ducks. We're very close, she and I."

"You look so wonderful. You haven't changed at all."

"What nonsense!"

"Okay, I'll shut up."

"I look a thousand years old. Can't be helped. I *am* a thousand years old. I was born in ninety-nine, didn't I say? God, it was a hell of a long time ago, I dare say." She gazed out the window, "My, what a windburst."

"Are you sure we aren't keeping you?"

"There's nothing to keep me from."

"What about lunch?"

"I think I had lunch. I don't remember."

She dared us to go down the hill to see the little house, her original house, to see the narcissus and daffodils. "Probably too hard a trip for you, hm?" We laughed—I was duly dared—and began the trip downhill. We talked about fencing. She seemed agile—bouncy even—reminding me of the way she used to move when she'd teach me how to walk up and down stairs in period skirts, always weighted with fish weights. "Never lift the skirt higher than the toe of the ascending foot and never touch it going downstairs. There's no necessity."

"You still walk like a billy goat," I teased.

"Well, I don't know about that. I can still move pretty well for my age. Not so bad. Not so bad, am I, Dimpy?"

We walked toward the chicken coops. Two bantam hens cackled wildly as Pat let Cujo out of the van to join us. My eye caught the narcissus; they were as beautiful as she had said—dotted along the hillside, blooming white gold against the green.

Then it truly was time to go. The trip uphill took longer. She showed her age.

"I'm stiff."

"From walking?"

"No, I'm just old. Aren't I, Dimpy? When did I say I was born?"

"Eighteen ninety-nine."

"My God, I must be ninety."

Pat empathized. "I'm getting close."

"How old are you?"

"Fifty-one."

"You have a long way to go. A long, long way to go." She stopped many times on the way up, breathing in: "Ooh, la la la la la la." Breathing out: "Ooh, la la la la."

We saw her to the door, said good-bye. I told her I loved her. She asked me back, "Anytime, please, anytime. Right, Dimpy? We're very close, she and I."

As we drove back to the city, I welled up. She may not have remembered our visit by that evening, but it didn't matter. She remembered me that day. And I remembered her.

TWENTY-SIX

We are healed with a suffering only by experiencing it to the full.

—MARCEL PROUST

It took me over three decades to separate from Mom. It took me twenty-six years to bury my dad.

In the summer of 1987 as I was lying down, reading, in our cottage in Jamaica, the rain was pouring straight down. It was a tropical afternoon rain, pounding on the roof, on the leaves, in a comforting tattoo outside, making the inside small, safe, cavelike. It was dark, that deep blue-gray dark that happens in Jamaica when the rains come.

My mother came in, quietly, feebly, her voice gruff from emphysema. Unable to see well, she was timidly negotiating the furniture. Remembering Rary in Chicago, Mom's terror was blindness. Depending on people, being a burden, preyed on her mind.

She told me of a friend who had encephalitis and had almost lost her eyesight. One night while her friend was dancing with a man she had never met, she said to him, "I just want you to know, I have encephalitis." The man stopped dancing and said, "I've never met anyone as honest as you in my life." Then he walked off and left her in the middle of the dance floor.

I looked at Mom carefully. I thought of her entering my room in Weston, in Encino, when she was forty, fifty, even sixty. Her gait had been full of energy, grace, a kind of lilt. Not like now. Her hair, now white, is short; her body, bent to see, is bent with pain. I call her Mom now. I stopped calling her Polly years ago, when the roles got sorted out.

We spent the afternoon and evening together, talking for hours—ending with a talk about her suicide attempts. She began by saying, "You know, Mariette, I've always been suicidal. It began, or at least the depression began, during the scandal in Baltimore." She was matter-of-fact. The divorce had leveled her. There were two or three attempts with Gainer—one in the bathroom in Texas with Fritz her dog—there was the attempt in Chicago, the attempt after Dad's death, the time in the garage.

"Was that the time I didn't come?"

"Well, you did come a few days later. We marketed, did some errands. You were very matter-of-fact," she laughed.

"What made you quit?"

"What's the use? I never could drown because I'm too good a swimmer. If I fell off a roof, I'd land on an awning. I never took enough pills, or someone always came home and pumped out my belly."

It was easy to listen to. Too easy. She reported it softly, matter-of-factly, as if recounting a menu in a middle-priced restaurant. No lifts or falls vocally. Quiet, in a monotone. She was talking about dying, about ending her life, as if she were reciting phone numbers.

"I've never been afraid of death. I've been afraid of dying without control, without dignity."

"Mom. Have you ever felt that you had an effect on people? That who you were mattered?"

She replied quietly, "No."

Like my mother, I lived for years thinking I couldn't affect.

While browsing in a bookstore, I saw a graphic of a leg from the knee down—a ribbed sock with a Mary Jane shoe walking through an alley. A disembodied arm was reaching in from the border of the painting, its hand shackled to the Mary-Janed ankle. I recognized that leg; I recognized that ankle. It took longer to recognize that the hand had become self-imposed.

Events large and small have helped me pry off that hand, one finger at a time.

The first was the movie, *Providence*. I went to see it with Patrick, sixteen years after Dad's death. A brilliant Resnais film, it's the story of a writer, played by John Gielgud, who views life through a debilitating paranoia, depicted by a greenish hue. He looks at his family with enormous distortion, imagining them impatient for him to die.

Gielgud's an alcoholic, a failed artist living in pajamas and slippers, lying in an ornate bed—all his needs by his bedside—constantly drinking. He is ill and in pain. Convinced that, "out there, in the icy universe, there's nothing," he thinks he has failed in the eyes of his children; he is angry, weeping for himself. He invents accusations for them: "When will you pull yourself together? You're always sniveling. Will we ever be free of you?"

But outside of his mind, life is beautiful. When you finally see the reality, the movie changes to vivid colors. The gardens become beautiful, populated by children, flowers, bikes. The family gathers in the sunshine, a cacophony of intelligent conversation. As they celebrate his birthday, he's given a knife of Ernest Hemingway's. He seems happy, fulfilled, then turns to the wine, "I think it's time for just one more . . ."

I understood that movie from the minute it started. When I saw what Dad must have been thinking, what he must have been seeing, when I lived in my father's brain for those two hours, I could not get out of my seat.

Providence's internal violence was cathartic, but I would recoil in movies if there was a hint of external violence. When I had to shoot Keir Dullea in *No Place to Hide,* I called Pat, trembling. He said, "Tell the director. That's all you have to do, just tell him what's going on." But I couldn't; I was full of some misguided shame, a fear of calling attention to myself: "Hey, look at me. I've had sadness in my life." It felt melodramatic.

Then I did two movies-of-the-week in succession that further loosened the grip.

The first was *M.A.D.D.: Mothers Against Drunk Drivers.* To research the movie, I went up to Sacramento for three days and lived with Candy Lightner. By walking around in her shoes, visiting the grave of her daughter, I realized Candy had been like me—totally apolitical. But her anger had started MADD. If anyone could get it through my noggin that one person could make a difference, it had to be Candy.

In the second movie, *Silence of the Heart,* I played the mother of a boy who commits suicide. I knew it was going to be tough, so I surrounded myself with help. When the filming was over, I found myself reverting to the behavior that followed Dad's death. For six months, I was irritable; I didn't want to get up in the morning; I plodded on with little energy. One day, when I was feeling passively suicidal, I called Joye Weisel—a friend and therapist—and told her what was going on.

"Are you angry at anybody, Mariette?"

"Oh my God, I guess I am."

All those early feelings about my parents had bubbled up. All those years of pronouncing myself wrong and them right, hanging on to their rightness at my expense.

Joye was right. I was not just angry; I was furious.

I think suicide is aggression turned inward. It is an accusation. If we could only face people and find out whether they're really accusing us, or why they're accusing us, or if they, themselves, feel accused—there might be less suicide.

A lot of people, especially in their teenage years, have contemplations of "wouldn't it be nice if this were all over." As I watched my father being wheeled out, part of me said, "My God, this works. Suicide really works. Don't mess around with it anymore." But another part of me wanted to die with him.

There is a history of stigma connected with suicide. Declared a sin, Christians and Jews alike have denied the bodies of victims the rite of religious burial. By the Middle Ages, suicide was against the law; survivors were punished. There once was a statute in Massachusetts that the body of the suicide victim had to be buried on a highway with a cartload of stones over it. All of this has served to make suicide hush-hush—low whispers behind closed doors, concealed weapons, hidden notes. The survivors are blamed for the death—by themselves, by others. And shame corrodes.

All these years I've carried memories of that O'Neillian night when Dad quit drinking. Guilty memories of my mother and me with our hair of snakes—taunting, tempting—feeling like accomplices. Logically, knowing it wasn't so; illogically, convinced that it was. It wasn't until recently that I discovered that Hemingway had shot himself exactly two years earlier than Dad on the same day, July 2. I don't know if it was a coincidence; I'll never know.

The first time I stopped skirting the details of Dad's suicide was when I was talking to René and Gary Spikowski, parents of a young suicide victim, while doing research for *Silence*. We started talking about the smell of the sheets, about death—with no limitations, no shame. I had never discussed the details with anybody, only my reactions to it. How do you talk about it so it doesn't appear maudlin, so it doesn't appear to be begging for attention?

It was so freeing that I got involved with suicide groups. I went on talk show after talk show on a relentless drive to exorcise the memory and redeem my father. Until I realized it was never going to go away, no matter how many talk shows I did. I could change how I reacted to it, but it was never going to go away.

At that time I was seeing Dale Sowers, a psychologist in New York, who kept trying to convince me that even though I was now listing the details, I still hadn't emotionally relived that night in Brentwood Gardens. He gently pushed and prodded, but I resisted. I lay on that couch and talked about Patrick, about Justine, about Sean—toe-dancing around the pit without a misstep.

Then, in the fall of 1988, I was asked to speak to about eight hundred psychiatric-social workers, teen workers, everyone involved with suicide at Harvard Medical Society, Dad's alma mater. I was very nervous, dealing with the demons, the voices nagging inwardly to, "Keep the family secrets." I got up, had my say, sat down, and eight hundred people stood up. I was astonished. I wasn't getting applause for doing a performance, for being someone else. I was simply saying this is my life: who I was, what happened, who I am now.

I knew that day the jig was up. I knew that I had to finish unwrapping that hand. If my marriage was going to last, if my relationship with my children was going to be full, I had to relive that July afternoon. I went to Dale and said, "Prop your feet up, because I'm going to tell you everything." So I poured it out, step by bloody step, without judging myself, without feeling that this was an indulgence, a bid for sympathy. I didn't even censor the sobs; I wailed full-out.

We had never had a burial service for my father. He had been cremated, then Mom had flown back East, asked Bill Snaith where to bury him, and he'd suggested the Gun Club. So Mom had buried Dad in the Weston Gun Club, ironically, under one of the blockhouse shooting stations where they stand on a slatted platform and say, "Mark! Pull!" while shooting clay pigeons.

On several occasions, I'd gone to the cemetery in Weston to visit Big John's plot, but I'd always avoided the Gun Club. It was hard to imagine myself thinking noble thoughts standing over a lump of shells at Shooting Station #7. Besides I didn't know if it was Shooting Station #7, or #6, or #3. I'd made halfhearted attempts to find out, then I'd get busy and comfort myself with the excuse that I was too far away.

When I moved to New York to do *The Morning Program* and no longer had an excuse, Patrick went to the Gun Club for me. First, he talked with new members who were too young to remember Dad. Then he talked with old-timers, "Oh yah, sure, I wasn't there, but John was. John, come on over here." John came over, but couldn't remember. Then someone recalled that the caretaker was still the same caretaker. Fortunately, he remembered. The ashes of my father were buried in front of the grandstand, either at Shooting Station #1 or #2. He wasn't sure which because the place had been redone. But he was absolutely sure it was Station #1 or #2.

I was taping the show at Disneyland in Anaheim, about to meet Snow White, when I got a call from Pat.

"We found your Dad."

"Where!"

"Don't worry. We know the area."

Although two members of the Weston Gun Club volunteered to find the exact location, I was still too busy. Besides, it was winter. Then spring, then summer. One day, when Mom called from Arizona, I asked if she wanted to be involved. She leapt at the chance.

'Okay, then let's set a date," I said. "How's June eleventh?"

"It doesn't matter, darling. I don't have another appointment for four years."

"Now, you sure you want to do this? You've already had a memorial service."

"Not like this one."

I knew I needed close friends around me, so I called Father Stan, who agreed to unofficially officiate. I called Arlene in Los Angeles ("I wouldn't miss it for the world"). I called Vicki ("I'm on the plane"). I called Dale ("May I bring my wife?"), I called Betty Silverstein, I called Annie. All seemed eager to be there.

Then I called Iris and Jack Bolton in Atlanta, friends whose son had committed suicide twelve years before, and asked if they would be there in spirit. ("What time is the service?" "Noon," "We'll stop what we're doing and hold our own service.") I called Joye in Los Angeles. I called my Uncle Jimmy; I called my cousin Wallace. All agreed to observe the noon hour.

Unfortunately, I didn't realize that the dates conflicted with Sean's summer camp until it was too late to stop the momentum.

Dad had always wanted to be buried underneath the apple tree in the back of the Newtown Turnpike house, but that presented a problem. I wasn't ready to knock on somebody's door and say, "Hi! Do you mind if I bury my father under your apple tree?" After talking to Mom, I bought two plots at Willowbrook in Weston, in a large and sunny area, banked by two large pines. One for Dad, one for Mom. The mortuary agreed to let me plant an apple tree behind the headstone.

But when I called the head of the Gun Club on June 5th, I learned they still hadn't located Dad's ashes. Since Mom had flown in ahead of the others, we decided to go to the Gun Club. Maybe she could remember.

So that Tuesday morning, over newspapers saturated with the massacre in Tiananmen Square, we made plans to drive to Weston. It was a joyous and chatty drive. As we came down the exit ramp from the Merritt Parkway onto the Weston Road, Mom was excited.

"Oh, look at that willow tree. Remember how Tony always wanted one?"

We drove by the Weston Market. We drove by Horace C. Hurlbutt School. We drove by Cobb's Mill. We drove by our old house on the Newtown Turnpike.

I said, "The river house is gone."

"How's Dad's rock garden?"

"Gone."

"That was his pride and joy. Well, at least, I can smell the lilacs. At least, they're still there."

"So's the forsythia."

"Good."

"So are the maples."

"Good."

"But the apple tree's gone."

We turned on Godfrey Road and drove past Big John's old house.

"Remember the Sunday barbecues at Big John's?" I asked. "Those big, thick sirloin steaks and those fabulous salads—and Tony would go home drinking the salad dressing from the jar?"

Mom was quiet. "I always loved that house," she said. "The architect was very famous."

"Who was it?"

"I don't know."

"That famous, eh?"

We drove by the Weins.

"Did you know they're considering making it into a retirement home?" I asked.

"What'll the poor bastards do?" Mom asked. Then she began to sing, "Fish gotta swim / Bird gotta fly / When you're eighty-two / It's time to say bye-bye." Mom was having a ball. "Boy, it's sure nicer talking to you in person than on the phone."

"You don't like to talk to me on the phone?"

"No. You always tell our phone conversations."

"I never do."

"Always. You told everyone I went into a decline when you used a nasty word on television."

"What nasty word, Mom?"

"Never mind, you know. You told everyone about *My Two Loves.* You always get that story wrong. You always misquote me."

"When do I misquote you?"

"Every time you tell the story."

"I called you in Arizona and said, 'Hi,' right?"

"I guess."

"Then you asked me what I was doing. I said, 'Well, I'm going to be in a movie-of-the-week.' You said, 'Oh, that's wonderful, honey, what's it called?' I said, *'My Two Loves.'* You said, 'Oh, that's a lovely title. What's it about?' I said, 'Well, it's about a woman who's lost her husband, is now widowed, and in her vulnerable state dips into bisexuality.' After a verrry long pause, you said, 'Is that so? Who's playing the other girl?' I said, 'Lynn Redgrave.' Then you said, 'Well, I hope you're not going to have to have an orgasm on screen.' I said, 'What?' You said, 'I find them disgusting, ridiculous, and totally unnecessary.' You did say that, right?"

"I still say that."

"Well, since I couldn't imagine you kicking back, smoking a cigarette, and watching *Pussycat Theater,* I said, 'Mom, when was the last time you saw something like that on television?' You said, 'Are you kidding? Jane Fonda had three in *Coming Home.*' "

Mom closed the window on the van, turned to

me, and said, "See, that's what I mean. She didn't have three orgasms, she had two, but if three's funnier, use it."

I laughed for about ten minutes. All the way to the Gun Club.

The difficulty of the task hadn't dawned on me until we were standing near Shooting Station #1—armed with shovels—and two members of the Weston Gun Club, who had volunteered to help dig, said, "About here." I was pleased that the sun had decided to hide behind clouds because I began to suspect we were in for a lot of digging.

"What was the canister like?" asked Pat. "What are we looking for?"

"A little brass box about this size," Mom extended her hands from a flexible twenty inches down to six, then back to twenty. "Gosh, Pat, I don't know. It was so long ago." She was just as precise when indicating the width. We were basically looking for a metal box of any size, black in color—due to the oxidation of the brass over a twenty-six-year period—and hopefully still in one piece.

But some enterprises benefit from divine backing and since our mission seemed benign in purpose, I had no doubt that we would find it.

We began to dig. After about a half hour, Pat struck something with a clang. We all froze. Dusting the earth, he revealed a large rock. We dug all day. As we dug, Mother kept trying to remember, "I'm sure it was Shooting Station Number One, but I was looking to the side of it." I prayed every time the shovel clanged, but we hit nothing but rocks. We continued to dig. And dig and dig. After another hour, Mom directed timidly, "I think we buried him to the right," then realizing the work it would entail, retreated. By late afternoon, we had destroyed one half of the lawn around Station #1 with nothing to show for it. No box. No ashes.

We were quiet most of the way home. Mom kept apologizing, "It seemed such a good idea. I wanted to bury him where he'd had so many happy hours," while I tried to make peace with the facts. "Do you think I should call it off? Should I let Dad be? Do you think Vicki can return her airline tickets?"

In frustration, I asked Mom, "Is there anything of Dad's in Arizona that we can bury?"

She thought for a moment, "His gun belt. I have his gun belt."

That did it. Ask for a sign, you get one. We decided to continue with the memorial service. If we couldn't lay his ashes to rest, maybe we could lay our minds.

The following night one of our Gun Club volunteers called several funeral parlors to find out what kind of a box Mom would have been given in '63. We were looking for the wrong thing, they said. The box would not have been made of brass, but of tin, and tin disintegrates. Give tin six to eight months underground, nothing would remain but the bones.

When they told Pat, he decided to return to Weston.

"They said the box would be gone, Pat. It's useless."

"Even so."

So the Thursday morning before the memorial service, Pat went back and tried again. He went to the right of Station #1, the untouched side, and started digging more gingerly. He kept thinking about Mom's "looking to the other side." Maybe the other side was the side that had not been disturbed, the side that was closer to Station #8. By early afternoon, he was still digging when he began to decipher the outline of a box. There was no metal; it was more like a rectangular shadow, a vague indentation occupied by remnants. He stooped down, inspected the loam, and made out pieces of bone, cradled in this small earthen sepulcher. The rains had driven the ashes into the earth long ago, but the pieces of bone were held as if by a sieve.

Pat called me from Weston: "I found your Dad."

hat Sunday, June 11, 1989—with the help of my other, my husband, my daughter, and all my od friends—I buried my father under an apple ee in Weston, Connecticut.

EPILOGUE

Mom is living near us now. She has irreversible emphysema and is down to eighty-six pounds, so she lives close, with her two friends, a part-time nurse named Rosie, and an oxygen machin named Thumper. It's not a perfect world, b we're all learning. There are days we feel the te sion. Days we think we win, days we know don't.

We learned the severity of her condition in t fall of '89 when her doctor called from Scottsda The family converged; decisions were made. The Patrick drove Mom up from Arizona, and she stayed with us for a while. I felt guilty about the hours I was spending away from her, rehearsing my one-woman show. I felt guilty about the days I'd be spending away from her, when we took the show on tour. But Mom was reassuring; she even asked Pat if he would bring her to a rehearsal. That Sunday she sat there and watched as I went through the entire show. Three verses into my last song, she got up and walked out.

She was crying. I saw it in her shoulders as she headed for the rehearsal room exit. I saw it in the way she struggled with the door. I hurried into the hall and found her sitting on a folding chair, sobbing.

"This is stupid. So stupid," she said with disgust. "I can't stop crying."

"It's okay."

"No, it's stupid. Really stupid."

She was teary in the car, teary when we arrived home. When we entered the house, she went directly to her room and closed the door.

At a loss, I followed Pat into our bedroom—analyzing, hypothesizing. "She's not drinking anymore. She's not smoking. She's not pushing things down. Do you think she's crying because I'm going away?"

He thought for a minute as he hung up his coat. "No, honey. I think she's crying because *she's* going away."

Shortly after, I walked back down the corridor, knocked on Mom's door, and entered. She was sitting at the end of her bed. "Mom, are you okay?"

"That was just stupid. So stupid. I just couldn't stop crying."

"Was it the rehearsal hall? Did memories flood back? The times you drove me to LeGallienne's, to Claire Oleson's, to the White Barn? Other rehearsals we shared together?"

She welled up. "All I can think is that I won't be around to watch you perform anymore. That there's no more future. It's as if I'll never be able to tell you all I want you to know. I'm happy here. It's crazy and chaotic and I'm happy. It's like . . ."

"Mom. Are you trying to tell me that you want to live?"

She looked down at her robe; her thumb caressed the border. She spoke so softly, the word was almost inaudible. "Yes," she said.

At eighty-four, my mother finally wanted to live.